THE BURLINGTON BIKE PATH AND WATERFRONT PARK

An Environmental Handbook for the Post Auto Era

By Rick Sharp

Onion River Press
191 Bank Street
Burlington, VT 05401

ISBN: 978-1-949066-30-2

Publisher's Cataloging-in-Publication Data

Names: Sharp, Frederick Philip, author.

Title: The Burlington bike path and waterfront park : an environmental handbook for the post auto era / by Rick Sharp.

Description: Includes bibliographical references. | Burlington, VT: Onion River Press, 2019.

Identifiers: LCCN 2019911613 | ISBN 978-1-949066-30-2

Subjects: LCSH Bicycle trails—Vermont—Burlington. | Rail-trails—Vermont—Burlington. | Cycling—Vermont—Burlington. | Outdoor recreation—Vermont—Burlington. | Sustainable development—Vermont—Burlington Metropolitan Area. | Urban renewal—Vermont—Burlington. | Burlington (Vt.)—Buildings, structures, etc. | Burlington (Vt.). Department of Parks, Recreation and Waterfront. | BISAC TRANSPORTATION / Bicycles | TRAVEL / United States / Northeast / New England (CT, MA, ME, NH, RI, VT)

Classification: LCC F59.B9 .S53 2019| DDC 974.3/17—dc23

Printed in the United States of America

THE BURLINGTON BIKE PATH
AND WATERFRONT PARK

An Environmental Handbook for the Post Auto Era

By Rick Sharp

ONION
RIVER
PRESS

191 Bank Street
Burlington, Vermont 05401

TABLE OF CONTENTS

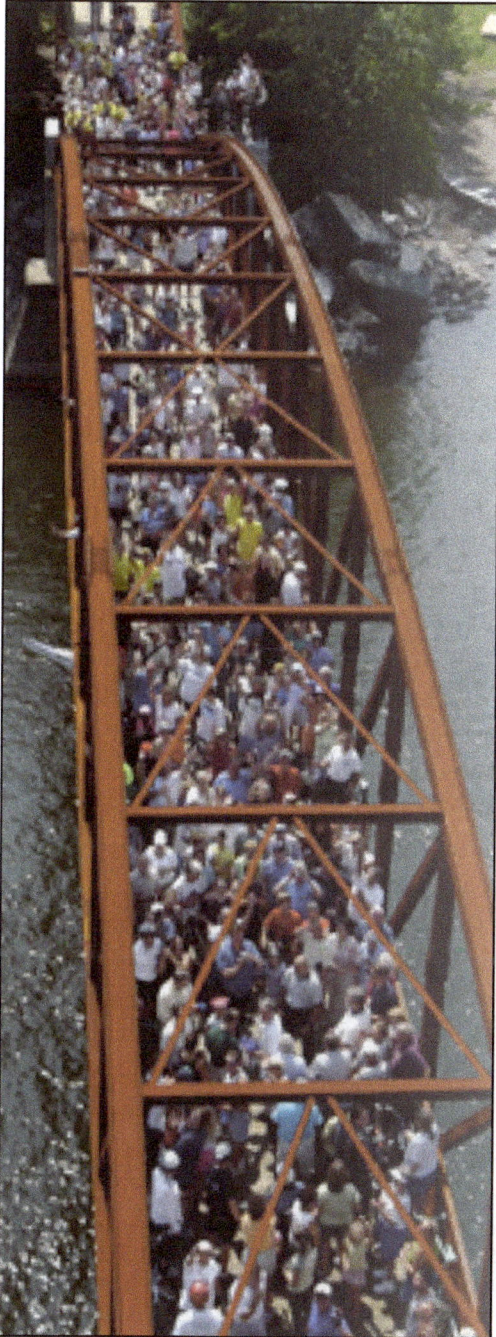

PREFACE

Have you ever pedaled a bicycle along a path on an old railroad bed? Did you ever wonder how that old rail bed became the bike path you enjoy today?

This is the story of the landmark U.S. Supreme Court decision that made that conversion possible - an epic battle to create one of the first urban bike paths in the country from an abandoned railroad bed in Burlington, Vermont. Interestingly, it weaves through the early careers of two of the most prominent Vermont politicians of the late 20th and early 21st century: U.S. Senator Bernie Sanders and former Vermont Governor Howard Dean, both of whom later ran for president of the United States.

This is my personal story of how I became an environmentalist and went on to thwart two proposals for a hotel, luxury condominiums and parking garages on the Burlington waterfront, eventually replacing those proposed developments with the bike path and waterfront park we all enjoy today. Finally, it is a peek into the future, including a different way of life untethered to the automobile, the infrastructure investment necessary to create a walkable/bikeable city, possible alternatives to automobiles such as bicycles, electric bicycles, electric scooters and Segway®PTs, and the sweeping changes coming with autonomous vehicles.

Starting in 1980 with an idea to repurpose an abandoned railroad bed along the shore of Lake Champlain in Burlington, Vermont to create a bike path, a small group of ordinary citizens banded together to pursue that pathway all the way to the U.S. Supreme Court in 1990. The issue was whether the Rails-to-Trails Act, enacted by Congress in 1983, would allow the conversion of this old rail bed to a multiple-use recreation path.

The legal dispute over the Burlington Bike Path was the first case in the nation to reach the U.S. Supreme Court after enactment of the Rails-to-Trails Act, which allows local municipalities or non-profit organizations to acquire rail beds throughout the United States for recreation paths upon abandonment. By the time the Burlington case got to the U.S. Supreme Court in 1990, it had over two hundred *amicus curiae* (friends of the court) legal briefs filed by other bicycle advocacy groups across the country in support of this conversion, including the influential Rails-to-Trails Conservancy.[1]

The U.S. Supreme Court ruled that the Rails-to-Trails Act would in fact allow the conversion of the old railroad right-of-way in Burlington to a recreation path over the objection of adjoining landowners. This decision set the precedent that has allowed the conversion of thousands of miles of old abandoned rail beds across the country to recreation trails.

This is my personal account of how a small group of people spearheaded the then wild-eyed idea of a 7.9-mile recreation path along the shore of Lake Champlain in Burlington, eventually converting this old railroad bed into the #1 Attraction for Burlington on Trip Advisor, the most popular

---

1. *With more than 100,000 members and supporters, the Rails-to-Trails Conservancy is the nation's premiere advocate for the conversion of unused railroad corridors to trails since its inception in 1986, with 2,130 open rail-trails to its credit as of 2019 extending over 24,000 miles. Their ultimate goal is to ensure that 90 percent of Americans have access to such trails within three miles of their homes — "connecting healthier people to healthier places".*

online tourist service provider of our times. The resulting landmark U.S. Supreme Court decision was something we had never anticipated. It always amazes me that the Bike Path in Burlington, Vermont was the test case nationally that established the rule of law that would allow the preservation of rail beds throughout the country forever.

And this is also the story of how the downtown Burlington waterfront was saved from a development project, including a luxury hotel and condominiums, that would have covered the lakeshore with buildings and parking garages instead of the park and bike path we enjoy today. The resulting park along the waterfront is the #2 Attraction for Burlington on Trip Advisor, with ample green space, a boardwalk and bike path along the lake's edge downtown instead.

This is the story of the struggle of a small group of environmentalists to save the land filled into Burlington harbor during the city's lumbering era from a development project vigorously supported by then Mayor Bernie Sanders and 12 out of 13 City Councilors. That struggle eventually resulted in a Vermont Supreme Court decision in 1989 preserving the filled land in Burlington harbor for public uses forever under a concept of law called the Public Trust Doctrine. The resulting park and bike path we enjoy today is truly the crown jewel of the Queen City.

But that isn't the end of the story. The completion of the Burlington Bike Path to the mouth of the Winooski River in 1990 inspired local bicycle enthusiasts to come up with an innovative solution to ferry bicyclists across the river to access the old Causeway built by the railroad out into Lake Champlain in 1901. Over a period of three years these bike advocates ferried over 40,000 people across the river, eventually leading to the construction of a new bridge just for pedestrians and

bicyclists championed by Governor Howard Dean and opened to the public in 2004, in order to allow bicyclists to travel from downtown Burlington all the way out to the Lake Champlain Islands free of automobile traffic.

The Island Line Trail along the old four-mile railroad Causeway out to the Lake Champlain Islands is a world class bicycle trail named to the Rails-to-Trails Hall of Fame in 2010. This trail system, built around an abandoned railroad line, has transformed Burlington into a bicycle mecca, attracting thousands of tourists and millions of dollars of business to the Burlington area each year. It has also vastly improved the quality of life in the Burlington area.

Finally, we will explore the future of the Queen City in the "Post Auto Era."

When Ira Allen first surveyed Burlington Bay in 1772, he believed Burlington would become "a place of consequence." It has indeed lived up to Ira's expectations. Over two centuries later, Burlington has also become a leading place of consequence in the environmental movement. These two landmark decisions and the resulting waterfront park and bicycle trail out to the Champlain Islands they made possible confirm and enhance that status.

I hope this book will inspire the environmentalist in everyone who reads it by setting the example of what can be accomplished with hard work and persistence in a quest for what might at first seem like an impossible dream.

To all you environmentalists I say:
Dream on! Be persistent! And may the
earth be your beneficiary.

TIMELINE OF BIKE PATH, WATERFRONT PARK AND ISLAND LINE

1901 Railroad line from Burlington through the Lake Champlain Islands is built in one year.

1901-1950s Railroad is operated for both freight and passenger service until the nation turns to automobiles.

1964 Rutland Railway declares bankruptcy. State buys rail line.

1964 String of Pearls proposal shelved.

1964 Railroad bed through the Islands is sold to adjoining landowners.

1968 Rendering plant in North End ceases operation. City creates Leddy Park.

1972 Railroad bridge across the Winooski River is removed for scrap.

1973 Rails removed from Winooski River south to rendering plant (now Leddy Park).

1975 Rails south of Leddy Park to North Beach removed.

1978 Triad plan for waterfront development is proposed.

1980 Pomerleau 18 story luxury condominium project is proposed.

1980 Citizens Waterfront Group (CWG) is formed.

1980 Plan for bike path is worked out and publicly proposed.

1980-1981 CWG organizes clearing projects on rail bed. College Street park is created.

1981 (March) Bike path referendum receives 75% support of city voters.

1981 (March) Bernie Sanders elected Mayor of Burlington on platform of "no enclaves for the rich on the Burlington waterfront".

1981 (July) Preseault v. Vermont filed in Chittenden Superior Court

1981 State law on railroad abandonment is changed through CWG efforts.

1982 Pomerleau plan for 18 story towers is withdrawn.

1982 Federal grant money obtained to pave 1.5 miles of bike path north of Starr Farm Road.

1983 Alden plan for luxury hotel and condominiums is announced.

1983 Railbanking provisions of the Rails-to-Trails Act is enacted by Congress.

1984 (March) $2 million bond for bike path proposed by CWG receives support of 55% of voters.

1984 (October) Lawsuit over public trust doctrine is filed in Chittenden Superior Court.

1984 (November) $750,000 bike path bond is approved by 67% of city voters.

1985 (April) Preseault v. Vermont is dismissed by Vermont Supreme Court for lack of jurisdiction.

1985	(April) CWG holds chainsaw party to clear log from rail bed north of Rock Point.
1985	(June) CWG proposal for 80-foot set back receives support of 45% of city voters.
1985	(July) Preseault files lawsuit against ICC in Federal District Court.
1985	(December) Alden plan for waterfront development fails to receive 2/3 necessary for approval.
1986	Alden plan is withdrawn.
1986	(June) Most of Bike Path from the Winooski River into downtown is complete.
1986	(November) Public Trust and a 100-foot setback referendum placed on the ballot by CWG receives 76% support of city voters.
1987	Railroad wins Public Trust case in Chittenden Superior Court. State and city appeal to Vermont Supreme Court.
1987	City voters approve bond funds for floating boathouse at College Street.
1988	Federal District Court rules for ICC in Preseault v. ICC, Preseault appeals to Circuit Court.
1989	Vermont Supreme Court rules that Public Trust Doctrine applies to filled land in Burlington harbor.
1989	Federal Court of Appeals rules for ICC in Preseault v. ICC, Preseault appeals to U.S. Supreme Court.
1990	U.S. Supreme Court confirms rail-banking provisions in Preseault v. ICC landmark case.
1992	Bike Path is complete.
1992	Colchester voters turn down bike path bridge across the Winooski River.
1993-1994	Railroad bed north of Airport Park in Colchester out to the Causeway is cleared for bike path.
1999-2002	Local Motion operates bike ferry carrying over 40,000 bicyclists across the Winooski River.
2001	Governor Howard Dean gets $3.5 million approved for bike bridge across the Winooski River.
2004	(August) Bike bridge across the Winooski River is dedicated.
2005	ECHO aquarium and science center opens on the waterfront.
2010	Causeway to the Lake Champlain Islands is named to the Rails-to-Trails Hall of Fame.
2011	(Spring) High lake levels and strong winds devastate the Causeway trail.
2012	(October) Causeway bike trail is finally reopened with FEMA funds.
2016	$1.5 million world class skate park opens on the waterfront.
2016-2020	$11 million reconstruction of the Burlington Bike path is completed.
2018	$6 million Community Sailing Center opens on the waterfront.
2018	Causeway is again washed out in May but temporarily restored by VTrans by July 4.
2019	Causeway closed for extensive repairs until May 2020. FEMA funds over $1.1 million of repairs.

CHAPTER ONE
Can't get there from here

When I arrived in Burlington, Vermont to study for the bar exam in 1978, the only point of public access to Lake Champlain in the downtown area was a small parcel of land at the foot of Maple Street called Perkins Pier. It was a beautiful sunny day in May. I rolled down Main Street in my 1968 VW Beetle containing all my worldly possessions. The sun reflected off the glimmering surface of the lake, beckoning me to come closer and touch it.

Sailboats were gliding to and fro in the foreground close to the lakeshore. Juniper Island was a green oasis in a blue-green sea that stretched 12 miles across the lake to the Adirondack peaks in upstate New York. "This is where I want to spend the rest of my life," I thought to myself. "Could anything be closer to paradise?"

I was intoxicated by the lake and the mountains and the city on the hill. As an adolescent growing up in Bellows Falls in southern Vermont, a trip to Burlington, where all the college kids attend the University of Vermont, was like traveling to Oz. And the fact that Burlington is the economic engine of the entire state was certainly appealing to me as a budding young attorney.

I had passed up the big salaries of law firms in Washington D.C. or Wall Street to return to Vermont, armed with a law degree from Georgetown Law School. My home town of Bellows Falls was just too small to return to. Many towns in Vermont like Bellows Falls are actually shrinking. When buildings burn down in Bellows Falls, they are replaced by parking lots. The High School now graduates half the students they did when I matriculated.

Burlington, Vermont's Queen City, had a lot more going on with five colleges, the state's strongest economy, and terrific skiing within a short drive. It looked like a much better place to settle down and start a law practice.

The day of my arrival, I wanted to actually touch the water. It was a warm spring day and I decided it would be great to take a dip in the shimmering lake. At the base of Main Street I discovered a large cement building blocking access to the lake. I later learned that this building was the central railroad station for Burlington until passenger service was abandoned in favor of automobiles in the 1950s.

I drove north on Lake Street, past the Pease Grain elevator, as far as I could, only to find derelict railroad yards, piles of scrap metal and huge oil storage tanks surrounded by earthen berms designed to contain an oil spill in the event of an accident. It was an industrial wasteland, like something out of that T.S. Elliot poem or F. Scott Fitzgerald's valley of ashes, in *The Great Gatsby* [2] — not exactly the shining city on the hill of my childhood fantasies.

---

2. *I was introduced to F. Scott Fitzgerald in an American literature class at The University of Southern California. He is my favorite author. His description of the faded, sun drenched, three foot irises of Dr. T. J. Eckleburg, oculist, peering out from a set of enormous eyeglasses on a billboard overlooking a valley of ashes in the Great Gatsby, is one of the most iconic images in American literature — something I never would have been exposed to if I had remained in Bellows Falls instead of getting a first rate education at a great university like USC.*

Aerial photo of the waterfront in 1980 with College Street at center right. Notice the last of the 6 Shell oil storage tanks at lower left. *UVM Special Collections.* Compare the wasteland above with the waterfront today on the cover.

I had never seen the ugly, decrepit side of Burlington in my travels there as an adolescent. We sang in a Glee Club gathering at Memorial Auditorium, or ran cross country at the Country Club. We stayed in a hotel across from City Hall Park called the Huntington and spent our time on Church Street when it was still a street with car traffic. We never ventured down to the lakeshore downtown. No one did.

I proceeded farther north on Lake Street in my search for somewhere to actually touch the water. Lake Street ended at an old hulking electric power plant belching black smoke, and beyond that 5-story industrial relic, a tank farm containing large stainless steel structures surrounded by chain link fences topped with barbed wire stretched to the horizon. I couldn't even get to the water, much less swim in it.

"That's too bad," I thought. "No way to even get to the lake." As the old Vermont saying goes: "Can't get there from here."

I turned south and drove along Battery Street past a row of dilapidated buildings to the newly restored Ice House Restaurant, turning toward the lake once again on King Street. The ferry docks stretched to the water's edge. It was obvious that there was no way to reach the lake there. I turned around and proceeded further south on Battery Street to Maple Street.

At the end of Maple Street there was a marina. A small peninsula penned in by large blocks of granite jutted out into the lake and a small patch of grass beckoned me closer to the lake's edge. I parked the VW and strolled out onto the peninsula. Huge stainless steel tanks with the same earthen berms surrounding them blocked most of the view to the south. More rail yards and a sewage treatment plant were visible between the tanks south of Perkins Pier. The stench of sewage being treated in open vats wafted northward from the plant on a stiff southerly breeze.

The water in the marina was foul with multi-colored oil sheens floating on top, and although I could walk down a boat ramp and touch the water, it was very unappealing for swimming. It was possible to dive into the lake off the granite blocks, but

Burlington Waterfront in 1975. Shell oil storage tanks in center. Moran belching smoke in lower right. Texaco tank at bottom right. *Courtesy of Special Collections and Archives, University of Vermont.*

Texaco oil storage tanks north of Moran Generating Station in the early 1970s. *Courtesy of NNECAPA.*

I thought twice about that after getting a good whiff of the sewage treatment plant close by to the south.

I recalled the last time I smelled that stench, emanating from what appeared to be a swimming hole in the middle of the New Mexico desert outside the stockade of Fort Courage, where they had filmed the old TV Series called *F Troop*.[3] It was a very hot day and we had travelled many miles in the sweltering heat. We had stopped at several water tanks for cattle along the roadside to see if we could take a quick dip to cool off, but they were all dry. Then we happened upon Fort Courage, lured to a restaurant there by the promise of bison burgers. The pond on the side of the road to Fort Courage was tempting indeed. Fortunately for us, we asked the waitress at the restaurant what the swimming was like in the pond on the side of the road lead-

ing to the fort. "That's a cesspool," she giggled. "You don't want to go swimming there."

With that in mind, I decided not to take a dip in Lake Champlain after all. And as it turned out my hunch about the quality of the water along the shore in Burlington harbor proved to be correct. At that time the outflow pipe from the sewage treatment plant ended inside the breakwater just off shore. When it rained hard in the summer, the combined sewer and storm water system in Burlington often spewed untreated sewage directly into the harbor. And, of course, untreated sewage dumped into Burlington harbor is not a new problem. Complaints date back to the 1930s from members of the Lake Champlain Yacht Club of foul smells from "pungent raw sewage dumped into the harbor not far from where teams cut and hauled ice in the winter."[4]

Years later the outflow pipe was extended at great expense out beyond the breakwater to get this discharge farther out into the lake and, inciden-

---

3. *F Troop was a satirical parody and somewhat wacky sitcom about U.S. soldiers and native Americans in the wild west during the 1860s, with a politically incorrect story line, that appeared on ABC TV from 1965 to 1967.*

4. *Vermont Life Magazine (Summer 1985).*

THE BURLINGTON BIKE PATH & WATERFRONT PARK

Oil storage tanks north of sewage treatment plant and east of Perkins Pier in 1978. *Courtesy of Thomas Hudspeth.*

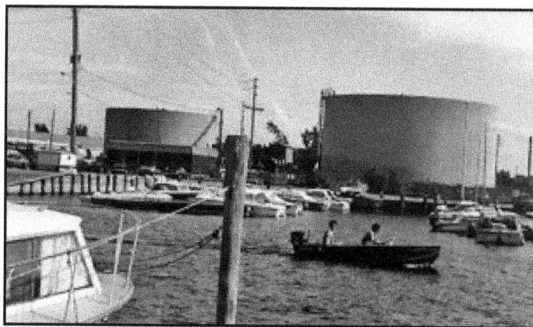

Oil storage tanks east of Perkins Pier in 1978 photo taken from the water. *Courtesy of Thomas Hudspeth.*

tally, closer to the drinking water intake pipes for Burlington. But the problem of untreated sewage discharges directly into the lake when storm water overwhelms the sewage treatment plant persists to this day. After five serious untreated discharges in the summer of 2018, city voters overwhelmingly approved a $30 million dollar bond to fix lingering problems and upgrade the treatment system by a 92% majority in November 2018. This still won't entirely eliminate untreated discharges, but it should reduce them. The city will undoubtedly need to continue to chip away at this persistent problem by diverting as much storm water from the sewage treatment plant as it can in the years ahead.

Needless to say, I was disappointed at not being able to even get to the lake, much less swim in it that day in 1978. I soon discovered that the beaches in Burlington were located far from downtown in the north and south ends of the city. I would have to be content for the time being with watching the sailboats whiz by offshore, propelled by a stiff southern breeze.

The Lake Champlain Yacht Club *(upper left)* in 1935 photo taken from just south of College Street in what can only be described as a junkyard on the waterfront. *Courtesy of Special Collections and Archives, University of Vermont.*

CHAPTER TWO
Howard's Call

During the summer of 1978 I lived on credit cards while I studied for the bar exam and delivered pizzas to pay the bills until I got the results. I also had to do a six-month clerkship to be admitted to the Vermont bar. I landed a job with the Vermont Agency of Environmental Conservation writing a summary of the federal Clean Air Act Amendments of 1977. I spent the next two years negotiating Assurances of Discontinuance to close down more than 40 dumps and deficient landfills around the state.

I got involved in Democratic politics and met a young physician named Howard Dean who had just finished his residency at what is now the UVM Medical Center. He lived just down the street in Burlington from State Senator Esther Sorrell, one of Burlington's leading Democrats at the time, who had taken him under her wing, acting as a mentor for his political interests.

One day in 1980 I got a call from Howard, who was very concerned about a proposal of the Pomerleau Real Estate Agency to build two 18-story luxury condominium towers on land controlled by the railroad on the waterfront just north of College Street. The towers were going to be located 30 feet from the lake's edge. The marina that would accompany the project would service only condominium owners. Howard was concerned that public access to the lake would be lost if a bunch of rich people moved into two luxury condominium towers that close to the lake.

The tallest building in Burlington and the entire state at the time, and still as of this writing, is Decker Tower on St. Paul Street. It is only eleven stories tall. So two eighteen-story towers on the waterfront would have been out of place and unsightly. The proposal generated a lot of opposition for this reason.

Howard mentioned a lecture by UVM Environmental Studies professor, Tom Hudspeth, at the Church Street Center on revitalizing the waterfront. Tom had spent part of a year on sabbatical studying waterfront redevelopment projects across the country. Howard and I attended the lecture. Tom described the Pomerleau proposal as a "mini-Aca-

Artist depiction of the two 18 story condominium towers proposed by the Pomerleau Real Estate Agency in 1980. *Illustration by Kevin Ruelle.*

THE BURLINGTON BIKE PATH & WATERFRONT PARK

pulco." He suggested converting the old abandoned railroad bed through Burlington's New North End into a bike path.

That sounded like a great idea to Howard and me. We spoke to Tom after the lecture. He offered to discuss the idea in more detail over a couple of beers, but Howard doesn't drink. I invited them to my law office nearby on College Street. After my stint with the Agency of Environmental Conservation, I found office space with Mark Kaplan, a Democratic State Legislator, and his dad, Jacob, and I began my law practice downtown. By the end of the evening we had formed the Citizens Waterfront Group (CWG), a public advocacy group for the creation of a multi-use path separated from car traffic all along the Burlington shore from Oakledge Park at the city's southern boundary to the mouth of the Winooski River in the north, as a means of ensuring public access to the lake as these development projects emerged in the early 1980s.

We then held a series of public meetings in my office to thrash out the details of the plan. Surprisingly, one of the most ardent supporters of the plan was a very charming older lady who taught music appreciation at Trinity College by the name of Dorothy Hunt. Dorothy attended the meetings religiously and took notes as the plan unfolded.

The Pomerleau proposal was just the latest in a succession of plans to do something, anything, with Burlington's derelict waterfront. Two years before the Pomerleau plan, a Montreal developer, going by the name of Triad Ltd, put forth a plan for 98 luxury condominiums, offices, shops, a restaurant, and a health club in an odd-looking structure resembling a prison covering almost all the flat land on the waterfront just north of College Street. The Triad plan also included a marina for the exclusive use of condominium owners. But Triad couldn't arrange sufficient financing. The Pomerleau Real Estate Agency took over Triad's option with the railroad.

"For several decades, Burlington's dilapidated waterfront has been a prime candidate for a major facelift," a *Burlington Free Press* reporter noted in August 1978. It appeared inevitable that *something* would be done there, but what? At one point, there were even plans to run an interstate highway through Burlington right along Lake Champlain.

The irresistible temptation of mid-20th century America was to build almost exclusively for the automobile. This plan, as well as another auto dominant master plan appearing on the next page, would have led to automobile dominance of the waterfront for decades. We are indeed fortunate neither plan was adopted. But other important space in the city was turned over to automobiles without a lot of thought. Automobile parking lined the overlook at Battery Park for years until that parking was replaced with grass. An automobile loop was created around the

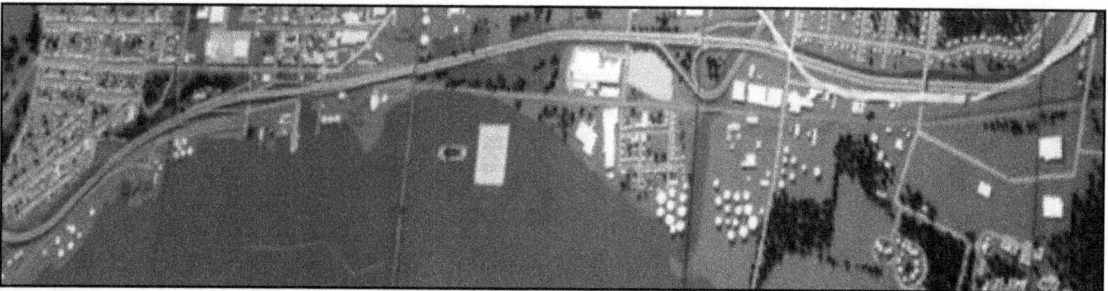

Be glad this never happened! This model, from the 1970s, shows a proposed elevated highway that would have run along the waterfront.

This plan was even worse.

heart of the downtown area during the so-called "urban renewal"[5] misadventure of the 1960s in Burlington. We still live with traffic problems caused by that merry-go-round.

In the 1950s there was a proposal to build a highway along the peaks of the Green Mountains to attract tourists — something similar to the Blue Ridge Parkway in North Carolina. Fortunately, that plan yielded to the Long Trail, reserved exclusively for hiking, instead. Our goal was to put the brakes on the dominance of automobiles in Burlington's urban center by rejecting these auto-centric plans in favor of a pedestrian/bike path along the lake instead.

Late in 1979 the *Burlington Free Press* reported the latest mega-deal for development of the waterfront as follows: "With smiles, handshakes, and congratula-

tions all around the table, waterfront developer Antonio Pomerleau, Central Vermont Railway official John Brudakin, and Mayor Gordon Paquette announced the sale of 12 waterfront acres to Pomerleau for a major condominium and marina project," The article didn't mention the smoke-filled room this deal was hatched in, but we could all just imagine.

Rather than cover the entire waterfront with condominium units, like the Triad proposal, the Pomerleau Agency planned to stack these units in two 18-story towers. Those two towers would have risen to a level close to that of Battery Park, but that would leave more space for landscaping around the towers. We attempted to get Pomerleau to move his buildings back away from the water to make room for the bike path. He agreed to move them back sixty feet from the water's edge — not enough room for a bike path along the water's edge in front of the towers.

Howard and I met with Mayor Gordon Paquette and unveiled our proposal for a bike path along the water's edge from Oakledge Park to the Winooski River. Paquette was not impressed. He was noncommittal, at best. Remember, he was in that smoke-filled room less than a year before greenlighting the Pomerleau plan. We appeared before the City Council and got a similar commitment to nothing.

It all sounded like such a pie-in-the-sky crazy idea. How could such a project be funded? What would it cost? How could the parcels necessary to create the path be assembled? There were no answers. Just a great idea

We knew we had our work cut out for us. We would have to fight off the Pomerleau proposal, popularize the concept of a park containing a bike path along the shore instead, get the public to support it, and in time, get the politicians to take us seriously. We would need to come up with projected costs and ways to fund the project. It would be a labor of love for me.

---

5. *Urban renewal was a misguided 1960s federal program to revitalize city centers across the nation by demolishing dilapidated buildings and slums and replacing them with more modern structures. The federal government supplied the funding that often led to wholesale condemnation of urban centers nationwide through eminent domain proceedings. In Burlington that meant bulldozing over 200 homes in the center city and the heartless displacement of hundreds of residents of "Little Italy," the heart of the Italian community downtown. The street grid downtown was sacrificed to a two-story indoor suburban-style shopping mall that finally failed in 2017. It also resulted in vacant lots in the city center for over 30 years, sucking the life blood out of downtown and resulting in a merry-go-round traffic pattern around the city core, great for automobiles, but very unfriendly to pedestrians and bicycles.*

THE BURLINGTON BIKE PATH & WATERFRONT PARK

CHAPTER THREE
My Environmental Rudder

But let me back track a bit here and tell you more about my life and the unlikely path that brought me to Burlington, Vermont as a committed environmentalist in 1978. I was born on Long Island in New York on September 2, 1952. My mom died when I was still an infant. Ironically, my dad moved my two sisters and I to Levittown when we were very young. (Ironic because Levittown was one of the first suburban mega-developments on Long Island built after the Second World War, relying entirely on automobiles — an evolution in human habitation patterns I severely critique in this book.). My dad moved us all over the place when we were kids. He was a silk screen artist who pursued jobs in Connecticut and then Los Angeles, before we finally landed in Bellows Falls, Vermont, in 1965, when I was in the seventh grade. Somehow my father's silk screen printing business evolved into a furniture factory that employed the whole family. The furniture factory was located on the property my dad bought in Westminster, just outside Bellows Falls.

My dad suffered from a severe case of hardening of the arteries at a fairly young age. He was a chain smoker and that undoubtedly caused or contributed to this condition. He was facing a series of life-threatening surgeries in which he might eventually have to have both legs amputated. A little over a year and a half after we moved to Vermont, he committed suicide with my rifle, leaving a huge hole in my life and a feeling of guilt because he had used my rifle to end his life. He was a gentle man

and a loving father, the only reliable, solid landmark in my life to that point, having moved about so much. Quite suddenly the Rock of Gibraltar of my life had vanished. It is so much easier to understand the mortal decisions he was wrestling with now as an old man in my 60s. It was a lot more difficult to understand at fourteen. I withdrew into a dark cloud for over a year and in a lot of ways became much more introspective.

After my dad died, my stepmother raised us on Social Security benefits. We didn't know it at the time — very few people in Bellows Falls are well off — but we were the poorest of the poor. I worked in the family furniture factory with my stepmother, my sisters and stepbrother. Despite long hours, we barely made a living in the factory. The Social Security checks each month made a big difference. At one point my stepmother cut her thumb severely on a table saw and treated the gash herself because we had no health insurance. For a long time, it looked like I would go to work full time in the factory after graduating from Bellows Falls High School.

Although I did well in high school, gaining the confidence of my peers as well, and leading my class in my senior year as Class President, Editor of the Yearbook and President of the Student Council, less than half of my graduating class went on to college. There was no way I was going to college without a lot of financial assistance. Fortunately, I received a full scholarship to the University of Southern California (USC). That was my one-way ticket out of Bellows Falls and the family furniture factory. None of my siblings or step-siblings went on to college immediately after high school, although my sister, Irene, later earned advanced degrees in psychoanalysis. My mother, my father and my stepmother did not go on to college. I was the first in my family to do so, and of course, that changed the course of my life forever.

After completing my undergraduate education at USC, I received a full scholarship to Georgetown Law School, an education worth several hundred thousand dollars. I felt that I owed a debt to society for the great education bestowed upon me. What could be better than helping to create a bike path along the Burlington shore as repayment for the debt I owed to society?

In a lot of ways, one's path through life seems much easier if that individual has a strong rudder. My environmental rudder was formed in the 1960s and '70s when it was common practice to dump raw sewage and industrial waste into waterways and pungent, dangerous pollutants into the air nationwide.

My earliest recollection of obvious careless man-made environmental degradation was at the age of fourteen during a climb to the top of Fall Mountain across the Connecticut River in New Hampshire from Bellows Falls. I spent a lot of time during the year after my dad's death by myself, exploring the environment and doing a lot of thinking about where my life was going. Looking down at the majestic gorge cut into bedrock by the Connecticut River

Cuyahoga River Fire Nov. 3, 1952. *Courtesy of Cleveland Press Collection at Cleveland State University Library.*

that became Bellows Falls, I saw that there was definitely something wrong. South of the paper mills downtown, the river turned a purple green color. It was common practice at that time to just open the spigots when the vats of dye used to color paper were spent and let the dye turn the entire river a different color. I was disgusted by that sight for days and began to think something had to be done to end that pollution. That was 1967.

Early in 1969 an oil rig in the Santa Barbara channel off the California coast blew out, spewing millions of gallons of crude oil that stretched out into an 800 square mile slick which soon washed up on pristine beaches, killing over 10,000 birds. Then the Cuyahoga River in Cleveland caught fire in June. *Time Magazine* brought national outrage to a boil with an article which described the Cuyahoga as a river that "oozes rather than flows" and in which a person "does not drown but decays." Actually, the 1969 fire was at least the 13th on the river, the first occurring as far back as 1868, but a river catching on fire so soon after the Santa Barbara oil spill was the final domino that set off the environmental tsunami that followed.

Interestingly, the photos *Time* used were actually from the largest Cuyahoga River fire in 1952, the year I was born, which caused over a million dollars in damage to boats, a bridge and riverfront offices. The 1969 river fire was out before photos were taken. So

THE BURLINGTON BIKE PATH & WATERFRONT PARK

Time ran the photos from 1952. The images said it all. Clearly, pollution of our air and waterways was out of control.

People across the nation finally became aware of the environmental degradation around them. This new environmental awareness actually started with Rachel Carson's eye-opening exposé, *Silent Spring*, (1962), revealing the dangers of uncontrolled and indiscriminate applications of pesticides, sometimes for frivolous purposes. Although *Silent Spring* became a best seller on the *New York Times* list, it took time for people to absorb its message. The events of 1969 brought Carson's message to center stage. Even popular music of the time took up the cause as Joni Mitchell pleaded: "I don't care about spots on my apples. Leave me the birds and the bees." *("Big Yellow Taxi," 1970)*. A series of protests sprung up in cities across the country in response to the devastation of urban neighborhoods as the national Interstate Highway system build out continued on mindlessly. People began to demand action to change these careless policies and practices and protect the environment.

By the time I graduated from high school in 1971 and set off to southern California for my undergraduate education, the environmental movement was well under way, with great progress being made in both water and air pollution. Vermont was the first state to ban billboards in landmark legislation enacted in 1968. The first Greenup Day in Vermont was on April 18, 1970. Thousands of volunteers scoured the roadsides throughout the state picking up trash and debris. Greenup Day in the spring each year is now a proud Vermont tradition. The first Earth Day on April 22, 1970, conceived as a teach-in on a few college campuses, brought out 20 million students, housewives, Boy Scouts and a diverse mix of ordinary Americans nationwide for rallies in recognition of the need to take action to protect the environment. Advocacy groups that would shape the environmental movement for decades to come sprang up like spring wildflowers: Friends of the Earth (1969), the National Resources Defense Council (1970) and Greenpeace (1971). The National Environmental Policy Act (NEPA) became the law of the land on January 1, 1970. The Environmental Protection Agency was established by President Richard Nixon later that year. The Clean Air Act also became law in 1970 and the Clean Water Act followed in 1972. Vermont enacted its landmark bottle bill requiring a deposit on all bottles and cans in 1972. And the landmark environmental law case of *Sierra Club v. Morton*[6] was decided in 1972.

In Burlington, in reaction to the Santa Barbara oil spill, the Lake Champlain Committee called for an end to oil transportation in barges on the lake in 1970. The city of Burlington also enacted zoning changes that year that made the 90 oil storage tanks on the waterfront "non-conforming" uses, imposing a 20-year deadline for their removal.

It's amazing that all that progress in the environmental movement in the United States transpired in a few short years just as I was coming of age as a young adult. Of course, at that time I had no idea how monumental these events were or how they would affect my life. I was a wild-eyed 19-year-old trying to avoid the draft while being exposed to a whole new world of ideas at a major university in California. Oil transportation on Lake Champlain was outlawed later in the 1970s. The five metal bollards offshore in Burlington, three off Waterfront Park north of downtown and two off Oakledge Park, are the only remaining vestiges of that era of oil transportation on the lake. *(See maps on pages 78-81.)*

---

6. *Sierra Club v. Morton, 405 U.S. 727 (1972).*

The second major event that set my environmental rudder for life occurred on a trip during spring break in 1972 from USC to the Colorado River. A friend of mine had acquired a small two-man rubber raft to float down the river. River rafting during spring break is a popular activity in southern California, and we soon ran into another larger group in a much larger rubber raft. We tied up with that group and floated down river for miles that afternoon.

One of the guys in the larger raft had eaten half a can of peaches before offering the rest to anyone who wanted it. I accepted and ate the rest of the peaches, leaving me with a can with a jagged top still attached. By that point we had separated from the larger raft and floated off.

Not wanting to risk puncturing the raft, I pitched the peach can with the jagged top into the river. The group in the other raft were horrified. They feverishly paddled back up the river to retrieve the can before it sank. Some unkind words were unleashed in our direction. I felt so embarrassed that I vowed to never allow another piece of trash to slip out of my hand and pollute the environment again.

The final event that directed my environmental rudder into bicycle paths was an undergraduate paper that I wrote on opening up the federal Highway Trust Fund to use for mass transit in my senior year at USC in 1974. I had started with the idea that too many of our resources were devoted to automobile transportation nationwide. I didn't have a car as an undergraduate at USC, not because of environmental awareness, but because I couldn't afford one. I hitchhiked across the country from Vermont to start my freshman year. My primary means of getting about campus was a bicycle. I had picked up an inexpensive second-hand ten speed and rode it everywhere, usually with no hands on the handlebar. Bicycles seemed like a much better way to get about an urban environment.

Living in L.A., I inhaled, on a daily basis, the smog generated by thousands of cars bumper to bumper on the traffic sewers they call freeways. The advantages of using a bicycle for transportation instead of a car became very apparent to me: less air pollution, less use of fossil fuels, more exercise, a healthier lifestyle and less congestion.

But there was no way to accurately measure the amount of resources being devoted to automobiles nationwide. So my professor urged me to narrow my focus to something manageable. I decided to write my paper on the effort to open up the Highway Trust Fund, financed by the national gasoline tax enacted by Congress in the 1950s, to use for mass transit. Up until that time, the fund could only be used for constructing roads for automobiles. Legislators from oil-producing states fiercely opposed using these funds for anything other than roads. Year after year they squashed the movement to open up the Trust and devote funds to mass transit.

In the meantime, the folly of this rigid policy had become apparent to most. In Washington, D.C. itself, whole neighborhoods downtown were in danger of demolition in order to make way for superhighways. People were standing in front of bulldozers, risking their lives to save their communities from the ravages of a very short-sighted national highway policy. Finally, in 1973 the dam broke and the Highway Trust Fund was opened to use for mass transit. My paper traced the movement in Congress that resulted in that legislation.

That sparked my interest in environmental law at Georgetown Law School, starting in 1975. William Rodgers was a leading environmental attorney who was teaching at Georgetown at that time. He had a major influence on the first Clean Water Act in 1972 which established the NPDES or National Pollution Discharge Elimination System that choked off liquid pollution at its "point source" and gradually cleaned the nation's rivers, lakes and streams over the next several decades. He had also written the textbook we used. He was highly respected. Out of his class of over 100 students there would only be five A's. I not only got an A, I shared the best exam paper designation from Rodgers with another student who had read the decision the exam was based on beforehand, while reviewing slip opinions working for the Environmental Protection Agency (EPA). In contrast, I had to figure out the correct answer on the spot. I was very proud to have shared the best exam paper designation from Rodgers with that other student who had read the case beforehand.

I considered my environmental law class to be the most important of all the classes I took at Georgetown — the apex of my academic studies there. That achievement focused my attention on environmentalism. It changed my self image and steered me into my lifelong pursuit of environmental issues. Later, in 1977, I ended up getting a job at EPA myself, my third year at Georgetown, drafting hazardous waste regulations under the Resource Conservation and Recovery Act (RCRA). I was completely committed to environmental law by the time I graduated from Georgetown Law in 1978.

As an environmental law student, I had read many of the opinions of Justice William O. Douglas from the U.S. Supreme Court. He was my hero - the voice of the environment itself. In his dissenting opinion in *Sierra Club v. Morton*, he argued that trees should have standing to bring an action in federal court to enforce environmental laws. It's worth going into some detail about that case here, both because it's one of the foundation blocks of modern environmental law and also because it demonstrates the strange and mysterious ways that environmental law moves forward, haltingly sometimes, but sometimes in lurches and surges.

The Disney Company had developed plans to build an Austrian-style alpine village in the pristine Mineral King Valley in northern California. Disney obtained a permit in 1969 for the project from the U.S. Interior Department over the objections of environmentalists, including the Sierra Club. Images of yodelers strolling about a cheesy Disney replica of an Alpine village with special appearances by Mickey Mouse, Pluto and Donald Duck were just too much for naturalists who had enjoyed this unspoiled remote valley for backwoods hiking and camping for years. And in order to get to the mountain site suitable for downhill skiing, the Disney company would have to build a roadway twenty miles long into this remote wilderness, along with a 66,000-volt powerline. The environmental community in California was aghast.

When Secretary of the Interior Morton refused to reconsider his decision to grant the permit without even holding a hearing on the matter, the Sierra Club brought a lawsuit in Federal District Court. The lower court ruled in favor of Disney, and the Sierra Club appealed that decision to the U.S. Supreme Court.

One of the most important issues to be resolved by the Supreme Court was whether the Sierra Club had standing to bring the suit. "Standing" is the legal right to launch a suit like this in the federal courts. The majority on the Court ruled that the Sierra Club had failed to prove that it was a party that would be sufficiently injured by the Disney company if it proceeded with these plans, thus throwing the Sierra Club out of court. Justice William O. Douglas wrote a stinging dissenting opinion in which he argued that trees themselves should have standing to bring such a suit. Otherwise regulations designed to protect the environment would be rendered meaningless. Here is the eloquent and brilliant heart of Douglas's dissenting opinion:

Inanimate objects are sometimes parties in litigation. A ship has a legal personality, a fiction found useful for maritime purposes. The corporation sole — a creature of ecclesiastical law — is an acceptable adversary and large fortunes ride on its cases. The ordinary corporation is a "person" for purposes of the adjudicatory processes, whether it represents proprietary, spiritual, aesthetic, or charitable causes.

So it should be as respects valleys, alpine meadows, rivers, lakes, estuaries, beaches, ridges, groves of trees, swampland, or even air that feels the destructive pressures of modern technology and modern life. The river, for example, is the living symbol of all the life it sustains or nourishes — fish, aquatic insects, water ouzels, otter, fisher, deer, elk, bear, and all other animals, including man, who are dependent on it or who enjoy it for its sight, its sound, or its life. The river as plaintiff speaks for the ecological unit of life that is part of it. Those people who have a meaningful relation to that body of water — whether it be a fisherman, a canoeist, a zoologist, or a logger — must be able to speak for the values which the river represents and which are threatened with destruction.

The voice of the inanimate object, therefore, should not be stilled. That does not mean that the judiciary takes over the managerial functions from the federal agency. It merely means that before these priceless bits of Americana (such as a valley, an alpine meadow, a river, or a lake) are forever lost or are so transformed as to be reduced to the eventual rubble of our urban environment, the voice of the existing beneficiaries of these environmental wonders should be heard.

Perhaps they will not win. Perhaps the bulldozers of "progress" will plow under all the aesthetic wonders of this beautiful land. That is not the present question. The sole question is, who has standing to be heard?

But before Disney could fire up the bulldozers and begin building the access road, the National Environmental Policy Act (NEPA) caught up with them, just in the nick of time (January 1970). NEPA requires an environmental impact statement to be filed prior to any federal action that might adversely affect the environment. Does that sound like something you just read? The voice of the environment through proper regulation. In the end, the environmental impact statement on the Disney Mineral King Project killed the development, mainly because of the damage that would be caused by the access road and power transmission lines. Disney was forced to abandon the project. The Mineral King Valley is still as pristine today as it was when Disney proposed its alpine village, and over 100 nations around the world have now adopted legislation modeled after NEPA's environmental impact provisions. The voice of Justice Douglas lives on in these echoes of his environmentalism.

I had read *Sierra Club v. Morton* in my environmental law class at Georgetown in 1977 and admired Justice Douglas for his innovative approach to the standing issue. He quickly became the hero of the emerging environmental movement and *Sierra Club v. Morton* became the handbook of the environmental community, setting out the road map for obtaining standing in future environmental lawsuits. One of the most important results of *Sierra Club v. Morton* was the inclusion of citizen suit provisions in amendments to environmental laws in the 1970s that ensured standing for citizen groups determined to enforce new environmental regulations for clean air and water.

In my third year at Georgetown I read an article in the *Washington Post* about Justice Douglas and his role in saving the Chesapeake and Ohio (C&O) Canal in Washington, D.C. from being drained and paved over to create a new freeway into downtown Washington. In 1954, after the entire country had fallen in love with the automobile, Congress approved a plan to drain a portion of the canal, which had fallen into disrepair over the years, and convert it to a freeway. The editors of the *Washington Post* wrote an editorial in support of the plan.

Justice Douglas cherished the quiet serenity of hiking along the canal, portions of which had been surveyed by George Washington over 200 years ago. He felt that the canal's historic significance and the natural environment it preserved in the heart of modern-day Georgetown, and for 185 miles along the Potomac River, made it an environmental treasure worth protection. He publicly challenged the editors of the *Post* to walk the length of the canal with him and reconsider their editorial support.

News of the hike spread, and by the time Douglas started he was accompanied by more than 50 other conservationists. By the time the hike was completed, Justice Douglas had convinced the editors of their error and they withdrew their support. The freeway plan was eventually abandoned and the C&O Canal was saved. In 1971 the C&O Canal was designated a National Historic Monument.

That story demonstrated to me that a single individual can make a big difference in preserving key portions of the natural environment, even in an urban setting. I was truly inspired by Justice Douglas and his environmental leadership both on the Supreme Court and in his personal life as well.

So when Howard Dean called me in 1980 and we learned of Tom Hudspeth's idea of a bike path along the old railroad right-of-way through Burlington's New North End, I jumped at the chance to repay my debt to society as a seedling of Justice William O. Douglas — a seedling that would one day stand as tall as one of his trees in *Sierra Club v. Morton*. I dedicated a substantial portion of my time to the bike path we proposed, with a single-mindedness that soon earned me the label "Mr. Bikepath" around town. Like a kamikaze pilot — and with the same apparent suicidal fervor — I was on a mission. The mission of my life.

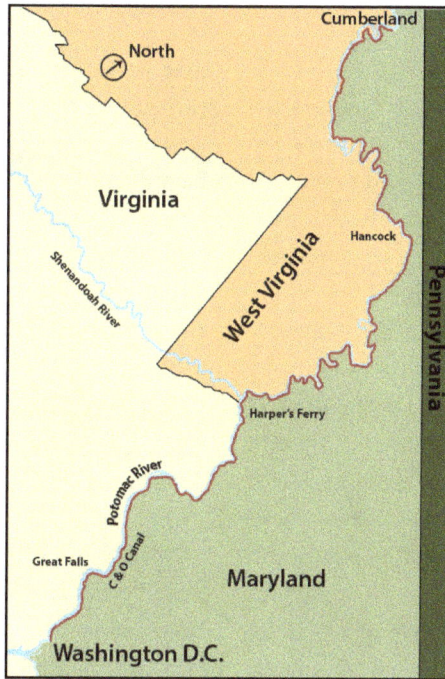

Map by M. Letourneau.

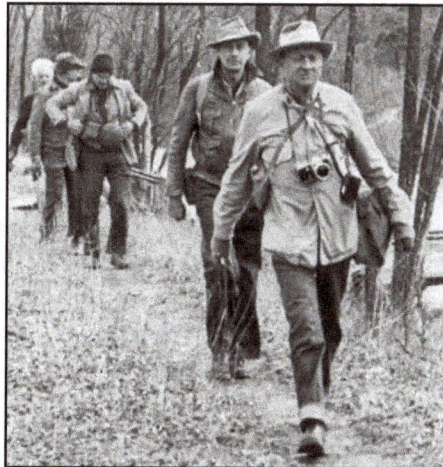

Justice William O. Douglas leads the tour of the C&O Canal. *Courtesy of the National Park Service.*

CHAPTER FOUR
The public campaign begins

Having made no progress at all with the Pomerleaus, Mayor Paquette or the City Council, we decided to take the bike path directly to the people of Burlington. The City Council refused to put the issue on the ballot because they knew our proposal would result in increased taxes, so we set about collecting petition signatures of five percent of city voters to get the bike path on the March 1981 ballot.

We passed out petitions to everyone who would take them. Dorothy Hunt, a white haired lady in her late 70s, compiled lists of her friends and distributed petitions to them. Dorothy was a long-time music professor at Trinity College, where she was sometimes mistaken for a nun because she was unmarried. Soft spoken, gentle, and devoted to the arts, she seemed like an odd advocate for a bike path. Yet despite her and her friends' advanced age, and it being very unlikely any of them would ever use such a path, Dorothy collected hundreds of signatures from friends at elderly housing complexes.

New North End residents Del and Karen Martin, Dan and Peg Mosely and Carol and Bill Parsons joined the petition collection process. We collected signatures at supermarkets and any other place we could approach Burlington voters. After two months of effort, we had collected more than enough signatures to get the advisory item onto the city ballot. And the process of collecting signatures had given us a great opportunity to spread the word about the bike path plan we were proposing.

We set about the task of informing the public of our plan. We called press conferences. We printed a flyer and delivered it to almost 15,000 residences throughout the city. Howard Dean and I took the lead as spokespersons for the CWG. We appeared before groups ranging from school children to the elderly to press our plan.

But our efforts also stirred up the ire of people living along the railroad right-of-way through the New North End. There was a lot of concern that the path would bring a criminal element into the back yards of people living along the old railroad right-of-way. We responded by pointing out that if someone wished to burglarize a house they would arrive on the street in a car or truck to haul the goods away. I always told these people that they would never see their TV going down the bike path balanced on the handlebar of a bicycle. "Criminals don't ride bicycles," I insisted. "Families do."

The Rails-to-Trails Conservancy performed a study in 2012 of the effect of rails-to-trails conversions on crime entitled: "Crime and Perceptions of Safety on Urban Trails". It concluded that "Although trail opponents often express fears that a trail will increase crime and cause safety issues, the actual documented impact of trails is that they reduce criminal activity, increase regular monitoring and improve the public safety of previously disused spaces."[7]

Many of the people who had expressed fear of increased crime due to the bike path later noted their proximity to the bike path after it was built, as an enticement in advertisements to sell their

---

7. *Rails-to-Trails Conservancy.*

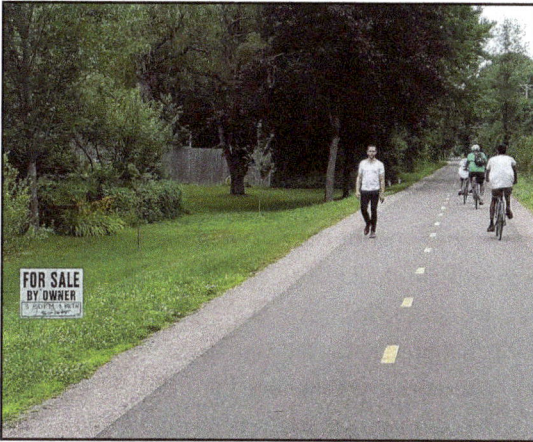

Home for sale sign on the Bike Path. *R. Masters.*

Aerial view of Preseault lakeside condominiums west of the railroad right of way. *A. Patterson.*

homes. Many homeowners along the Bike Path actually built pathways from their homes to connect to the Bike Path, and when they want to sell their homes they put for sale signs on the Bike Path. My bet is that many of those sellers got a premium for their home because it abuts the Bike Path. Local realtors I've spoken to confirm this. A 2012 study by the University of Cincinnati School of Planning found that rail to trail conversions boosted the desirability and value of homes in neighborhoods they connect to by up to $9,000 per home.[8] How times have changed!

In the end, the ballot item received the support of over 75% of city voters. We were elated. But our success at the polls stirred a sleeping giant, or Grinch, by the name of Paul Preseault.

The most important challenge to the creation of the path soon emerged in the form of a lawsuit initiated by Preseault, an adjacent property owner in the New North End. He owned a condominium development called Little Eagle Bay on both sides of the old railroad right-of-way just north of Rock

Point. Four of Preseault's units were waterfront condominiums located on the west side of the old rail line, with drop-dead views of the lake. One of those units was occupied by Clarke Gravel, the senior partner in Gravel, Shea and Wright, one of the largest law firms in Vermont at the time.

Gravel was aware of Vermont case law involving an abandoned railroad right-of-way in Barre in which the Vermont Supreme Court had reaffirmed the old English common law rule that abandoned easements or rights-of-way revert back to adjoining landowners. Since the railroad tracks through the Preseault property had been removed years before, Gravel reasoned that the rail bed had been abandoned. Prompted by our plan to convert the rail bed to a bike path, in July 1981 Gravel filed suit in the Chittenden Superior Court on behalf of Preseault, asking the Court to clear or settle the title to the rail bed, which Gravel claimed had reverted to Preseault and other abutting landowners. The suit named as defendants the state of Vermont, Vermont Railway, Inc. (VTR), and the city of Burlington.

Preseault was almost a caricature of a movie villain you love to hate — at least that's the way

8. *Rails-to-Trails Conservancy.*

many in town came to view him. Extremely litigious, he filed more than a dozen lawsuits against the city and others through the years. He was loud, short, pompous, and self-assured to the point of boorishness. He was a pugnacious bully, at least from my perspective. At any rate, he failed to see the value of a bike path running by the back door of his expensive condominium units, and he planned to kill the bike path idea in the cradle. We immediately realized the desperate situation in which we found ourselves. Without that one little section of the rail bed, less than seventy yards in length, the bike path plan we envisioned would be dead on arrival. There was no way around that link.

Preseault approached other property owners along the old rail bed through the New North End in order to bolster his case and probably to spread the cost out over a larger group of plaintiffs. He convinced the Episcopal Diocese, the Elks and about a dozen other property owners to join the suit with him. The Diocese has extensive holdings on Rock Point that are bisected by the old rail line, putting almost a mile of the railbed at risk. That made winning the lawsuit even more critical because there was no other path across Rock Point or the Elks property. Fortunately, almost all the other property owners along the railroad right-of-way refused to join the suit. Most of them supported the bike path plan.

To make matters worse, Preseault decided to demonstrate control over this section of the rail line by placing barriers in the pathway that people had been using for years to get downtown from their homes in the New North End. First he had a dumpster placed in the path next to his condominiums. Then Preseault moved the dumpster and had a huge log placed across the path. Bicyclists had to lift their bikes over the log to proceed up or down the path past Preseault's property.

The state of Vermont, VTR, and the city answered Preseault's complaint. But the initial legal opinion of Assistant City Attorney, John Leddy, prepared at the request of Alderman Allen Gear, on the likelihood of success in this litigation was only fifty percent. (*See Appendix 1.*) We got Leddy to ask the Superior Court to allow us to remove the log Preseault had placed across the path while the lawsuit proceeded. At a hearing on July 27, 1981, Judge Hilton Dier ruled that the status quo would be maintained throughout the pending suit, and we were thus barred from removing that damn log for nearly four years. But that didn't stop Preseault from blocking the path with steel rebar in November that year, prompting the city to once again ask the court to order him to comply with the "status quo" order and remove the rebar.

In the early 1980s, the railroad still stored rail cars on the tracks north of downtown, all the way to North Beach. North of North Beach the steel rails had been removed, but there were ties in the rail bed that made the path usable by only the heartiest bicyclists who had to bump along over the ties. We organized several tie removal parties during the summers of 1981 and 1982. Del Martin got his Boy Scout troop to assist. We pried up hundreds of ties with crow bars and hauled them away, starting in Leddy Park and heading south.

We also focused our efforts to reclaim the waterfront for public uses on a small peninsula at the foot of College Street once we found out the city owned that parcel. This little spit of land used to flood in the spring each year. In the summer, people would drive their cars out onto this parcel, drink beer and smash the bottles on rocks along the shore. On June 15, 1981 the CWG received permission from the City Council to improve that spit of land into a pocket park. We got excavation crews to bring loads of material they dug up at excavation sites around the city to the foot of College Street to raise the peninsula out of the flood plain. We had over 200 loads of urban excavation material brought to the site. Although over 60 acres of land have been filled into Burlington harbor over the past 200 years, by 1981 it was clearly illegal to fill in the lake without a permit from the Army Corps of Engineers. That spit of land was clearly below the high water mark of the lake. The Corps could have ordered us to remove the fill we brought in or they could have fined us. In the end they just ordered us to stop bringing in any more material. We then got a volunteer to run a backhoe to rearrange cement fragments into makeshift shoreline protection for our new park.

We used some of the railroad ties from Leddy Park to frame a pathway out onto the peninsula, composed of used bricks we recycled from the urban rubble. By the end of the summer we had converted that little peninsula into a very pleasant park. Robert Bensen planted lilacs from his yard and Dorothy Hunt brought the usual lemonade and cookies and donated a locust tree. Merten Lamden also assisted in these efforts. We capped off the urban rubble with top soil and seeded the whole peninsula.

Once the park was completed, we asked the City Council to deed this small park over to the Parks Department. This was the very first piece of that ugly industrial wasteland downtown to be reclaimed for public use. We were very proud of our grassroots effort. A line sketch of the park we created at the foot of College Street became the logo we used on all our newsletters and communications with members thereafter.

Rob Swanson, a freelance photographer who frequently worked for the *Burlington Free Press* in the 1980s, took this photo of the College Street park while it was still under construction. Note the brick walkway framed by railroad ties from Leddy Park and the piles of top soil ready to be spread. Note the old Pease Grain building, the gas station that is now Burlington Bay Market and Cafe and the Follett House prior to its restoration later in 1981.

At about that time a family of beavers showed up on the waterfront downtown and started gnawing down cottonwood trees that grew like weeds along the shoreline. When they had cleared out most of the smaller, tender, younger trees, they started gnawing on a couple of tall cottonwoods located at the foot of College Street. Howard Dean obtained a couple of sections of chain link fence and wrapped them around these large cottonwoods to prevent the beavers from felling them. That did the trick and the trees were saved. They grew in around the chain link fence and those trees dominated the foot of College Street well into the 21st century when they were finally removed by the Parks Department. Tall Cottonwoods become a danger to the public from falling branches in high winds as they age. The Cottonwoods needed to come down.

citizens waterfront group

This is the line sketch of the park we created at the foot of College Street which we used on all our letterhead throughout the 1980s. The Burlington Boathouse was built on a barge permanently anchored off the end of this peninsula in 1987.

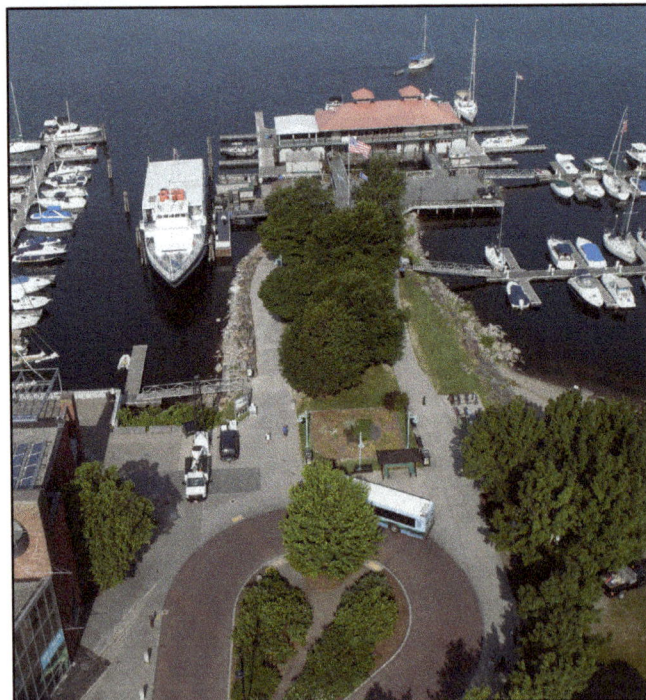

This is a photo of this peninsula in 2019 with the Spirit of Ethan Allen and the Burlington Boathouse in the center. *A. Patterson.*

This peninsula has become the focal point of the Burlington waterfront downtown with the ECHO museum anchoring activities on the south side of a traffic circle where a free bus now shuttles people up College Street to the Church Street Marketplace and UVM. The Burlington Boathouse was built on a barge that was anchored at the end of the peninsula in 1987.

Dock space was created just south of the Boathouse for the Spirit of Ethan Allen cruise boat. Charter sailboats are now available in front of ECHO and the Boathouse, and the marinas on both sides of the peninsula provide needed dock space, a lot of activity and income for the city. This is truly remarkable; more than we ever thought possible when we created that College Street park in 1981.

CHAPTER FIVE
The Emergence of Bernie Sanders

After formulating a plan for a multi-use pathway we had labeled the Burlington Bicycle Path, from Oakledge Park to the mouth of the Winooski River, we all assumed that city officials would quickly take up the cause and commission a study to determine the cost of construction and funding sources available to complete the path. We quickly learned that was not the case, and that we still had a lot of work to do to move the path along.

Howard Dean and I went to see Mayor Gordon Paquette. He made it clear that he did not intend to spend city money on a study to identify a route for the pathway through downtown and the south end, or to determine the cost of such a project. He also made it clear that there were no funds available for paving or construction. We left the meeting with Mayor Paquette scratching our heads. That lead to the petition collection process we initiated to get the bike path referendum on the March 1981 ballot along with the election for mayor and city council.

Howard Dean and I were both life-long Democrats and we assumed that Mayor Paquette, also a Democrat, expected our support. In fact, I think he took it for granted. The race for mayor quickly became very heated, with the emergence of a left-wing candidate running as an independent with the support of a new political party calling themselves the Progressives. That candidate was Bernie Sanders.

Bernie Sanders was an odd-ball long shot candidate for mayor of Burlington in 1981. He is a self-avowed socialist and he isn't a Vermont native. He has a thick Brooklyn accent and unkempt curly hair receding from a bald spot in the middle of his head. He wore horn-rimmed glasses that dominated his face and exaggerated his many expressions. He had hardly worked a day in his life, but he purported to represent the disadvantaged and working poor. He had run for governor and the U.S. Senate as a Liberty Union candidate, but was unable to attract more than 4% of votes cast in those elections. He was not considered a serious challenge to Paquette.

But as the campaign progressed and the debate sharpened, Sanders' fiery rhetorical skills began to receive notice. And Sanders began to voice strong oppo-

Bernie Sanders celebrates his victory by 10 votes in the race for Burlington mayor in 1981. *Rob Swanson. Courtesy of The Burlington Free Press.*

sition to the Pomerleau plan to build two eighteen story luxury condominium towers on the waterfront north of College Street. At one of those debates Sanders loudly proclaimed "No enclaves for the rich on the Burlington waterfront." And in fact, his opposition to the Pomerleau plan became one of the centerpieces of his campaign for mayor.

I followed the campaign with great interest and found myself agreeing with Sanders' position on the waterfront and his strong opposition to the Pomerleau plan. Dick Bove, the owner of a well-known local Italian restaurant, had joined the race for mayor after a tiff with Mayor Paquette. The Progressives characterized the Democrats as the "old guard" and out of touch with the interests of the new emerging younger political scene in the city. Democrats had controlled the mayor's office in Burlington for most of the 20th century. Paquette had been mayor for a dozen years, after thirteen years on the City Council. The Democrats had grown stale over that period of time.

In some respects the fact that Paquette failed to capitalize on a bike path plan put forth by two young upstart Democrats says it all. The bike path ballot item was forward thinking and would have been embraced by an administration open to new ideas. Bernie Sanders was the new idea on the ballot with the bike path. The bike path referendum on the March 1981 ballot probably helped propel Sanders to a whisker of a victory over Paquette.

In the end I too abandoned the old guard Democrats. Paquette hadn't done anything for the bike path. Believing his rhetoric, I thought maybe Bernie Sanders would. I became one of the ten people that put Bernie Sanders over the top to become mayor of the city of Burlington in the March 1981 election. Little did I know what I had unwittingly helped unleash on the city. The Progressives soon turned into the dominant political machine in Burlington,

leaving Democrats like Howard Dean and me on the outside looking in.

Immediately after the election of 1981, Sanders found himself with a full plate of political worries as the Democrats scrambled to contain the Progressive movement and the Sanders Administration. Everyone assumed that Sanders' surprising success would be short-lived and that the Democrats would recapture the mayor's office in the following election. They were badly mistaken.

Howard Dean and I assumed Sanders would be a natural ally in our quest for creating the bike path along the lake based upon his rhetoric during the campaign. After things settled down a bit, we went in to see Sanders. We expected a much more favorable reception than the one we had received from Mayor Paquette, but we were wrong.

Bernie Sanders knew that Howard Dean and I were both Democrats, and he immediately took a defensive posture. He listened to our plan but failed to take up the cause. There would be no funding for a study to create the bike path and no funding for construction. To be fair, Sanders had his hands full battling the Democrats on the City Council. But his interests were largely elsewhere, devoted primarily to his socialist agenda of eat-the-rich and redistribute their wealth to the poor. He put a lot of effort into promoting the arts and building the most powerful political machine the city had ever seen. Howard Dean and I were the enemy. So our plan for the bike path received lip service but very little support.

On October 5, 1982 the CWG published a detailed plan for construction of a bike path from Oakledge Park to the mouth of the Winooski River, calling for a $2 million bond to fund the path if no other funding sources were identified by 1984. (*See Appendix 2 for the text.*). We called a press conference to announce and distrib-

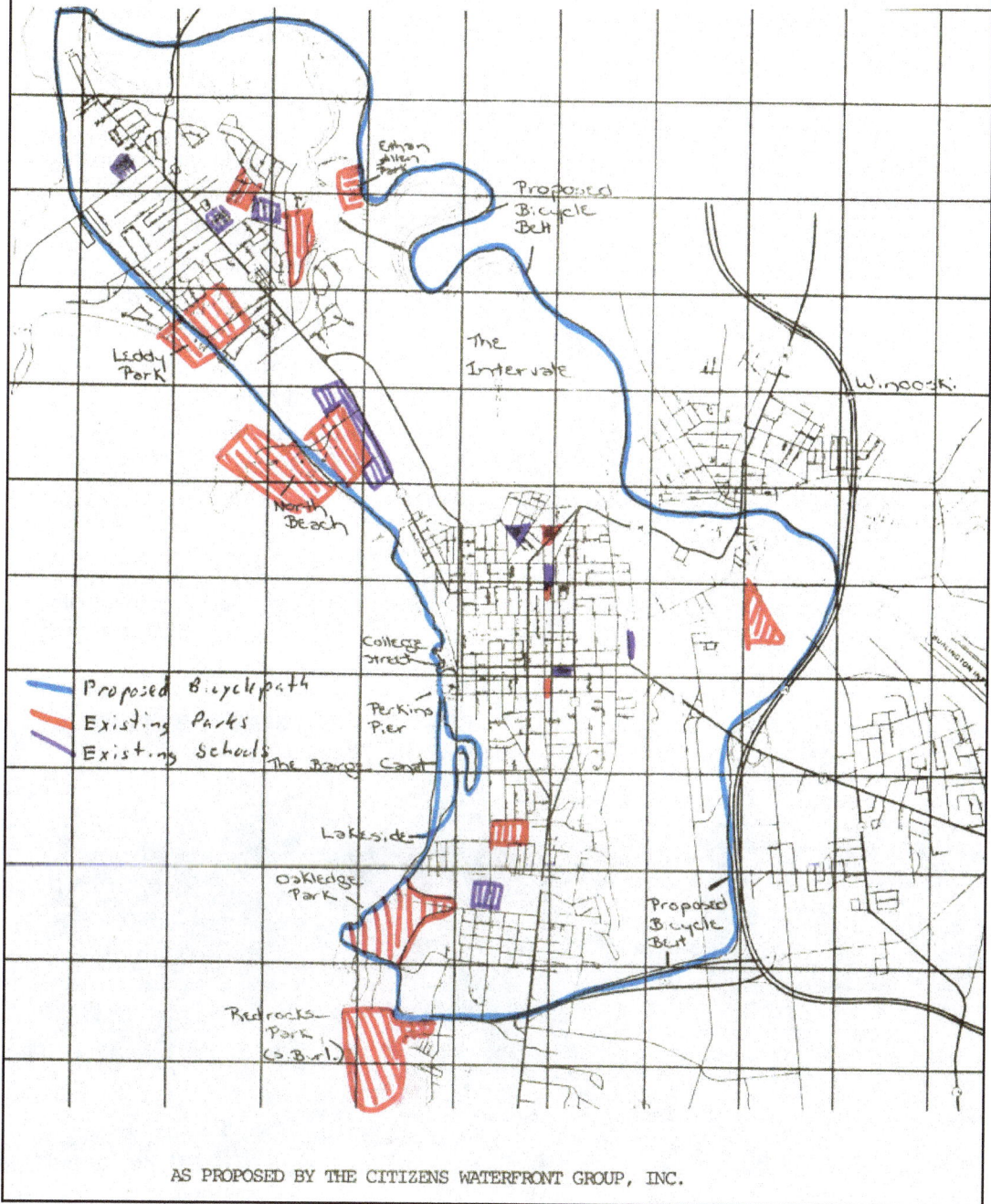

THE BURLINGTON BICYCLEPATH

Ethan Allen Park

Proposed Bicycle Belt

The Intervale

Winooski

Leddy Park

North Beach

College Street

Perkins Pier

Proposed Bicyclepath
Existing Parks
Existing Schools

The Barge Canal

Lakeside

Oakledge Park

Proposed Bicycle Belt

Redrocks Park (S.Brl.)

AS PROPOSED BY THE CITIZENS WATERFRONT GROUP, INC.

The cover of our detailed plan depicts the bike path we proposed. The full plan appears in Appendix 2.

ute our detailed plan and to challenge the Sanders Administration to come up with an alternate source of funds. We used the hand-drawn image of the proposed path connecting parks and schools across the city that appears on the previous page for the cover of the plan.

The Pomerleau plan failed to gain widespread support due to opposition to 18 story towers on the waterfront, and the whole idea of devoting some of the most important land in the city to "an enclave for the rich." I suspect that Pomerleau had the best legal advice money could buy, and that his attorneys were telling him that the railroads' ability to convey their holdings on the waterfront was somewhat in doubt due to a concept of law called the Public Trust Doctrine. (*See Chapter Eight.*) Pomerleau withdrew his plan late in 1982. In December 1982, Bernie Sanders repeated his opposition to any development that would have little public access, as reported in the *Burlington Free Press*. He said that the city must not be put "on the defensive" by the plans of another developer, but he failed to embrace the detailed plan for a bike path and park along the

water's edge that we had proposed two months earlier on October 5.

We had made little progress on the bike path in almost two years, and the whole plan was seriously in doubt due to Preseault's lawsuit over the portion of the railroad right-of-way running by his condominiums.

Howard Dean knew most of the Chittenden County delegation to the legislature on a first name basis. We quickly put him to work on legislation to change railroad abandonment law in Vermont. As the old saying goes, "There's more than one way to skin a cat." The Barre case dividing an abandoned railroad bed between adjoining landowners was based upon old English common law that had evolved over centuries. What to do with an easement after it is abandoned? The English solution was to turn it over to adjoining landowners. U.S. law evolved from English common law. But common law can be changed by statute.

Howard Dean got Representative Polly Rowland to sponsor legislation that would prevent railroad rights-of-way throughout the state from

The four condominium units on the left are the original Preseault units. The two on the right are the units added after our request for rezoning in 1982. *A. Patterson.*

THE BURLINGTON BIKE PATH & WATERFRONT PARK

reverting to adjoining landowners upon abandonment.[9] The state owns most of the abandoned rail beds in Vermont. It acquired these rail beds from the Rutland Railroad when it went bankrupt in 1964. This legislation, enacted in 1981, preserved these rail beds forever, allowing them to be converted to recreation paths until they are needed for other transportation purposes. And of course, that is exactly what the federal Rails-to-Trails Act did nationwide in 1983. We were ahead of our time.

Preseault caught wind of the legislation we had proposed. He had lobbyists amend it so that it wouldn't affect his litigation. It didn't matter in his case, as it turned out, because of federal preemption, but this legislation changed the common law in Vermont on abandoned railroad rights-of-way forever.

Unfortunately, in the early 1960s policy makers in Vermont government didn't understand the importance of preserving these railbeds for recreation and future transportation purposes. Perry Merrill was the State Commissioner of Forests and Parks in the early 1960s. He couldn't see the value in preserving the old railroad bed out through the Lake Champlain Islands. Instead he got the legislature to approve a bill to sell the rail bed through the Islands to adjoining landowners for $50 an acre! Augh! (*See Chapter Fifteen.*)

We also attempted to attack the problem of preserving the railroad right-of-way from a zoning perspective. When we became aware of Preseault's plan to develop more condominium units on the west side of the rail bed south of his four existing units, we attempted to get the railroad right-of-way, and all the property west of it in that area, rezoned as recreation/conservation so that Preseault couldn't build on it.

Howard Dean and I made a request for rezoning to the Planning Commission and the Waterfront Board. They refused our request. In a November 1982 article in the *Vermont Vanguard*, I was quoted as saying, "I can't believe they're doing this," turning down the proposed rezoning. City Attorney John Leddy had advised the Planning Office to hold back on the rezoning because he felt there was a 50-50 chance the city would lose the suit with Preseault.

At one point Bernie Sanders vetoed a resolution from the City Council that referred the request to the Planning Commission because it didn't include the Community Economic Development Office (CEDO), where he would have more control over the bike path. That kind of turf war with the Sanders Administration continued until the bike path was completed. In the end, the Waterfront Board and the Planning Commission both rejected our request for rezoning. Eventually, Preseault built two more condominium units between the rail bed and the lake on the lot we had requested be rezoned.

Developer Rod Whitter also wanted to encroach on the railroad right-of-way when he put forth a plan to develop condominium units at North Shore. We got into the negotiations with the city there and made sure his units were set back from the rail bed through his property, with no units built on the west side of the rail bed.

The only other property along the shore that was eventually lost to the development of lakefront condominiums west of the Bike Path was the development at Harbor Watch south of the Lakeside neighborhood. (*See page 75 for an aerial view of Harbor Watch.*) Otherwise the Bike Path did exactly what we had intended from the start — it provided public access to the lake all along the Burlington shore forever.

---

9. *30 VSA § 711.*

CHAPTER SIX
Federal Railroad Law to the Rescue

Of course, we knew nothing about federal law applicable to abandoned railroad rights-of-way when confronted with the Preseault litigation. In pursuing these types of projects, it is often necessary to get into unusual areas of the law that one would never have had a reason to look into otherwise. We learned that under federal law, in order to start or terminate railroad operations you need a certificate from the Interstate Commerce Commission (ICC). As things turned out, federal jurisdiction over railroads was critical to protecting the rail corridor through the New North End, as it has been across the country.

So bear with me as I go through some fairly arcane background that proved to be all-important for our case. In 1964, in order to preserve rail freight service to western Vermont, the state of Vermont purchased the line of the strikebound Rutland Railway Corporation from Bennington to the Lake Champlain Islands and leased a portion of that line to a new railroad operator, Vermont Railway, Inc. (VTR). The state and VTR requested and obtained ICC approval for the new operation. In Burlington, VTR's ICC-authorized operations extended into the New North End, to provide rail freight service to the Burlington Rendering Company, a slaughterhouse located on a large tract of land (now the site of Leddy Park) between Lake Champlain and the Ethan Allen Shopping Center. In 1968, the rendering company relocated (undoubtedly a relief to nearby homeowners), ending the need for rail freight service in the New North End, although VTR continued to use the tracks for rail car storage.

In the early 1970s, in preparation for the 1976 Bicentennial, the state of Vermont began planning the Vermont Bicentennial Steam Expedition, which consisted of a steam-powered train operating over the old Rutland Railway trackage south of Burlington. This section of track had not seen passenger train operations since the early 1950s. Not surprisingly, safety was a prime concern. When track inspections detected serious flaws in some of the rails south of Burlington, the state began an urgent search for replacement rails. The dormant line in the New North End contained exactly the type of rails needed, so the state authorized VTR to take up the rails north of North Beach and use them for the urgently needed track repairs. But the state and VTR neglected to obtain ICC approval for removing the rails, which meant that the line legally remained part of the national rail network. So even though the rails had been removed, the rail line past the Preseault property was deemed to still be under federal jurisdiction of the ICC; it had never been formally abandoned. Federal law preempts state law. It took quite a bit of archival legal digging to unearth all of these facts. But suddenly the great Clarke Gravel didn't seem so invincible any more.

And even better for our cause, we learned that a recently enacted 1983 federal law on railroad abandonment encourages the conversion of old railroad beds to recreation paths. At the apex of the railroad building era in 1916 there were more than 270,000 miles of railroad tracks criss-crossing the nation.[10] Then Americans fell in love with the automobile and built roadways that eventually allowed the trucking industry to eclipse the rail system as the primary means of transporting goods nationwide. The slow decline of the railroads began.

By the 1960s many railroads, including those in Vermont, curtailed or abandoned operations. In the early 1970s major railroad companies across the country were facing the same fate. Rail lines were increasingly abandoned. According to the Rails-to-Trails Conservancy "our nation's rail corridor system, painstakingly created over several generations, was at risk of becoming irreparably fragmented."[11]

We were the first wave of what later became a national movement. As railroad lines were abandoned across the country, constituents begged local politicians to help convert them to trails instead of overgrown eyesores that attracted homeless encampments. Recognizing that once these rail corridors are lost, they would be almost impossible to reassemble at a later date (as in after the gasoline runs out and we need to go back to rail transportation at some point in the future), in 1983 Congress enacted the so-called "Rails-to-Trails Act."[12] This landmark legislation calls for "banking" these old railbeds and allowing municipalities or nonprofit groups to acquire them upon disuse for rail service and convert them to recreational uses which, of course, preserves them for future transportation uses if necessary. Just in the nick of time for us.

That seemed to change the entire complexion of the Preseault litigation. Suddenly the chance of success seemed much better than John Leddy's initial assessment of 50-50. Preseault initiated negotiations with the city and the state. He offered 10 feet out of a right-of-way that was 70 to 120 feet wide for the bike path. We were sure Preseault would build more lakeside condominiums on 110 feet of the 120 foot wide right-of-way if we compromised at ten feet. Our group was adamantly opposed to this offer after learning that the Rails-to-Trails Act would allow the conversion of this rail bed to a recreation trail. Alderman Allen Gear led the negotiations for the city. He directed John Leddy to counteroffer with 10 feet for the pathway with 10 feet on either side which could not be built upon. Howard Dean pleaded with the Diocese to withdraw their opposition, but they refused. Preseault turned down the additional restrictions, and the Elks Club finally pulled the plug on the negotiations, refusing to grant the city any easement for a bike path at all.

Robert Devost was a strong supporter of the bike path. He lived in the New North End at that time. He published a small neighborhood weekly newspaper called *That Paper*, including a string of articles about the progress of the lawsuit, or the lack thereof, and the negotiations as they dragged on, which Howard Dean and I fed him. I have kept some of those editions, so I will be quoting from them periodically.

At the start of the lawsuit, Gravel had requested a gag order preventing the parties from discussing the case in the press. I had filed a Motion to Intervene as a party in the litigation on behalf of the CWG. Judge Hilton Dier ruled that the CWG lacked standing to join the suit and denied us party status. The gag order was clearly a prior restraint of free speech prohibited by the First Amendment to the Constitution, but it didn't apply to me since I was not representing a party to the litigation, so I didn't bother to complain.

---

10. *Rails-to-Trails Conversions: A Review of Legal Issues (2006) by Andrea C. Ferster, Legal Counsel to the Rails-to-Trails Conservancy.*

11. *Id.*

12. *16 U.S.C. § 1247 (d).*

I sat in on all the hearings and John Leddy insisted that the hearings be held in open court so I could hear the proceedings. It is common for judges to hold hearings in their chambers with only the parties' attorneys, and that's exactly what Dier did at first. Gravel and Dier were old friends. I got the impression they socialized with each other on the golf course or elsewhere outside of the courtroom. It was an old boys' club. Leddy was a young attorney about my age. I think Gravel thought he was going to roll right over him in this litigation. John Leddy is the son of former U.S. District Judge, City Alderman and Parks Commissioner, Bernard J. Leddy, the namesake of Leddy Park. Though well-educated and competent, he knew nothing about railroad abandonment law at the start. He was a quick study and didn't let Gravel or Dier push him around. He insisted that Dier hold the hearings in the open courtroom.

I kept feeding my account of the hearings to CWG members through newsletters. Devost published updates in *That Paper*. As a party to the litigation, Preseault was prohibited from responding. We tarred and feathered him in the press and turned him into the Grinch that was attempting to kill the bike path in its cradle. I must admit we all enjoyed exposing Preseault for the selfish, money grubbing developer that he was.

Gravel finally asked Dier to lift the gag order so his client could participate in the public debate. Dier told Gravel from the bench, "You'd have been better off to have kept him in [the litigation]." Gravel reluctantly agreed, "That would have shut him up," he observed, referring to me of course. Gravel then wrote a letter to *That Paper* outlining Preseault's claim to the rail bed, which was published late in 1982. It went over like a lead balloon.

By that point Preseault's reputation in the community was substantially tarnished. He was an airline pilot, a profession that requires a level head and a steady hand, but he was a real hot head. He ran his rental condominium units at Little Eagle Bay just north of Rock Point like a warden runs a prison, with rigid rules that often led to disputes with tenants and litigation. Over a period in excess of thirty years he pursued legal process against the city over this railroad right-of-way through eleven reported decisions.

I took a case against him for assaulting one of his tenants who just happened to be a six-foot-three-inch-tall Burlington Police Officer. Preseault blind sided my client with a closed fist when he went to open the door to his rental unit to retrieve his possessions as he was moving out. Preseault was short and balding. My client could have pulverized him. But he stayed cool. The jury ended up awarding my client a $41,000 punitive judgment against Preseault, one thousand for damage to furniture caused by Preseault's men and $40,000 for being a mean S.O.B. of a landlord.

On August 11, 1983, Judge John Martin, who had taken over the case from Judge Dier, dismissed Preseault's lawsuit in the Chittenden County Superior Court, ruling that under federal law only the ICC had jurisdiction to decide whether the rail line through the New North End should be abandoned. Preseault appealed to the Vermont Supreme Court, but the handwriting was on the wall. The Burlington Bike Path was like a snowball rolling downhill. The idea kept picking up public support and momentum in its inevitable evolution into the number one attraction for the city on Trip Advisor.

CHAPTER SEVEN
The Alden Plan

With the Pomerleau plan out of the way, by 1983 a new plan for waterfront development downtown emerged. Paul Flinn was the chief spokesperson for the Alden Group, as he had been for Triad Ltd. He put forth what would become the most dangerous of the three plans proposed for redevelopment of the downtown Burlington waterfront in the late 1970s and early 1980s.

Flinn and his colleagues hired the renowned architectural firm of Benjamin Thompson to draft his plan. Thompson was widely acclaimed for his previous waterfront development projects in Baltimore Harbor, South Street Seaport in New York City and Faneuil Hall in Boston. All three of those projects were mega-developments with a waterfront boardwalk and swanky buildings crowding up to the water's edge in those major cities on the east coast of the United States. All three projects turned into stunning success stories by converting ugly industrial junkyards on the waterfronts of those cities into thriving tourist attractions. By the time Thompson turned his attention to the Burlington waterfront he had achieved almost godlike status.

The Alden plan made a big splash at its debut in Contois Auditorium at City Hall early in 1983. The hall was packed to the rafters with local citizens, most of whom listened carefully with open minds. I was one of them.

The initial plan included the usual bevy of luxury condominiums crowding up to the shoreline, abundant retail and office space, two large parking garages and a seven-story 200 room hotel that they euphemistically called an "Inn" jutting out into the lake just north of College Street, with a marina offshore for those with the means to own a condominium or stay at the posh Inn.

There was very little public space in front of most of these structures and none at all in front of the hotel. But the initial plan also included a seven-acre park to be filled into the lake at the foot of College Street that would double as a breakwater for the marina. This plan left no space for the bike path we had proposed and nothing for the waterfront park we had envisioned. Instead the bike path was depicted as a glorified sidewalk on the west side of Lake Street behind the dumpsters for the hotel and condominiums in what was labeled a "transportation corridor." I was somewhat dismayed right from the start, but I bit my lip and tried to keep an open mind in an attempt to influence the project as it evolved. A copy of a concept plan labeling elements of the project appears on the next page.

Public comments on the new plan for waterfront development ranged from strong support from the business community, including the Lake Champlain Regional Chamber of Commerce, the Burlington Business Association and most business owners in town, to outrage from the left. The Green party was strongly opposed and quickly expressed a preference for more open space. Bea Bookchin was perhaps the most outspoken of the far left who wanted a more environmentally friendly waterfront plan. Initially Mayor Sanders concentrated his criticism on affordable housing, the arts and public space.

The Alden plan was the opposite of what the Citizens Waterfront Group had proposed. We had previously called for ample park space with a bicycle path meandering along the water's edge in front of any development on the waterfront. I met with Paul Flinn early in the public review process and pleaded with him to set his buildings back at least 80 feet from the lake in order to leave space for a bike path with trees and green grass for the public to enjoy.

I showed Flinn the hand drawn maps reproduced on Page 40. It's amazing how close these drawings are to how the waterfront eventually came out. I argued that the Alden development would actually be more appealing with park space along the lake's edge and a public way that would invite people into his development project. I noted that the views from the hotel and condominiums would be preserved forever because no other building would be built in front of his project. Flinn listened politely but refused to give an inch.

Why should he? By that point he had the leaders of all three political parties behind his project. Everyone in the city was sick and tired of the junkyard the railroads had maintained on the Burlington waterfront for almost 100 years. They were eager for change — overeager as far as I was concerned. Flinn viewed me as an environmental gadfly who could be easily dispensed with. He underestimated me.

I followed up my meeting with Flinn with a detailed letter to Charles Shea, also a partner in Gravel, Shea and Wright, the lead attorney for Alden, on April 1, 1985, explaining our vision for a park and bike path along the lake in front of the Alden development. As

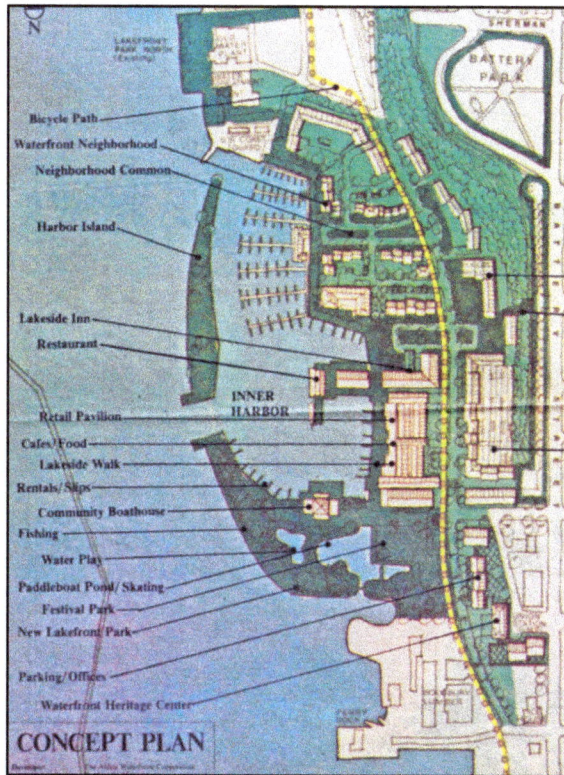

CONCEPT PLAN

a compromise, I suggested an 80-foot set back from the water's edge and even suggested that the issue be placed on the next city ballot. I offered to drop my opposition to the Alden plan in the Chittenden Superior Court and support the plan publicly in exchange for an 80-foot setback. (*See Appendix 3.*) Shea rejected my offer, of course.

After two failed attempts to redevelop the waterfront, the Triad proposal in 1978 and the Pomerleau plan in 1980, most people seemed to think that Alden was the last chance the city would

get to redevelop the waterfront into a more attractive, inviting destination. I wasn't convinced this was the right development for Burlington.

In order to pick up the Mayor's support and appease the Progressives, Flinn initially agreed to add affordable housing, a public boathouse and an arts center to his plan. Mayor Sanders began calling the Alden project a "people oriented" waterfront. "Rich people oriented," I thought. What ever happened to "no enclaves for the rich on the Burlington waterfront"? I knew our plan was in trouble at that point.

Unlike Howard Dean and I, Tom Hudspeth is a Progressive and supported Mayor Sanders. He favored the Alden plan. Then in a letter to Paul Flinn dated July 17, 1985, even Howard Dean came out in support of Alden. Howard is a politician, after all. And he correctly read the will of the majority of city voters on Alden.

As you know, I've spent a tremendous amount of time on the various issues surrounding the development of the Burlington waterfront. While I have not always agreed with the Alden Corporation, I believe the Alden Corporation has presented by far the best plan, and in fact a plan which is so good that it is unlikely to be duplicated. It is my view that if the Alden Corporation does not develop the waterfront,

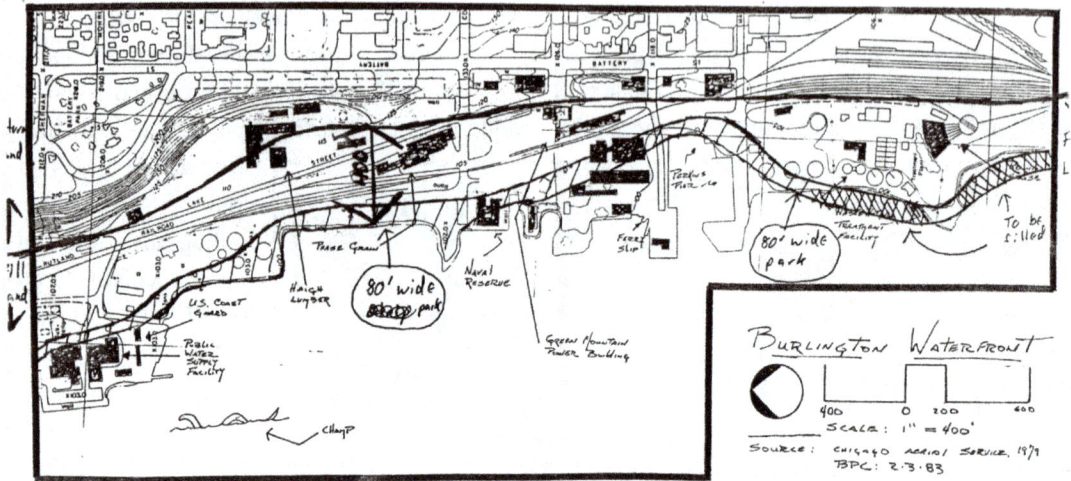

Filled land owned by the state is all existing land *west* (down on this map) of the dark black line

Natural Land

BURLINGTON WATERFRONT

SCALE: 1" = 400'

SOURCE: CHICAGO AERIAL SERVICE, 1979
BPC: 2·3·83

it will lie undeveloped for some years, and then will give way to a far less people oriented waterfront. (See Appendix 4.)

That left me all alone out on a limb with the Greens and a few far left environmentalists in opposition to the Alden plan. It was beginning to look like a hopeless cause.

I began to think more carefully about where the water's edge met the land. In order to prevent flooding of the new development at the high-water point in the spring when the lake sometimes rises to as high as 103 feet above sea level, it would be necessary to import a lot of fill and literally raise the

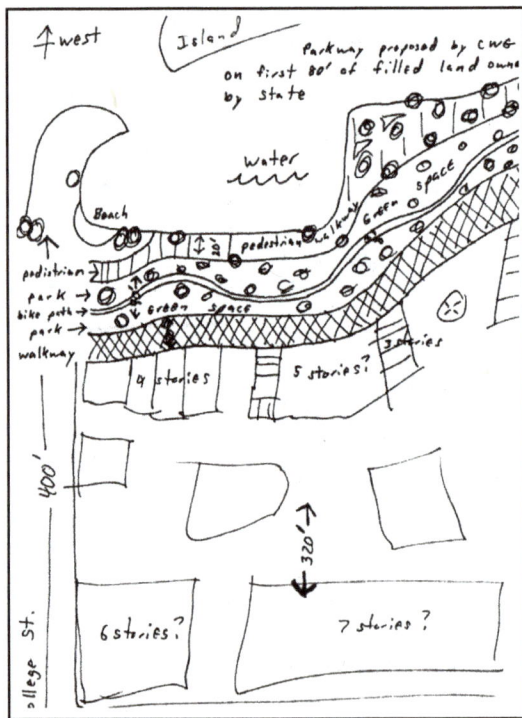

The hand drawn maps of the waterfront appearing on this page are maps I showed to Paul Flinn, offering to settle for an 80 foot wide park along the lake's edge in front of the hotel and condominiums.

ground floor of all buildings to be constructed out of the flood plain. The surface of Lake Champlain routinely varies between a low point of about 92.5 feet above sea level late in August to a high of 102 feet in the spring.[13]

---

13. *In 2011 the lake exceeded its previous all-time high and actually got to 103.2 feet above sea level, flooding the Maritime Museum building at Perkins Pier and the ferry dock property with three or four feet of water.*

THE BURLINGTON BIKE PATH & WATERFRONT PARK

It quickly became apparent to me that the key question would be: where does private property end and where do public waters of Lake Champlain begin? My free legal education was about to pay an unexpected dividend. University of Vermont professors Tom Hudspeth and Jean Flack assigned a healthy group of eager college interns to work with me from their environmental studies classes. I taught legal research and writing to first year students at Georgetown as a law fellow during my third year there in 1977. My UVM students were as good as first year law students at Georgetown.

Together we began a search of case law defining where private property ends and the public right to enjoy the waters of Lake Champlain begins. It took some time and the students went down some rabbit holes, especially at first, but in the end they hit pay dirt. Jen O'Hara and Shep Johnson were particularly helpful in this effort. They compiled a memorandum of relevant case law that pointed the way to the litigation the city and the state eventually pursued all the way to the Vermont Supreme Court. They eventually uncovered a series of cases involving the conveyance of building lots along the lake's edge in Colchester for housing developments: *State of Vermont vs. L. John Cain.*[14] This case clearly established that the state of Vermont holds title to all lands under Lake Champlain below the "mean low water mark" of the lake (about 94 feet above sea level). Private property owners along the lake own the lakeshore down to "mean low water." However, under the Vermont Constitution and subsequent case law, the public has the right to boat over this private property up to the "mean high water mark."

According to this case law, the property developer in the Colchester cases owned the bed of the lake exposed during low water in the summer, but he could not just fill in the lake to bring his property up above the flood plain in the spring because that would interfere with the public right to boat and fish up to mean high water protected by the Vermont Constitution. Very interesting.

We also uncovered a case called *Hazen vs. Perkins.*[15] That case involved a dam that regulated the level of Lake Morey. The private owner of the dam in that case ran a saw mill on the lake for over 120 years generating power for the mill by adding or subtracting boards to a sluiceway in the dam as he saw fit. This raised and lowered the level of Lake Morey by several inches. Property owners along the lake shore complained and the resulting case wound up in the Vermont Supreme Court in 1918. The Supreme Court ruled that "The bed or soil of such boatable lakes in this State is held by the people in their character as sovereigns in trust for public uses for which they are adapted." Thus, lakebeds are to be used solely for the benefit of the public. The Court also held that the Vermont legislature "cannot grant to private persons for private purposes the right to control the height of the water level on boatable lakes…for such a grant would be inconsistent with the exercise of such a trust."

And best of all, the Vermont Supreme Court cited a U.S. Supreme Court case out of Chicago in 1892 called *Illinois Central Railroad vs. Illinois,*[16] which turned out to be an incredibly important ruling for our purposes.

---

14. *State of Vermont v. L. John Cain, 126 Vt. 463 (1967).*

15. *Hazen v. Perkins, 92 Vt. 414 (1918).*
16. *Illinois Central Railroad v. Illinois, 146 U.S. 387 (1892).*

CHAPTER EIGHT

The Public Trust Doctrine

Illinois Central Railroad v. Illinois is the landmark decision of the U.S. Supreme Court regarding land filled into a lake in the United States. It relies heavily on old English common law that proclaimed tidal marshes (referred to as moors in England) to belong to the monarchy. But it also imposes on the monarchy a duty to preserve such tidal lands for the public good. By analogy, the U.S. Supreme Court held that the bed of Lake Michigan belongs to the people of Illinois (as opposed to the monarchy) and must be preserved and devoted to public uses under what the Court called "the Public Trust Doctrine".

According to the findings in the Illinois case, the Illinois legislature conveyed the title to lands filled into Lake Michigan in Chicago to the Illinois Central Railroad in 1873. The railroads were very powerful in the latter half of the 19th century. They got similar legislation enacted in a lot of states in the early 1870s, including Vermont.

The great Chicago fire of 1871 resulted in a large volume of demolition material that had to be disposed of somewhere. Most of that material was dumped into the lake east of Michigan Avenue. The Illinois Central Railroad took possession of filled land and began conveying title to filled land to third parties at a considerable profit. By 1875 the composition of the Illinois legislature changed drastically and the new legislature began to view the action of the earlier legislative body, and the undue influence of the railroad, as suspect. They repealed the 1873 legislation granting the railroad title to land filled into Lake Michigan and the railroad took them to court to challenge that revocation.

In 1892 that case reached the U.S. Supreme Court. The Court ruled that the Illinois legislature did not have the power to convey title to land filled into Lake Michigan because the bed of the lake belongs to all the people of the state of Illinois and must be used for public purposes under the Public Trust Doctrine. And that's why the Chicago waterfront is now public park space with bicycle paths and public uses and will always remain so.

We immediately understood the applicability of the *Illinois* case to the Burlington waterfront. If the Public Trust Doctrine applies to the bed of Lake Michigan, it would similarly apply to the land filled into Lake Champlain during the lumbering process that preceded the arrival of the railroads to the Burlington waterfront in the latter half of the 19th century. Further research revealed that the Vermont legislature had enacted legislation very similar to the Illinois law of 1873 the following year, in 1874.[17] But the Vermont law had never been reversed or challenged! Alden would be the test case.

I quickly assigned the UVM interns the task of determining how much of the land along the Burlington shoreline was filled into the lake. They uncovered some great maps dating back to the early part of the 19th century that revealed extensive filling of the lake.

---

17. *27 VSA § 1003.*

The oldest map of the Burlington shore downtown uncovered by the interns was an 1810 map drawn by John Johnson *(reproduced below)* depicting a smooth shoreline with no wharves, docks or filling.

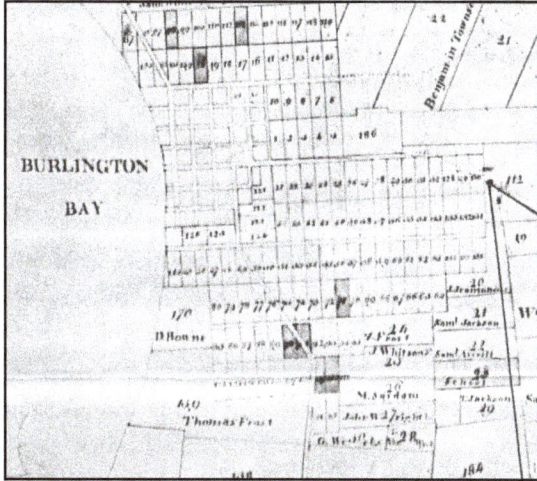

The 1830 map of Burlington drawn by Ammi B. Young *(below)* depicts a single wharf (the Salt Dock) at the end of Wharf Street (now Maple). Battery Street was called Water Street at that time. Main Street was called Fayette Street and King Street was called Pine Street.

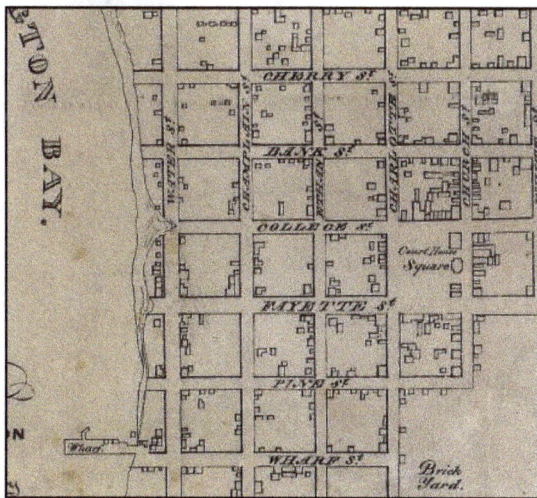

The 1853 map the interns uncovered *(below)* depicts four wharves: one north of Main Street, one at Main Street, Nyes Wharf at King Street and South Wharf at South Street (now Maple). Extensive filling has occurred between Main Street and

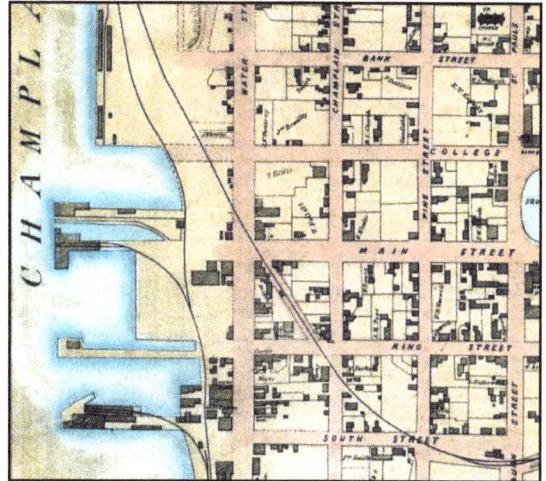

King Street and north of College Street.

By the time Burlington was incorporated as a city in 1865, Water Street had been renamed Battery Street, Fayette Street was renamed Main Street, Pine Street became King Street and South Street was renamed Maple Street. Most of the remaining filling in Burlington harbor occurred during Burlington's days as the third largest lumber port in the world in the 1870s when all the trimmings off the logs and sawdust were poured into the lake to create more flat space to stack lumber during Vermont's long winters when the lake freezes over.

According to City Assessor Jim Howley approximately 60 acres have been filled into Burlington harbor over the past 200 years.

The Burlington area was uninhabitable during the Revolutionary War prior to 1783. British gunboats dominated the lake during that period and would burn down any structures erected by the rebel colonists before the battle of Yorktown in 1782. Shortly after the treaty with Britain established the border with Canada 40 miles to the north, the hamlet of Burlington was established on the east shore of Lake Champlain. Burlington grew up on commerce on the lake in the latter part of the 18th century and the early part of the 19th century.

Of course there were few roads in Vermont at that time. And no railroads. The only way to move goods in or out of Burlington was by water. Lake Champlain was the superhighway of that time period. So when the Champlain Canal opened in 1823, connecting Lake Champlain to the Hudson River, that was like extending that water superhighway all the way to New York City. After that date it was common to load goods onto ships in New York harbor and unload them on the Burlington waterfront, greatly reducing the cost of manufactured goods for residents of northern Vermont.

The Erie Canal opened in 1825, extending that water superhighway all the way to the Great Lakes. Burlington became the leading port on Lake Champlain and quickly grew due to commerce on the lake.

The first dock in Burlington, called the Salt Dock, was located where Perkins Pier is today.

The Stone Store at the corner of Maple and Battery Streets today is one of the oldest surviving buildings dating back to that period. It was built by Timothy Follett in 1827 to store goods unloaded at the Salt Dock. It was the Walmart of the early part of the 19th century for Burlington.

Follett is a very interesting character who played a key role in Burlington's development, leaving behind not only the Stone Store but also perhaps the most important architectural gem in the city today, known as the Follett House, on College Street. It's worth taking a moment to introduce the man as a major character in the early history of Burlington.

Timothy Follett was born in 1793 in Bennington. His mother moved him to Burlington to study at UVM. He entered the University at age 13. He graduated at 17. He was admitted to the Vermont bar at age 21. He was Chittenden County State's Attorney by the time he was 26 and appointed as a Superior Court Judge by the time he was 30 — quite a meteoric rise through the legal profession.

But Follett was an opportunist at heart. He quickly realized the opportunity to become rich on commerce on Lake Champlain in the early part of

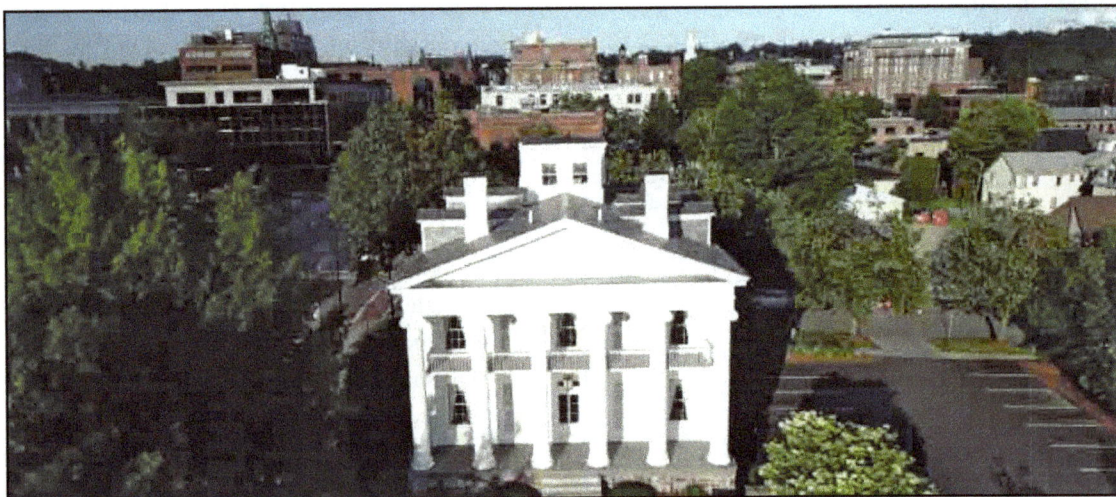

The Follett House in 2019. *A. Patterson.*

THE BURLINGTON BIKE PATH & WATERFRONT PARK

the 19th century with the opening of the Champlain and Erie Canals. So he resigned his judgeship and went into the shipping business on Lake Champlain.

In addition to building the Stone Store in 1827, his firm designed and built the unique canal boats of the time that allowed them to sail Lake Champlain but still navigate the canals, with their low bridges, by being able to quickly take down the masts in order to get under bridges on the canal. The *Lois McClure* that docks in Burlington harbor today is a replica of the canal boats built by Timothy Follett's shipping firm in the early part of the 19th century.

With the riches accumulated from lake commerce Follett built what is now known as the Follett House in 1840, the most beautiful and ornate home in the entire state at that time. It is the beautiful Greek Revival building on College Street currently occupied by the Pomerleau Real Estate Agency, designed by the famous architect Ammi B. Young, who also designed the State House in Montpelier and some of the most important structures on the Dartmouth campus in Hanover, New Hampshire. Young also drew one of the earliest maps of downtown Burlington in 1830. *See page 43.*

The Follett House soon became the center of social activity in Burlington. Follett threw lavish parties there throughout the 1840s. It was sort of the Gatsby House of Burlington for several decades. In 1849 Follett started the Merchants Bank in order to fund construction of the Rutland & Bur-

Burlington Harbor in the 1870s.

lington Railroad. Unfortunately, Follett's railroad went bankrupt in 1853 due to competition with the Central Vermont Railroad. Follett was forced into bankruptcy as well and he lost his house on College Street. He died penniless in a sanitarium in 1857. His home on College Street was acquired by a rival railroad president who continued to use it as the focal point of the community for several decades thereafter. The house fell into disrepair in the later days of the 19th century and barely survived the wrecking ball of urban renewal in the 1960s. It was finally restored to all its former glory by the Pomerleau Real Estate Agency in 1981.

But I digress. I can't help recalling that story because it's such an important part of the history of downtown Burlington.

Turning our attention back to the waterfront, it's important to understand that Burlington grew into the largest city in Vermont by the middle of the 19th century due to the lumber mills located on the waterfront. Large portions of the Green Mountain Forest were cut down in the early part of the 19th century. Logs were floated down the Winooski River to be milled on the Burlington waterfront. After the Green Mountain Forest had been decimated, logs were imported from Canada. There was a steep tariff on lumber from Canada, but no tariff on raw logs. So the lumber mills began importing whole logs from Canada. Burlington's population doubled between 1860 and 1870. By the 1870s Burlington was the third largest lumber port in the world, right behind Chicago, Illinois and Albany, New York.

During the long winters in Vermont it's not possible to ship lumber on the lake because it is frozen over, or at least it used to freeze over. So all winter long the lumber produced by the saw mills in Burlington harbor had to be stacked to await the spring thaw.

Burlington is located on a steep hill and there was little flat land on the waterfront to stack lumber. So in order to create more flat land on the waterfront to store lumber, they threw all the sawdust and trimmings from the milling process into the lake. Perhaps 90% to 95% of the land filled into the lake during that period is sawdust and trimmings from the milling process. Over time about 60 acres of land in Burlington harbor was created by filling in the lake.

According to our research, all that filled land is subject to the Public Trust Doctrine. Since the Public Trust Doctrine requires this filled land to be preserved for public uses, it quickly became apparent to us that hotels and condominiums have no place on the filled land in Burlington harbor. A home is certainly the most private of uses imaginable. Condominiums are homes and hotels are temporary homes. Thus, we reasoned, hotels and condominiums should be prohibited on the filled land in Burlington harbor under the Public Trust Doctrine.

And as it turned out, fortuitously for me, the Assistant City Attorney in the early 1980s, working for Mayor Sanders, was John Franco, who was doing research into the law of where private property meets the public interest in Lake Champlain at the same time my interns and I were. And lo and behold, Franco uncovered the Public Trust Doctrine at the same time we did.

Franco and Sanders were interviewed by Debbie Bookchin, Bea Bookchin's daughter, who was working as a reporter for the *Rutland Herald* in the early 1980s. Franco just couldn't resist revealing his findings on the Public Trust Doctrine reported in an article in the *Rutland Herald* on August 24, 1983.

According to this article, most of the prime lakefront property Alden planned to build on was filled land. Thus, the Canadian National Railroad, the eventual successor of the railroad which was granted title to the filled land by the Vermont legislature in 1874, might not actually hold clear title to this land and might be unable to sell the land for commercial use:

According to Franco and waterfront expert Lawrence Sager, the legal doctrine governing the lakefront hails back to English Common Law.

It is known as 'jus publicum' pronounced 'use publicum' and was designed to protect the public interest in navigable waterways by prohibiting anyone from filling in land and claiming it as their own private property.

"What's pretty clear in New York and I suspect in Vermont, is that you can't just come in and plunk down a bunch of fill and change the water mark," said Sager, a New York University Law School professor. "If that were true then you'd have a magical way of increasing your land."

To protect the public interest the doctrine places the land in a public trust guarded by the state.

"The bottoms of navigable waterways such as Lake Champlain are owned by the people — the public, with the state acting as a public trust." Franco said.

The state is allowed to convey title to the land for a use consistent with the public good such as railroad shipping.

But once that use is finished, "then there is a reversionary interest back to the public," he noted.

THE BURLINGTON BIKE PATH & WATERFRONT PARK

According to Franco, that means that the state in 1874 did not have the power to give the railroad an unconditional deed to the land.

"Research suggests the state is not competent to convey outright [an] interest in the lake bottom. It's just not anything you can sell," Franco said, noting that for legal purposes the fill-land is the same as the lake bottom.

Franco said numerous legal cases around the country, including an 1892 landmark Supreme Court case in which the State of Illinois tried to deed away a lake bottom, support the public interest over private interests.

Franco was citing the same case we had uncovered in our research — the Illinois case — as the "landmark" decision. Bingo. Unfortunately for John Franco, Bernie Sanders got sucked into the Alden plan later that year. After he extracted a vague commitment to affordable housing, a boathouse and some art display space from Flinn, Sanders went over to the dark side and became the primary proponent of the Alden plan. Suddenly John Franco wasn't so sure that the Public Trust Doctrine meant that private uses, such as hotels and condominiums, couldn't be built on the filled land in Burlington harbor. Sanders had silenced him.

Curiously, despite the Sanders Administration's assertions about the Public Trust Doctrine in the *Rutland Herald* on August 24, 1983, by February 1984 CEDO Director Peter Clavelle insisted in a *Vanguard Press* article: "The reality is that it [the waterfront] is private property and it will be developed. Obviously Alden can go ahead without the City's participation."

In response, I wrote a letter to the *Vanguard*, published on February 12, 1984, that called out the Sanders Administration:

The real truth is that the Alden Corporation does not own the "fill" land on the Burlington waterfront (almost half of the land it acquired from the Central Vermont Railroad). All the "fill" land in the Burlington harbor is owned by the State of Vermont and it is held in trust for the people under a principle of law known as the public trust doctrine.

The mayor, Peter Clavelle, the "progressive coalition," and Assistant City Attorney John Franco all know this. Why then would the mayor's director of Community and Economic Development make such a statement?

Because the Sanders administration is attempting to assist the Alden Corporation in building on our land. Then the mayor and the "progressive coalition" will be able to take credit for development of the waterfront.

Fortunately, there is an alternative. It's called the Burlington Bicyclepath — a 9.1 mile parkway at least 80 feet wide all along the water's edge from Oakledge Park to the mouth of the Winooski River.

Rather than entering into a "pseudo partnership" with the Alden Corporation, I think the City should be negotiating an arm's length business deal with Alden that will preserve public lands for the public. I for one don't want to give our land to private developers.

— Rick Sharp, Burlington

The Sanders Administration would keep up this charade for almost two years, insisting that the Public Trust Doctrine was a mysterious concept that they had used as leverage in negotiations with Alden. They not only failed to inform the public of their right to the filled land in Burlington harbor. They actively worked to deny the power of the Public Trust concept.

CHAPTER NINE
Funding the Bike Path

New North End residents had been using the old rail bed through their community as a means of getting about in a north/south direction since the rails had been taken out in the 1970s. Hearty bicyclists bumped along over railroad ties south of Leddy Park for years. Del Martin used the rail bed to commute from his home on Fern Street in the New North End to his job at General Electric south of the barge canal by bike since he bought the home in 1967.

The Parks Department put down a 6 1/2 foot wide paved pathway from Leddy Park north to Starr Farm Road sometime in the 1970s, depicted in red on this map. When the city received a $33,000 block grant in 1982 under the federal revenue sharing program popular in the 1980s, New North End residents who supported our pathway, and CWG members city-wide, came out en masse at neighborhood meetings and got the grant devoted to paving the portion of the railroad right-of-way north of Starr Farm Road all the way to the bridge abutment at the Winooski River, depicted in orange on this map. The paving of that section was completed in the spring of 1984. That got the ball rolling. The portion of the rail bed south of Leddy Park, depicted as rail ties on this map, was tied up in the lawsuit with Preseault. We pried up rail ties there in 1981 and 1982.

By 1983, the Community Economic Development Office, CEDO, and the entire city was on board in support of converting the old railroad right-of way into a bike path, and there were a lot of other people looking for additional funding. We searched high and low but could not identify any other source of funds available

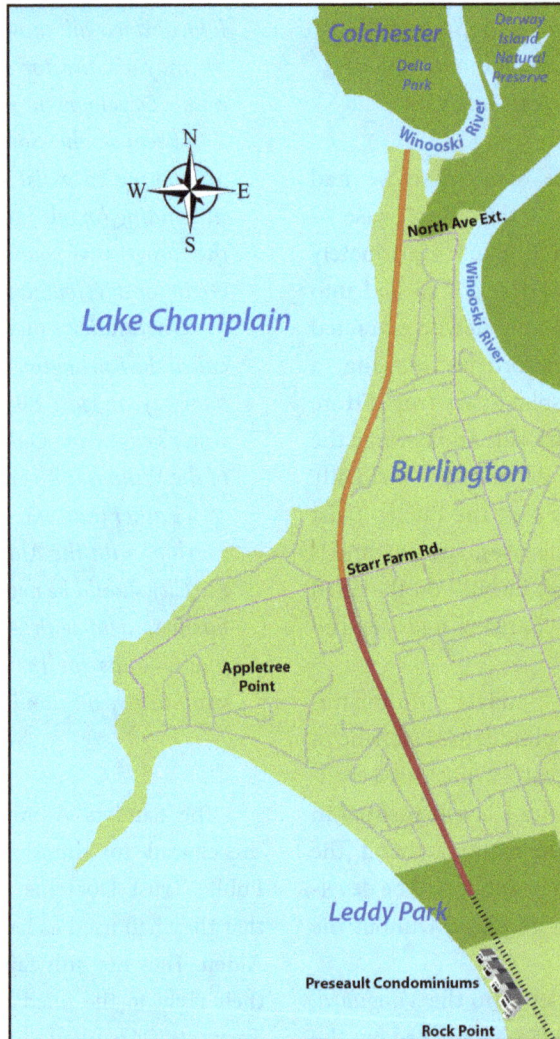

Map by M. Letourneau.

VOTE YES ON #4

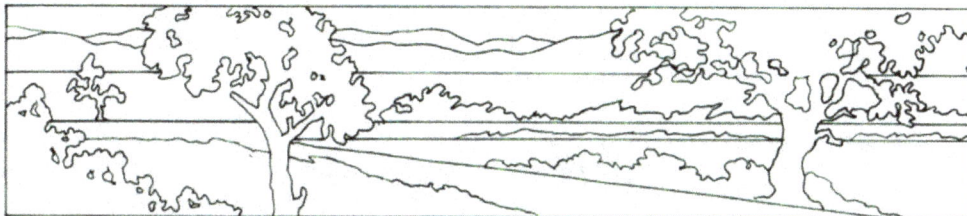

THE BURLINGTON BICYCLEPATH

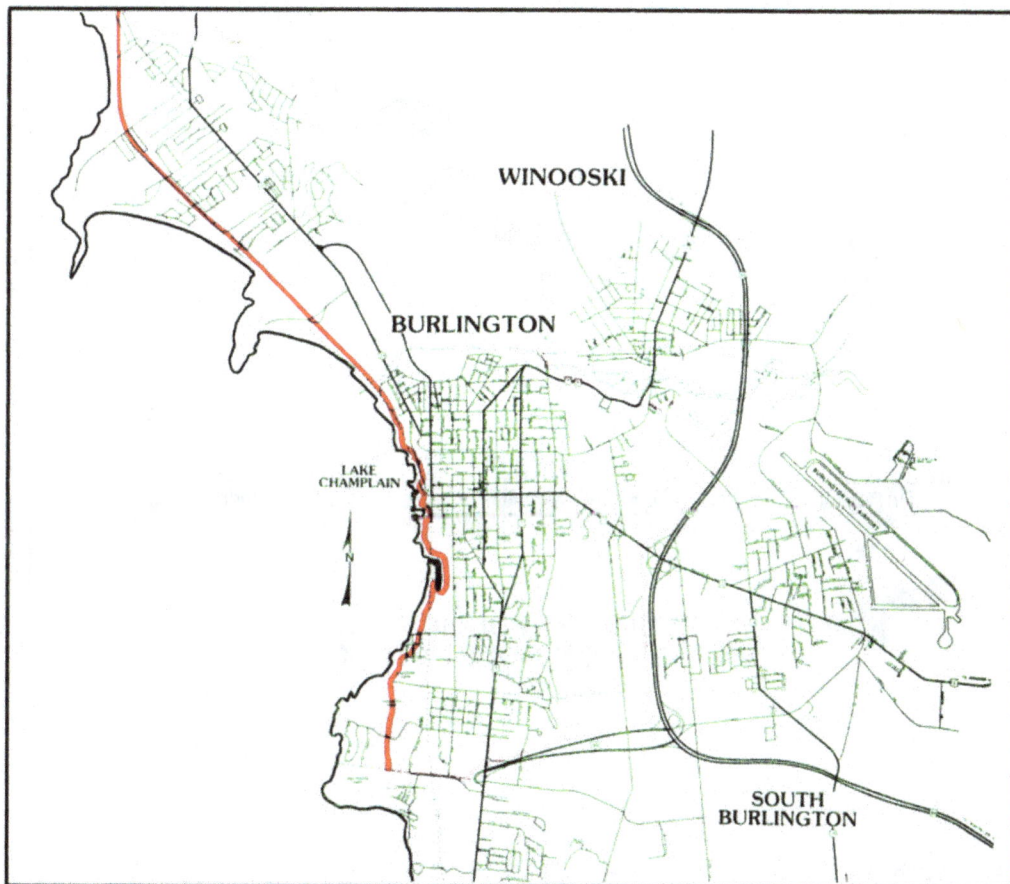

THE BURLINGTON BICYCLEPATH

Depicted on the reverse side (in red) is the Burlington Bicyclepath proposed by the Citizens Waterfront Group, Inc. The proposed pathway is more than just a bicyclepath, however. Only eight feet of a proposed strip of land at least 80 feet wide along the water's edge would be paved for use as a bicyclepath. The remaining 72 feet or more would contain a nature trail for strolling, a bridle path for horseback riding, natural areas, trees, playgrounds and plazas for viewing the lake without interference from bicyclists. The bicyclepath would also be used for cross country skiing in the winter.

IN REALITY A 9.1 MILE PARK

The proposed parkway would extend from Oakledge Park (Cliffside) at the City's southern border, to the mouth of the Winooski River at our northern boundary. It would link City parks at Oakledge, Perkins Pier, North Beach and Leddy Park. Later the parkway could be extended to Red Rocks Park in South Burlington and finally encircle the entire City along I 189, I89, through the Intervale and back to the mouth of the Winooski River (depicted in pink on the reverse side) — 26 miles in all!

Just imagine a Burlington Marathon run along this scenic route!

VOTE YES ON #4

On March 6th, voters will be asked to authorize the City Council to issue bonds (borrow from the public) up to $2 million for acquisition and development of this waterfront parkway. The exact cost of the parkway will depend upon the route selected and the amount of funding available from grants and private sources.

To the greatest degree possible land rights and development will be obtained from other sources first. Bond funds would be spent only when all other sources of funding are unavailable or exhausted and only after the City Council approves the specific expenditure. Ordinary citizens could propose specific expenditures and the public would have a full opportunity to review and comment upon all expenditures before any public funds are spent. If the parkway costs less than $2 million, the remaining funds would not be spent.

SAVE OUR WATERFRONT FOR THE PEOPLE

City voters have often supported public bonds for worthwhile projects, including $2.4 million for expansion of the Fletcher Free Library, $12 million for the new water filtration plant and $55 million for the woodchip burning plant.

Two million dollars is a small sum to pay to insure public access to the entire Burlington Waterfront for all time. This figure represents only a single year's tax revenues from a ten-acre site on the waterfront if developed in accordance with plans submitted by the Tri-ad Group, the Pomerleau Agency or the Alden Corp. The McNeil generating station will pay $2.1 million per year in lieu of taxes beginning in 1986. Thus, the entire parkway can be constructed for less than one year of revenues from the Alden development or the McNeil plant.

Our City is at a crossroads. One road leads to widespread public access to the lake. The other leads to a lakefront of private enclaves, expensive and exclusive, and accessible to only a few. On March 6th Burlington voters will be presented with an alternative to the Alden waterfront plan.

PLEASE SUPPORT PUBLIC ACCESS.
VOTE YES ON QUESTION #4.

For more information about the proposed parkway write Rick Sharp, Citizens Waterfront Group, P.O. Box 191 Burlington, Vermont 05402

Proposed Bike Path Would Ensure Public Access To City's Lakefront

City officials throughout the country have long since recognized the need to set aside sanctuaries that are insulated from the frenetic pace of urban living where people can go to commune with nature and with themselves.

Large parks and commons are characteristic features of many of the nation's metropolitan areas and such cities as Boston have established waterfront parks where the public can merely enjoy the scenery or take part in recreational activities. Such facilities enhance the quality of life in the inner cities.

Public access to Lake Champlain, Burlington's most important scenic and recreational asset, has for years been limited to beaches and small sections of the waterfront where downtown meets the lake. Had Burlington officials known years ago that the situation would develop, they might well have considered the possibility of setting aside public access areas before lakefront property was acquired by individuals and skyrocketed in value. To at-

Editorial

tempt to establish large parks or recreation facilities on the lakefront today would be impossible because of the high cost of such projects.

But the Citizens Waterfront Group Inc. has developed a feasible proposal that would create an 80-foot bicycle path and promenade that would run along the lakeshore from Oakledge Park to the mouth of the Winooski River. Eight feet of the strip would be paved and it would be open to the public for bicycling, jogging, cross-country skiing or strolling. Motorized vehicles would be barred from the path. It would link Oakledge, Perkins Pier, North Beach

and Leddy parks. Ultimately the group thinks the system could be tied in with the Winooski Valley Park District to form a circumferential path.

City voters will be asked to approve a bond issue of up to $2 million in the March 6 city election to begin the work on the project. Money would be used to buy property, protect the shoreline from erosion, paving and sprucing up the existing portion of the path which runs along the old Rutland and Canadian railroad right-of-way in the North End. Some members of the group believe that work on certain phases of the project can be done by disadvantaged youth.

Members of the group have acknowledged that the price tag is largely a guess. But they have pledged to monitor the costs carefully to insure that the money is spent wisely and well.

Because quality of life is an essential ingredient in the atmosphere of any city, the Free Press recommends that the voters approve the bond issue as an important step toward that end.

---

for paving an abandoned railroad right-of-way.[18] We had no idea what it would actually cost to install such a bike path, but without funding it was obvious the bike path was going nowhere. Of course, the lawsuit with Preseault had to be resolved and the path through the downtown area was unresolved, but that didn't stop us from moving forward with a request for bond funding.

With no funds forthcoming from the Sanders Administration to study the course of the path or the cost of construction, we were forced to pick a figure out of thin air. Two million dollars sounded like a number that would do the job. But of course,

a bond would have to be paid back out of property tax dollars.

A two-thirds majority is needed to pass a bond in Burlington, so we had our work cut out for us. Mayor Sanders opposed the bond because it would mean a substantial increase in property taxes. Most of the City Council agreed with him. And of course, our proposal was an easy target because we had no study to indicate what such a pathway would actually cost. Despite repeated requests for a study, the Sanders Administration had failed to produce these figures by late 1983. And I think the bike path had become a bit of a turf war over who would get credit for the path.

Once more, just as we had done in 1981, we collected enough petition signatures to get the two-million-dollar bond on the March 1984 ballot. We put out a flyer that we distributed to every house-

---

18. *That would not be the case today. There are transportation funds available at the state and local levels and most municipalities would be happy to fund or find funds for paving an old abandoned railroad bed to create a recreation path. Contact the Rails-to-Trails Conservancy for more information.*

hold in Burlington. A copy of the flyer for the two-million-dollar bond appears on the previous pages.

As you can see, we were proposing an ambitious vision for a bike path within an 80 foot strip of park space along the Lake Champlain shoreline. Recreation would be the focus of the path with bicycling in the summer and cross country skiing in the winter. We envisioned playgrounds, natural areas and plazas for viewing the lake. We even foresaw nature trails, bridle paths and a marathon.

This flyer was distributed door to door to almost every household in Burlington by an army of volunteers. It was well received even though it would result in an increase in real property taxes citywide. We sent letters supporting the plan to the *Burlington Free Press, That Paper* and the *Vanguard Press*. We also made passionate arguments for the bond in radio and TV appearances and at gatherings at UVM. We even received a favorable editorial from the *Burlington Free Press* on February 17, 1984. (*See previous page.*)

Somehow that wild idea we had started with four years before had become a "feasible proposal" supported by the *Burlington Free Press* Editorial Board. As I pointed out before the vote, "Two million is a small amount to pay to ensure public access to the waterfront for the next hundred years. This figure represents only two years of tax revenues for a single ten-acre site on the waterfront. The city spent more than a quarter of a million dollars on a parking lot at North Beach last fall. For the price of eight parking lots, the public could have unlimited access to the waterfront in Burlington."

Mayor Sanders would not support the bond, conceding that the bike path was a good idea, but contending that it did not justify a two million dollar bond without a full study of the potential costs. But Sanders refused to conduct such a study. As I pointed out at the time, in 1984, this was an Orwellian case

of "double think", or double talk at any rate. Sanders had us in a Catch-22.

In summary, I wrote that "Our City is at a crossroads. One road leads to widespread public access to the lake. The other leads to a lakefront of private enclaves, expensive and exclusive, and accessible to only a few. On March 6, 1984, Burlington voters will be presented with an alternative to the Alden waterfront plan."

But in the end, though it received a solid majority, with 55% support from city voters, the bond vote failed. It didn't reach the crucial two-thirds level necessary for passage.

Nonetheless that was a great showing. A majority of city voters actually favored raising their own property taxes enough to pay for a two-million-dollar bond for a bike path. That proved how popular the bike path concept had become in only a few short years.

Fortunately for us, the bond vote got the attention of the Mayor and the City Council. The Sanders Administration finally completed a study of the path[19] and in August Mayor Sanders announced his support for a $750,000 bond to be included on the November 1984 ballot. The City Council agreed. And of course, that was a presidential election year, so a lot more people came out to vote that fall. My college interns that semester registered hundreds of students and helped get them out to vote for the bike path bond.

The $750,000 bond received 67% support, just barely making it over the high hurdle for city bonding. That wasn't enough to get the job done correctly, but it was all we could get. It had to do. Compromises needed to be made to complete the path from one end of the city to the other. (*See Chapter Thirteen*). But we were well underway with a funding source firmly in hand at last.

---

19. *The Boehm Report. See Appendix 6.*

THE BURLINGTON BIKE PATH & WATERFRONT PARK

CHAPTER TEN
The Chainsaw Party

Preseault's lawsuit progressed at a snail's pace through the Vermont state court system before finally reaching the Vermont Supreme Court. On April 19, 1985 the high court affirmed the decision of the Chittenden County Superior Court and dismissed Preseault's claim, ruling that the Interstate Commerce Commission (ICC) still had jurisdiction over the rail line through the New North End, even though the rails had been removed. A certificate is required from the ICC to abandon a railroad. Since no abandonment certificate had ever been issued, the rail bed through the city's New North End was declared to still be an active railroad. That meant that the state courts had no jurisdiction over Preseault's claim. So the Court dismissed Preseault's lawsuit.

However, that decision didn't end Preseault's pursuit of this issue in the courts. He just moved the battle to the federal courts. But it was our cue to remove the dreaded log that had blocked the pathway through Preseault's property for over four years. With the dismissal of the case in the state court there was no longer any outstanding order prohibiting us from removing the log.

I sent an invitation to CWG members for a chain saw party. On Saturday morning April 27, 1985 a group of perhaps twenty CWG members assembled in Leddy Park. I brought my chainsaw and met Dorothy Hunt, Karen and Del Martin, Dan and Peg Moseley and Alderman Allen Gear in a wheelchair in the parking lot beside the old rail bed in Leddy Park.

From the left: Dorothy Hunt, Rick Sharp, Dan Moseley, Allen Gear and Karen Martin. *Photo M. Shadroui.*

The photograph on the previous page was snapped as we waited for the rest of the group to assemble.

Once everyone had arrived we strolled south down the railroad right-of-way with several lawn chairs, two bottles of champagne and the chainsaw, to Preseault's property several hundred yards away. We had previously removed all the railroad ties in the rail bed so it was fairly easy for Alderman Gear to wheel along in his wheelchair.

When we arrived at the log, Dorothy produced a poem she had written for the occasion. She started reading it, asking us all to join in at the end of the poem with a loud Hurrah!

> *This Saturday morning*
> *The weather is fine!*
> *Elated bike-pathers,*
> *We all form a line,*
> *And march to the spot*
> *Where the hated log stands.*
> *A chain saw is brought*
> *And it's run by Rick's hands.*
> *Hurrah!*

With the poem complete I started the chainsaw and began slicing through the log. Preseault came running up and tackled me while the saw was still running. It's an indication of just how volatile a man he was that he was crazy enough to attack someone running a chainsaw. Very dangerous.

I quickly got my finger on the kill switch and shut off the saw before anyone got hurt. Fortunately, I had completed the cut and the log was in two pieces that could be moved much more easily. Preseault was livid. He launched into a tirade that went on for some time, calling me every foul word he could think of. Mrs. Preseault soon appeared and positioned herself between me and the log and vowed that I would have to roll it over her before it could be removed.

The police arrived soon thereafter. I was pretty sure they wouldn't arrest an 81-year-old lady and an alderman in a wheelchair. We made it clear that we didn't want an altercation with Preseault and that he had attacked me, not the other way around. Preseault insisted that we had no right to remove the log from his property. We pointed out that the railroad right-of-way was not his property, according to the Vermont Supreme Court, and that he had no right to place the log across the pathway to block it. A *Burlington Free Press* article dated May 1, 1985 quoted me as saying, "Mr. Preseault has no more right to place a log there than to park his car on the Statehouse lawn." Then Preseault argued that it was, nonetheless, his log.

Several members of the CWG offered to cut the log up and remove it onto his property. Preseault didn't take kindly to that offer. The Burlington Police resolved the dispute by telling us that the log would remain where it was until the city removed it. Allen Gear offered to introduce a resolution to remove the log at the next city council meeting. He then added "I wish we had two chain saws". As it turned out, we didn't need two.

In order to avoid further confrontation, we left the log in two pieces with a gap wide enough to get Allen Gear's wheelchair through, and then we strolled back up the bike path to Leddy Park. Sometime during the following night, both sections of the log somehow got pushed over the steep embankment adjacent to the bike path. When I returned to the area the next day the pathway was clear. I had no part in the disappearance of the log. I suspect someone who had long since grown tired of lifting his or her bike over the log took a cue from our handiwork and finished the job.

We had made our point. The log never returned to block the pathway again.

THE BURLINGTON BIKE PATH & WATERFRONT PARK

The following week Robert Devost, the editor of *That Paper* published an article with the following headline:

SHARP CLAIMS "FINAL VICTORY" IN LEGAL BATTLE OVER BIKE PATH; PRESEAULT SUMMONS POLICE TO BLOCK LOG CUTTING CELEBRATION: ALDERMAN GEAR TO INTERVENE WITH CITY TO REMOVE LOG

The Vermont Supreme Court affirmed the decision of the Chittenden Superior Court on Friday, April 19, 1985 and dismissed the legal action over the railroad right of way between Leddy Park and North Beach. It now appears the bicycle path will be preserved for public use forever due to legislation that got through the Vermont legislature in 1981. It wasn't quite the Cuban Missile Crisis or the peaceful march on Selma, but there was a bit of high noon drama on the bike path last Saturday April 27th.

Last Saturday (April 27th) a small group of neighbors and friends, some belonging to the Citizens Waterfront Group, (CWG) a group long active in the preservation and development of the city-wide bicycle path, gathered at Leddy Park before walking to the bike path area where the infamous 'Preseault (blockade) Log' was located and soon after hoped to chainsaw into history what should be the last physical and legal obstruction to block the city-wide bike path concept.

Unfortunately, that wasn't the end of the legal struggle. Having been thrown out of state Court for lack of jurisdiction, Preseault petitioned the ICC, arguing that a "de facto" abandonment had occurred when the rails were removed years earlier. Since this was the first case to come before the ICC under the provisions of the newly enacted 1983 Rails-to-Trails Act, the state of Vermont and VTC were the "trailblazers" in setting the rules and procedures for rails-to-trails conversions nationwide. That took a lot of time, but in the end the ICC found that without the abandonment certificate, the line through the New North End was part of the national railroad system protected by the railbanking provisions of the Rails-to-Trails Act.

But that still didn't stop Preseault. He appealed that decision to the Court of Appeals and finally on to the U.S. Supreme Court, accumulating a total of eleven federal and state court decisions before he was through, and in the process, establishing the main body of federal law on railroad abandonments nationwide. *More on the outcome of that landmark decision in Chapter Fourteen.*

Although Dorothy Hunt contributed so much to the creation of the Burlington Bike Path, she was well into her 80s before it was complete. We could always count on Dorothy to get 20-25% of the signatures we needed for petitions, often from elderly housing complexes through people she knew personally. She also became a cheerleader for the group and its unofficial secretary. Although she was not capable of contributing physically to our work projects, she faithfully showed up with lemonade, cookies and other refreshments. The Dorothy Hunt Special Collection at the University of Vermont contains most of the minutes, notices and plans of the Citizens Waterfront Group during those early years. It's a treasure trove of how we created the Bike Path, thanks so much to Dorothy Hunt. I got to know her quite well at afternoon tea and she will always have a special place in my heart.

CHAPTER ELEVEN
The 80 Foot Setback

Having failed to convince Paul Flinn, from the Alden Group, to push his development back 80 feet from the lake's edge in order to leave space for the bike path and a waterfront park, we set our sights on creating this setback by going to the voters once more.

A special election had been called for June 11, 1985. We saw the opportunity to get our proposal for an 80-foot setback on the ballot. By that time Mayor Sanders and most of the City Council were firmly in the Alden camp.

We asked the Board of Aldermen to put an advisory item on the ballot for an 80-foot setback at a meeting on May 13, 1985. Democratic Aldermen Rowell and LaFayette voted in favor, but the Progressives and the Republicans were firmly opposed. It was soundly defeated.

Once again we resorted to a petition drive to get this measure on the ballot. The theory was that if enough voters supported a setback, the Alden Group would be forced to respond by giving us the space we needed for a waterfront bike path.

We pointed out that other communities throughout the United States had enacted shoreline protection measures to ensure public access to the ocean. California had enacted legislation to protect access to beaches along the Pacific Ocean waterfront. Ogunquit, Maine had the Marginal Way — a public pathway along the Atlantic Ocean coast that allows visitors to stroll along the shore. This pathway is extremely popular with tourists and locals alike and is often credited with increasing tourism

and boosting business at local shops and restaurants along the Way.

We reasoned that similar setback provisions along the Lake Champlain shoreline in Burlington would attract tourists and provide an economic boost to local businesses. This argument fell on deaf ears in the Burlington business community. Mayor Sanders quickly dismissed our efforts as an attempt to kill the Alden plan. Most members of the City Council followed suit, signing on to a Resolution to oppose the 80-foot setback. (*See Appendix 5.*)

We pushed on undeterred. Again we delivered flyers door-to-door to almost every household in Burlington. Mayor Sanders and leading members of the Board of Aldermen, Republican Will Skelton and Progressive Gary DeCarolis, signed a full page ad in the *Burlington Free Press* and distributed a flyer in opposition to our proposal city wide.

I saved a copy of the flyer "Paid for by the Committee for a Better Burlington" and I have reprinted it in full on the next page.

The argument put forth by Mayor Sanders and this tri-partisan group of city leaders was that our plan would "kill" the Alden development, which they claimed provided more public space than the 80-foot set-back. They failed to note, however, how much of that land would provide real public access to the lake shore. Although their flyer and the *Burlington Free Press* ad indicated that Alden "agreed to move the location of the inn 50 feet from the shore", instead of projecting out into the harbor as originally planned, the revised plan also included an over-

If you really want a people-oriented waterfront in Burlington... vote **no** on Question #3.

Question #3 is a non-binding referendum which asks voters whether buildings should be set back at least 80 feet from the water's edge.

On the surface, that might sound reasonable.

But the truth is...we could lose open space, and the requirement could kill the Alden Waterfront Plan. We could miss the best chance we've ever had to develop a people-oriented waterfront.

Here a few of the specific reasons why the Alden Waterfront Plan is a better deal for Burlington residents:

• The Waterfront Plan includes almost twice as much land for open park space as would be provided by the 80-foot set-back ballot question. The 80-foot strip would produce approximately 4 acres of open space, but the Alden Plan includes more than 7 acres of open space.

• The Waterfront Plan provides for a pedestrian promenade along the water's edge and a bike path in a separate location. Unlike the proposal for an 80-foot set-back, the Alden Plan recognizes the fact that you can't mix pedestrians and bicyclists.

• In the Waterfront Plan, buildings would be set back an average of 50 feet from the water. Only a few buildings like the community boat-house and a portion of the outdoor cafe would be closer. In response to public comments, the Alden Corporation agreed to move the location of the inn 50 feet from the shore. This variety of building set-backs is a much better design than having a straight wall of buildings 80 feet from the water.

Alden's Waterfront Plan includes a good mix of public spaces, cultural activities, and commercial uses. If built, the waterfront area will be an environment which is inviting to Burlington residents throughout the year.

It has already received intense public review... and approval. After the public hearings, 75% of the people responding to the survey approved the plan. The Board of Aldermen have also approved the conceptual plan.

It's a large project with many elements, and it's a complicated project. Many steps have to be taken before the plan becomes a reality.

An enormous amount of time and energy have gone into developing the project so far, and many Burlingtonians believe it would be one of the most exciting and people-oriented waterfront developments in the country. Let's keep the project moving ahead. We hope you will vote **no** on Tuesday, June 11th.

Thank you for your consideration.

Mayor Bernard Sanders

Will Skelton
President, Board of Aldermen

Fred Bailey
Chairman, Aldermanic Waterfront Committee

Gary DeCarolis
Member, Aldermanic Waterfront Committee

George Thabault
Member, Aldermanic Waterfront Committee

Right-of-Way Could Help Create a Park for All Seasons

Vermont Perspective

By Rick Sharp

On June 11, Burlington voters will have an opportunity to direct city planners and the board of aldermen to preserve at least 80 feet of space along the waterfront for a public park and bicycle path that will one day extend from Oakledge Park to the mouth of the Winooski River.

This ballot item would require an 80-foot setback from the water's edge for any future private development on the so-called "filled lands" in the Burlington harbor. Filled lands are lands which were filled into the lake over the past 200 years. The filled lands in the Burlington harbor stretch from the barge canal to approximately a quarter mile north of the Moran Generating Station.

The State of Vermont owns the bed of Lake Champlain and holds it in trust for the people of our state. Thus, the state actually owns the filled land in the Burlington harbor, although the railroad currently uses this land for public transportation purposes under a grant from the Vermont Legislature in 1874.

The railroad has plans to transfer its interest in the filled lands to private developers who intend to build hotels and condominiums within 20 feet of the lake's edge.

Although I generally support the Alden plan for waterfront development, I also feel very strongly that at least 80 feet of this filled land, which belongs to all of us, should be preserved for park space, open to the public.

The filled land in question is some 400 feet wide at the foot of College Street where Alden plans to construct its project. The 80 feet proposed for preservation as park space is less than a quarter of this filled land.

For comparison purposes, 80 feet is slightly more than a normal city street. Preservation of this strip will cost city taxpayers absolutely nothing — it already belongs to us. The Alden Corporation could still build upon the remaining 320 feet of public property in the harbor, assuming it can obtain all necessary permits for construction.

The issue of who owns filled land in public lakes was resolved by the U.S. Supreme Court almost a century ago when the City of Chicago attempted to reclaim lands filled into Lake Michigan by the Illinois Railroad. The City of Chicago was successful and today the Chicago waterfront is a public park with beaches and bicycle paths open to the public year around. Burlington should follow this example and preserve at least a portion of this filled land for public space.

This is probably the last opportunity voters will have to voice their preference for park space over private development, for this issue is about to be resolved without public input behind closed doors in a court of law.

Voters should know that this ballot item is only advisory. It is not binding upon city planners or the board of aldermen. It will, however, give one support for an argument before the court that the people of Burlington want more land along the shore preserved for park space.

Voters should also know that this ballot item will not affect existing structures on the waterfront. These structures would be "grandfathered in."

The difference between 20 feet and 80 feet is the difference between Vermont and New Jersey. Eighty feet is the absolute minimum space needed to create green park space along the waterfront and preserve the quality of life we all cherish here in Vermont.

It has been suggested that this 80-foot greenstrip be planted with sugar maples. In the spring, the city could establish a maple sugar harvest festival with the collection of sap by local residents, possibly with horse-drawn carts or sleighs, along the meandering path which would be used as a bicycle path in the summertime.

In effect, this waterfront park would become a "maple gateway" to Vermont's Queen City. This maple gateway park would be in keeping with Vermont's unique maple tradition. And just imagine the colors in the fall! Truly, this would be a waterfront for all seasons.

Rick Sharp is a member of and attorney for the Citizens Waterfront Group, Inc. He lives in Burlington.

---

hanging third through seven stories in the hotel that would approach to within 25 feet of the lake's edge. It would be easy to close off a boardwalk within 25 feet of the hotel. That would not be park space, we argued. That would be an outdoor patio for the hotel.

And in the end, the island Alden proposed as the majority of the public space in their plan was withdrawn. The battle lines for the all-important vote in December were becoming entrenched.

On June 5, 1985 the *Burlington Free Press* published my opinion piece advocating for the 80-foot setback.

I was trying to walk a tightrope in this editorial, aware that a majority wanted development on the waterfront (seventy five percent according to the Sanders Administration). Eighty feet along the water's edge would do the job and still allow development. The comparison to a New Jersey development was meant as a contrast to the maple-lined pathway we were proposing. As I wrote back then, "Just imagine the fun of a maple sugar harvest festival with horse-drawn sleighs collecting sap along the same path used by bicyclists in the summer time." It's unfortunate that the city didn't plant more maple trees along the Bike Path as we suggested. Vibrant foliage along the path would have drawn even more tourists (leaf peepers) in the fall.

But in the end, with the business community, Alden, the Mayor and most of the City Council firmly opposed, the 80-foot setback measure garnered only 44% support.

The next day the headline in the *Burlington Free Press* shouted: "Waterfront Setback Defeated". I have quoted extensively from the article below:

"I think that's tremendous," exulted Charles T. Shea, one of the principals in Alden....

Sharp said, "I think that we did very well, considering that the two strongest political parties in the city were working very hard to defeat the proposal. It is a setback for the bicycle path and a setback for the quality of life in Burlington."

"I'm quite surprised by the results," Sanders said. "I'm just delighted that the people of Burlington were able to see through what appeared to be a reasonable and progressive measure."

In an impromptu news conference in the city clerk's office, where he had been waiting for vote totals, Sanders declined to predict whether the negative vote would silence Sharp.

"Rick Sharp is Rick Sharp," Sanders said. "He will do what he chooses."

Sharp said he will continue his fight. "It's not over until they start the construction," he said. "This fight will be continued in the permitting process."

Current zoning law requires buildings to be at least 30 feet from the water's edge. Alden officials said only two of their buildings, a boathouse and a cafeteria, would be closer than 50 feet.

"According to the plans I've seen," Skelton said, "the average of 50 feet is sufficient. The waterfront will always be open to the people. I've seen areas where there are large open setbacks, and generally they're cold and unused."

Sharp accused Sanders and Skelton of having distributed a flier that was "very deceptive" by claiming the closest building would be 50 feet from the water, when the third floor overhang of a proposed hotel would be within 25 feet.

Alderman Gary Decarolis, I-Ward 3, a member of the aldermanic Waterfront Committee, said the vote reflected both the sophistication of Burlington voters and a support for the Alden plan that has been consistent over the last two years.

It's interesting to note that the percentage of voters we attracted to the 80-foot setback is almost identical to those that ended up opposing the six million dollar bond for the Alden project later that year. So the skirmish over the 80-foot setback turned out to be an accurate barometer of the vote to come on Alden.

Mayor Sanders and I clashed over other issues as well. I led the opposition to a Progressive initiative for rent control, and I opposed a bond billed by the Sanders Administration as a measure to close the landfill in the Intervale. The Mayor's plan would

not have closed the landfill for five years. I argued that the bond was not a plan to close the landfill as soon as possible, but was actually a scheme to keep it running for five more years.

I had attempted to close the Burlington landfill as a young attorney at the Solid Waste Division of the Vermont Agency of Environmental Conservation. I knew the impact the landfill was having on the wetland in the Intervale. It should have been closed in 1980 when I was closing down failing landfills leaching into wetlands statewide. But the head of the Solid Waste Division, Dick Valentinetti, had refused to allow me to force Burlington into an Assurance of Discontinuance. Burlington has a lot of political clout in the legislature. That concerned Valentinetti. He didn't want to lose support in the Burlington delegation in the legislature, by closing down a cheap and convenient place to dispose of the city's garbage, so he muzzled me.

During discussions of the bond to "close" the landfill, some neighbors complained that there were rats stalking the place "as big as cats". As a joke, one of my law clerks bought a large inflatable rubber rat and left it on my desk one day to greet me when I returned from court. Mayor Sanders was having a press conference about the landfill bond later that day at City Hall. I deflated the rat and tucked it into my jacket pocket as I left for the press conference.

The Mayor's staff had placed a boom box in front of the stage at Contois Auditorium to play their theme song, "Let's Close Down The Dump". The TV cameras were all there. I just couldn't resist blowing up the rat and placing it down front next to the boom box for all to admire.

Mayor Sanders turned bright red, marched to the front of the auditorium, grabbed the rat, took it back to where I was seated and threw it at me. I couldn't resist. "Assault with a rubber rat," I declared. The mayor wasn't amused.

Those efforts did not exactly endear me to Mayor Sanders. He refused to talk to me at all. And although I had nothing to do with what was going on at the City Council, as a Democrat, I was viewed as the enemy. Sanders actually crossed the street to avoid me if he saw me coming down the sidewalk in front of him.

So obviously, even though I was one of the main proponents of the bike path plan that now had almost universal support, I had no input whatsoever in the planning process for construction. After the failed $2 million bond vote in March, 1984, CEDO contracted with landscape architects Boyle/Boehm Association to do a formal preliminary study of possible alternatives for construction of the bike path and costs associated with the various possible routes. The so-called Bohem Report, *see Appendix 6*, identified numerous alternative routes for the path once it left the railroad right-of-way just north of downtown. Each alternative was analyzed for ease of construction, obstacles remaining and cost estimates. It identified two alternative routes from Texaco Beach to the Alden project, one hugging the remaining railroad track and the other along the water's edge, and numerous possible routes south of College Street, for getting around the barge canal area in the south end, routing through the Lakeside neighborhood and the oil storage tanks just north of Oakledge Park.

But when it came to property that Alden had under contract with the railroad, only one alternative was depicted in the plan. It was simply noted that the bike path "traverses the Alden Waterfront Corporation's property and is planned to follow the east side of Lake Street," no doubt at the direction of the Sanders Administration.

Instead of running along the lake in a park, the pathway would be relegated to a glorified side-walk down the east side of Lake Street behind the dumpsters for the hotel and condominiums, the parking structures and 210,000 square feet of retail and office space. CEDO Director, Peter Clavelle, insisted that the proposed bike path belonged in a "transportation corridor" sandwiched between the remaining rail track on the west and Lake Street on the east. Clavelle argued that locating the bike path in an 80 foot strip along the lake's edge would result in an unsightly "Chinese Wall" of buildings along the waterfront. I had no input in the process leading up to the Boehm Report and didn't even become aware that the Sanders Administration had finally ordered a study of possible routes for the path until the report was released late in the summer of 1984.

Of course I voiced my opposition to the placement of the pathway through the Alden development. But my voice meant nothing at that point and I received almost no attention at all.

Things were not looking good for a waterfront bike path at that point, with the Mayor and all three political parties firmly behind the Alden plan. And to make matters worse, in October 1984, Republican Attorney General John Easton, in the middle of an election campaign for Governor, announced that the state of Vermont and the city of Burlington had found a way to short circuit the Public Trust Doctrine. The state, the city, the railroad and Alden joined forces and filed a collusive lawsuit in Chittenden County Superior Court to "settle" the public trust issue looming over the Alden project. They would get the court to rubber stamp an agreement that would approve whatever Alden put forth as a plan on the filled land in Burlington harbor.

It was indeed a strange alliance between conservative factions of the statewide Republican Party and the Progressives led by Mayor Sanders. And there were no objections raised by the Democrats either. I was all by myself out on a long limb when I filed a Motion to Intervene in this lawsuit to present a much different view of the Public Trust Doctrine as applied to the filled land in Burlington harbor.

I argued that the Public Trust Doctrine prohibited hotels and condominiums on the filled land because these uses were clearly private. What could be more private than a home like a condominium or a temporary home like a hotel room? The other side argued that the Public Trust Doctrine could encompass a wide range of development options. They cited case law in California approving retail shops on land filled into tidal marshes.[20] And Mayor Sanders even went as far as to argue that if the people of Burlington anointed Alden as their preference, even though it contained hotels and condominiums, such a vote trumped any argument that those uses were in opposition to the Public Trust Doctrine.

In short, black could be turned into white with the sleight of hand of a misinformed popular vote! It was indeed fitting that this absurd double speak argument was being peddled by Bernie Sanders in the year 1984. In an editorial that we passed out at neighborhood planning meetings I noted: "Now the Administration's position is that the public trust law is 'mysterious' and they can't tell the people what it means or even if it exists at all! Big Brother has closed the Neighborhood Planning Assemblies to informed public interest groups willing to educate the people about the public trust…George Orwell was right. 1984 is upon us."

In the end, my Motion to Intervene failed on the basis of a lack of standing to bring such a suit on behalf of those opposed to the Alden plan. Thus, the sizeable minority of Burlington voters who were opposed to Alden were denied a voice in the lawsuit that would settle the issue of the Public Trust Doctrine as applied to the filled land in Burlington harbor. The same legal argument that had prevented the Sierra Club from halting the Disney alpine village in the Mineral King Valley in California had been effectively used to toss us out of court.

However, I was allowed to file a Bench Memorandum with the court as an *amicus curiae*, or friend of the court *(See Appendix 10)*. My Memorandum relied heavily on *Hazen v. Perkins* and *Illinois Central Railroad v. Illinois (See pages 41 and 42)*. I also insisted that the Vermont Constitution itself requires the preservation of the bed of boatable lakes for public purposes. Central Vermont Railroad (CV) argued that wharfing statutes enacted in 1827 and 1874 conferred "fee simple absolute" title to these wharves and the land filled into the lake between them. I argued: "The shortcoming of CV's approach is its failure to adequately analyze these grants within the broader context of public policy and the public trust doctrine. In effect, CV has focused on the bark of the tree and failed to adequately examine the entire public trust forest."

We wouldn't find out who would ultimately prevail until 1989. In the mean time the Alden plan was on the fast track.

---

20. *City of Berkeley v. Superior Court of Alameda Country, 26 Cal 3rd 515 (1980).*

CHAPTER TWELVE
The Alden Vote

That set the stage for the Alden vote on December 10, 1985. Mayor Sanders had prevailed in every tactic we had employed to head off the Alden plan and move the buildings back from the water's edge to leave space for a waterfront park and bicycle path. He had all three political parties behind him, the entire City Council, the business community and a sizeable majority of city voters. The Sanders Administration claimed that 75% of city voters supported the Alden plan.

The Alden plan had undergone substantial refinements by that point. Mayor Sanders had wrangled a commitment for a boardwalk out of Alden, but not much more. The Inn had been pulled back from extending out into the lake, relocated to a position just north of College Street, approaching as close as 25 feet to the lake's edge on the third through seventh floors. One hundred fifty luxury condominiums were planned for the filled land farther north that eventually became the event space used today for the finish line of the marathon and concerts like the Grace Potter Grand Point North event and a host of other festivals throughout the summer each year.

The seven-acre island and the majority of public space initially proposed by Alden was gone. If a boathouse was to be built, the city would foot the bill. A second phase of the revised plan included two parking structures for 1,200 cars, 175,000 square feet of office space, and 45,000 square feet of retail space, filling almost every inch of filled land in that portion of Burlington harbor. The bike path was relegated to a sidewalk along the west side of Lake Street. This is the revised plan, printed in the *Burlington Free Press* on October 6, 1985. Note that

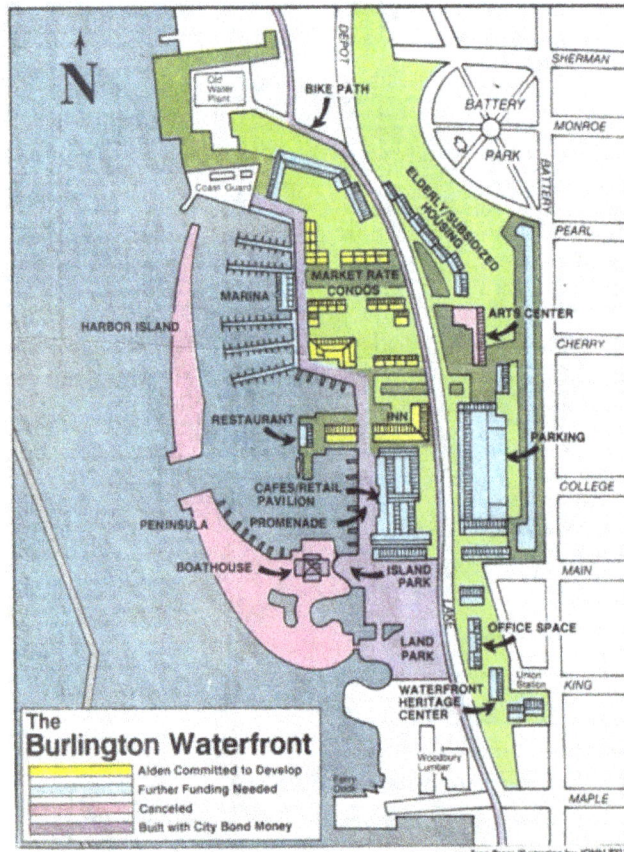

The
Burlington Waterfront

Alden Committed to Develop
Further Funding Needed
Canceled
Built with City Bond Money

Free Press Illustration by JOHN PYLE

it incorrectly depicts the Inn and restaurant jutting out into the lake, a scheme Alden had abandoned several months earlier.

The Community Economic Development Office (CEDO) worked closely with the Alden Group to promote their plan. But they had failed to secure a $17.5 million federal grant to sweeten the pot and help make the project economically viable. So with Mayor Sanders' support, Alden was forced to turn to city voters for the six million dollar gap that needed to be bridged to go forward with the revised project. That money would instead have to come from the city in the form of a bond. In order to reduce the tax burden on city voters and make the project more palatable, CEDO came up with an innovative way to finance this bond called Tax Incremental Financing or TIF.

Under the TIF plan, new taxes generated by the Alden project (over existing taxes) would be devoted to paying off the bond. That would cleverly dodge an immediate impact on real estate taxes citywide, but it also meant that very little new taxes would be available from the project for years to come. Nonetheless, Mayor Sanders and CEDO sold the bond as a painless way to finally turn the wasteland on the waterfront into a "people oriented" wonderland. But the only wonder was why a socialist like Bernie Sanders would devote six million dollars of funds backed by the full faith and credit of the city and all those tax revenues for years to come, to a project with very little public space that covered the waterfront wall to wall with structures to service the well-to-do. It didn't make a lot of sense, given Sanders' rhetoric about the "one percent" at the top, but by that point Sanders was fully committed. It was like a stampede of lemmings running headlong off a cliff. Politically there was no turning back.

Bea Bookchin, an outspoken Burlington environmentalist, called out Mayor Sanders in an article in the *Burlington Free Press* published on Nov. 26, 1985, headlined "Sanders Denies Sellout to Alden on Waterfront." Bookchin said that Sanders was supporting "an enclave for the rich" and that the "project is everything Bernie Sanders said it would not be." Sanders reacted defensively, saying "There's an illusion that all we have to do is keep pushing a developer. We feel we pushed him as far as we can go, and we feel we got significant concessions." Sanders also claimed that I had been "grossly inaccurate" in describing the plan.

We had done our very best to put the brakes on the project, or at least modify it, to get our bike path and waterfront park up front by the lake, but clearly we had failed miserably. All indicators were that our bike path plan was about to get flattened by the bulldozers of the Alden plan.

Nonetheless, it's always tough to get a bond passed because it requires a two-thirds majority. But Mayor Sanders was in command of the most powerful political machine the city had ever seen and he had the backing of the City Council, the business community and Alden. Gene Bergman, one of the leaders of the Progressive Party who later defeated me twice in campaigns for Alderman in Ward 2, was actually opposed to the Alden project, but he sat on his hands and said nothing publicly in opposition to the plan. Similarly, even if the majority of Progressives were opposed to the plan, they did little or nothing to slow down Mayor Sanders or make their opposition public. That task fell to me, Bea Bookchin and the Greens almost exclusively.

And of course Mayor Sanders was in control of the timing of the Alden vote as well. So in order to ensure a low turnout at the polls and overwhelm the vote with their political machine, a very odd date was selected for the Alden vote: December 10, 1985.

That date would pretty much exclude the student population in Burlington because they would be in the middle of exams with no time to pay attention to environmental radicals like Rick Sharp, Bea Bookchin and the Greens. That date for the vote would also minimize participation generally as people began to focus on Christmas shopping.

It was a masterful orchestration indeed that promised to achieve the difficult task of obtaining a two-thirds majority. I knew we were outnumbered and outmaneuvered and that we would be marginalized by the process going into the December vote, but there was little I could do about that.

And to make matters worse, and tip the scales even further in their favor, CEDO came up with a brilliant, if devious, plan to limit the discussion and cut off almost every avenue for us to lob informative projectiles at the Alden plan. They set up six separate "dog-and-pony" shows to explain the Alden plan to the public in advance of the vote, one in each of the six wards of the city at that time. And of course the format for those public hearings was controlled by CEDO.

The agenda would begin with a presentation by the Alden Group, followed by the endorsement of CEDO before the discussion would be opened up to the public. I requested time to present our alternative of a bike path and waterfront park along the lake's edge and to reveal the Public Trust Doctrine we had unearthed through extensive research, but CEDO would have no part of that. They did everything they could to silence me.

The final insult in that process was a rule that they imposed to ensure that I would be unable to mount an effective opposition at those dog-and-pony shows. After Alden and CEDO painted a rosy picture of the plan at the beginning of each public hearing and they opened the meeting up to public comment, they decided to restrict comments or questions to people living in that ward, until everyone living there had an opportunity to comment.

Only then would anyone like me or Bea Bookchin or a Green, who didn't live in that ward, be allowed to speak. By that time it would be late at night and the majority of those who turned out for the meeting, as well as the press, would be long gone.

Since Bea and I could only live in one ward and Bea wasn't an attorney and couldn't effectively explain the Public Trust Doctrine, it was a foregone conclusion that we would be effectively silenced.

That's when I had an epiphany. If the powers that were running the public hearings were going to completely shut me out, my only recourse was to make copies of the article by Debbie Bookchin in the *Rutland Herald* with those great quotes from John Franco about the Public Trust Doctrine, and hand them out to people as they came into the room to attend the public hearing. As they sat down to wait for the hearing to start, they had plenty of time to look over the article, and that would prompt them to ask about the Public Trust Doctrine. And best of all, it wasn't me espousing the rights they all held under the Public Trust Doctrine. Why should they believe a young environmental attorney fresh out of law school who held no elective office in the city, versus the legal experts hired by Alden and the authority of the CEDO office? It was much more effective to have the information coming out of the mouth of the Mayor's handpicked Assistant City Attorney — John Franco.

The first of the six public hearings was scheduled at the Burlington Electric Department in Ward 6. Since I was a resident of Ward 2, I would be prohibited from speaking until everyone in the ward had spoken. I showed up about 15 minutes early with a stack of copies of the *Rutland Herald* article and began to give them out to people as they filed in. They all sat down and naturally began reading the article as they waited for the hearing to begin, just as I planned. Once Paul Flinn realized what I was doing, he became enraged. His face turned bright red and he grabbed me by the arm and ushered me out to the hallway.

"What the hell are you doing?" he demanded.

"The last I knew Burlington is a part of the United States," I replied. "There is a thing called the First Amendment to the Constitution. If you aren't going to let me talk at this hearing, I have no choice other than to hand out copies of this article."

I turned, went back inside, and continued to hand out copies of the *Rutland Herald* article. Flinn was dumbfounded, but there was absolutely nothing he could do.

That changed the course of the hearing, of course. When Peter Clavelle began his presentation at the conclusion of the talk by the Alden people, he felt obliged to address the Public Trust issue right off the bat. John Franco spoke as well. And of course he emphasized that the Public Trust Doctrine was not clear cut, that it did not mean there could be no development on filled land and that the issue was extremely complex. In Franco's opinion, as part of the Sander's team, the Alden plan would fit within the concept of public trust, if that's what the people of Burlington wanted.

I had to wait until the meeting was almost over to contribute my thoughts, and of course I pointed out that Franco had been very clear about the Public Trust Doctrine back in August of 1983, before Sanders had silenced him. I told those left in the room that I believed the old John Franco was right. Public meant public. Condominiums and hotels were some of the most private uses of property imaginable and simply could not be permitted on the filled land under the Public Trust Doctrine. And it didn't matter if Burlington voters anointed the Alden plan. Under the Public Trust Doctrine, the filled land belonged to all the people of the state of Vermont, including people from my home

town of Bellows Falls. The people of Burlington could not change that. Private uses like hotels and condominiums could not magically be converted to public uses even with a two-thirds majority of city voters.

For the most part my argument fell on deaf ears, but at least we had effectively raised the issue and begun to change the course of the debate over Alden. Of course, the press had already left by that point, and I was speaking to a half empty room, but I had forced Clavelle and Franco to address the Public Trust issue. I went home that night feeling that I had actually accomplished something.

The question remaining was whether any of that would make a difference in the outcome. I felt like I was standing in front of a freight train headed down the tracks at full speed. Even if I was right about the Public Trust Doctrine, it might not matter if the bond passed by the necessary two-thirds. With that vote in hand and a collusive lawsuit to rubber stamp the argument that hotels and condominiums are in the public interest, it would take a cold day in hell for us to prevail.

I attended each of the six public hearings and repeated the process of handing out copies of the *Rutland Herald* article at each one. Clavelle was forced to address the Public Trust Doctrine at each meeting, and we started to pick up some press with this argument. I'm sure Paul Flinn was beginning to feel the heat. Was it possible that his plan could be derailed by an environmental gadfly?

At a meeting of the Board of Aldermen on November 18, 1985, I argued that the state of Vermont should seize the land filled into Burlington harbor under the Public Trust Doctrine. I knew I was making progress with that argument when the Sanders Administration produced a letter from Assistant Attorney General J. Wallace Malloy immediately afterward questioning whether the state could seize land under the Public Trust Doctrine and warning that litigation to settle the matter could take years.

On November 19, 1985, the *Burlington Free Press* reported:

> Opponents of the bond say public access would be greater and cheaper if voters rejected the bonds and the state seized the land from the railroad under the "public trust doctrine."
>
> Rick Sharp, a bond opponent, argued Monday the city could ask the state to seize the land, which the state conveyed to the railroad in 1874.
>
> But moments after Sharp finished his argument, City Attorney Joseph McNeil produced the attorney general letter, which says the "public trust doctrine" may not apply.
>
> "Because of the continuing uncertainty as to whether the public trust doctrine applies at all to the filled lands in question, it continues to be our position that the proposed use of the properties be reviewed closely. We have satisfied ourselves that, regardless of whether the doctrine applies to this land, the provisions in the (agreement) are satisfactory to insure that the public interest has been protected and even enhanced," the letter said.
>
> Sharp, an attorney, called the letter "an attempt to head us off at the pass" but said the attorney general cited no legal cases in saying the "public trust doctrine" was unclear. Sharp said he has two cases that show the state could take the land and use it for the public's benefit.[21]

As the vote drew closer, we knew that we didn't have to convince everyone. All we needed to do was raise enough doubt to prevent the proponents from obtaining a two-thirds majority. And as time wore on, it became apparent to me that Mayor Sanders had actually made a major tactical error by setting up the vote all by itself in a special election scheduled for December 10, 1985.

If the Alden issue had been one of a number of items on a larger ballot, with candidates running for office at the same time, the attention of the press would have been spread out, covering all those other issues and candidates. By holding the Alden vote by itself, the attention of the entire city was focused upon this one issue.

For two months before the Alden vote, the press ran a piece on Alden almost every day. The *Burlington Free Press*, the *Vanguard Press*, the local TV stations and the radio programs all focused exclusively on Alden. I barely had time to practice law during this period. Every day I was doing an interview with one arm of the press or the other. Clavelle, Sanders and Franco had their hands full responding to questions raised by our small group of radical environmentalists. In frustration, toward the end of the campaign Clavelle finally lost it one day, asking the press, "Who the hell is Rick Sharp to get all this attention?" I knew I had gotten under their skin at last.

And I knew we were touching a nerve with the public when former Alderman, Maurice Mahoney, joined the cause along with another local and well-respected attorney by the name of Sandy Baird. Then sitting Alderman Paul Lafayette came out in opposition to Alden. We had finally cracked open the City Council. This was no longer just Rick Sharp, Bea Bookchin and the radical left environmentalists in the Green party. Mahoney, Baird and Lafayette were respected

---

21. *Hazen v. Perkins*, 92 Vt. 414 (1918).
   Illinois Central Railroad v. Illinois, 146 U.S. 387 (1892).

THE BURLINGTON BIKE PATH & WATERFRONT PARK

Democratic voices. We had opened up a fissure in the Democratic Party.

We all met in my law office downtown in the evening to plot our strategy, just as we had met so many times before as the Citizens Waterfront Group. Our new group was called Citizens for a BETTER Waterfront. We knew we would need to put out a leaflet and deliver it door-to-door to inform voters of the problems with the Alden plan and counter a pamphlet put together by a coalition of downtown business associations featuring Mayor Sanders' endorsement. Together with Alden, these business groups had raised over $9,000 as of November 25 and hired Paul Bruhn, the respected former Chief of Staff at Senator Patrick Leahy's office, to run an advertising campaign to promote the Alden plan. We had only raised $80 by that point.

Our flyer was drafted by a committee to set forth a wide variety of arguments against the Alden plan. It was intentionally written to raise unanswered questions. And we were in a hurry to get it out as the vote approached. "Our Waterfront is Not for Sale!" screamed our headline. "Please vote NO on the Waterfront bond issue on Dec. 10, 1985. Sponsored by Citizens for A BETTER Waterfront."

We went to print before all the facts were in and made some mistakes. We seriously debated distributing it anyway. It had cost $400 to print 8,000 copies. The Sanders Administration was accusing us of playing loosely with the facts. In the end we did the right thing, corrected the errors and reprinted the flyer. I paid the additional $400 out of my own pocket. The incorrect flyers sat in boxes in my office undistributed for weeks afterward. A copy of the two flyers is attached as *Appendix 7.*

In addition to the Public Trust Doctrine, we argued that the TIF mechanism would actually create a "tax dead zone" for twenty years. All the tax revenues derived from the Alden development would be devoted to paying back the bond, which would swell to over $13 million dollars over its term. We also noted that the Alden development would cost tax dollars for police, fire protection and maintenance expenses. And we argued that Alden would have an impact on the schools and result in gentrification of neighborhoods close to the development.

But perhaps the most important development late in the weeks leading up to the Alden vote was the opposition of the School Board. Due to a quirk in the TIF legislation, the Alden bond would be repaid not only out of tax revenues that would have gone into the general fund. It would also be repaid with funds that would otherwise have gone to the schools. The School Board was already facing a $1.5 million deficit at that time and its members were livid that the Alden project would cut off additional tax revenue to the schools for twenty years or more. "We're being asked to vote on a vision of the waterfront, and I think we should have one," said one school board member, "but I don't think we can sacrifice the vision we have for the schools." In the end, the Burlington School Board voted eight to three to oppose the Alden plan.

Our final tactic was to hold a public information meeting of our own at the Fletcher Free Library on December 2, eight days before the vote, and a last walk on the waterfront on December 7, led by Alderman Lafayette. The meeting at the Fletcher Library was well attended and, best of all, it was captured on video tape by the local public television station. A transcript of the meeting appears as *Appendix 8.* The video was digitized almost thirty years later and is available from CCTV.

A final depiction of what Alden was firmly committed to building going into the vote on December 10 appeared in the *Burlington Free Press* on December 1, 1985. Depicted on the next page.

In the end our tactics worked. The bond received the support of a majority of voters, with 53.4% in favor and almost 46.6% opposed, but it failed because it did not achieve the necessary two-thirds. Our small vocal minority had saved the majority from themselves. As was stated in a Pogo comic strip years ago, "We have met the enemy and he is us."

We celebrated in my office until late that night. We had actually defeated the most powerful political machine the city of Burlington had ever seen!

In the wake of the vote, the *Burlington Free Press* wrote a feature article on me, fittingly headlined, "Rick Sharp Puts Image on Line for Environment," published on December 15, 1985. *Appendix 9.* Reporter Mark Johnson led the article off with: "[Rick Sharp] has been dismissed as a dreamer, a political gadfly who pops up to spoil the plans of Mayor Bernie Sanders. His credibility has been challenged, his

ideas labeled absurd, and his motives questioned." Now, Johnson noted, he is "a political force that cannot be ignored."

Johnson quoted me: "I think there are a lot of people who don't understand where I'm coming from or why I'm doing what I'm doing. I do not like being opposed to bond issues. My public image in this community has been damaged. I guess I place the quality of the environment over my self-interests or looking good." I went on to note that "I see myself as one of those seedlings of Justice Douglas who has been transplanted to Burlington, Vermont and who is going to create that same green strip…. It's good to dream a little bit." I concluded.

Johnson noted that I was known around town as "Mr. Bike Path." But I conceded that "I know I will be the goat of Burlington if there isn't any development on the waterfront in the next three to five years."

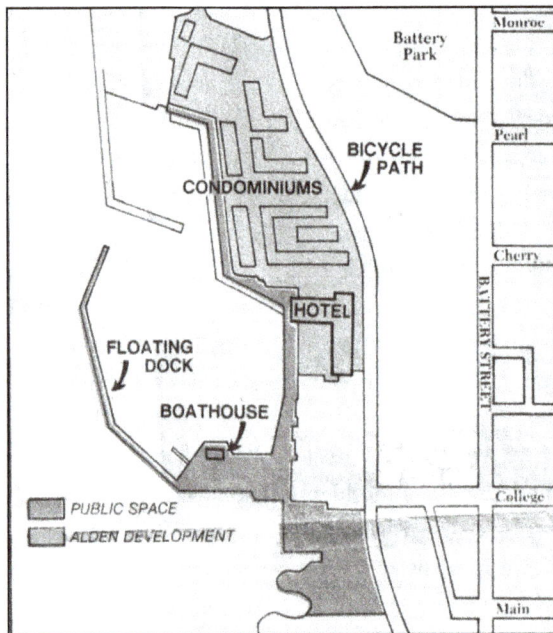

Election night December 10, 1985. The press conference at City Hall. Murray Bookchin, Rick Sharp and Sandy Baird. *Courtesy of Rob Swanson.*

CHAPTER THIRTEEN
After Alden

With the Alden vote in the rear-view mirror, we quickly set our sights on capitalizing on the Public Trust Doctrine we had popularized. We had successfully taken an obscure doctrine of law and transformed it into a household word.

But in the process we had also alienated a lot of people. Mayor Sanders certainly was not among my admirers. As reporter Peter Freyne noted in an "Inside Track" article in the *Vanguard Press* twelve days after the Alden vote on December 22, 1985,

> The bitterness over the defeat of the $6 million bond issue to get the Sanders — Alden waterfront hotel and condo project rolling was evident at this week's meeting of the board of aldermen.
>
> Sanders once again shouted angrily at Rick Sharp, one of the leaders of the team that beat Bernie on this one. But while Sanders has a bottomless pit of venom to unleash on Sharp, he has so far spared one of his closest political colleagues, Ward 2 Alderman Terry Bouricius, the customary public tongue lashing.
>
> You see, Terry, like Sharp, also voted "No" on the bond question. Bouricius says that before we put condos for the rich on the lakefront he'd like to see rent control become a reality in the Queen City.

Although some leading Progressives had opposed Alden, their opposition was never voiced publicly during the long debate leading up to the vote on December 10, 1985. Republican support for Alden was understandable, since Republicans usually favor development. The Greens loudly opposed Alden. Paul Lafayette, Maurice Mahoney and Sandy Baird were all leading Democrats publicly opposed to Alden. Where were the Progressives? They had been silenced by Bernie Sanders.

So the question of the day became what would now become of the derelict waterfront? An article in the *Burlington Free Press* on December 12, 1985 indicated that Governor Madeline Kunin and Mayor Sanders would both support pursuit of the Public Trust Doctrine. There really wasn't any other path for Sanders at that point. But a lawyer for the railroad (Earl Opperthauser) was bitterly opposed to that outcome and couldn't resist taking a cheap shot at me in the press:

> The governor and Sanders said they would support an effort to seize the land from the railroad through the 'public trust doctrine.' Bond opponent Rick Sharp has said that since the railroad property is land reclaimed from the lake by filling, the legal doctrine of 'public trust' says the land should revert to public ownership if the railroad is no longer using it.
>
> Opperthauser disagreed flatly.
>
> "(Sharp) is all wet...and if he isn't all wet we'll stay there forever," Opperthauser said.
>
> "You can't confiscate land in this country for nothing. Maybe you can in Russia or Nazi Germany, but not in the United States of America," he added.

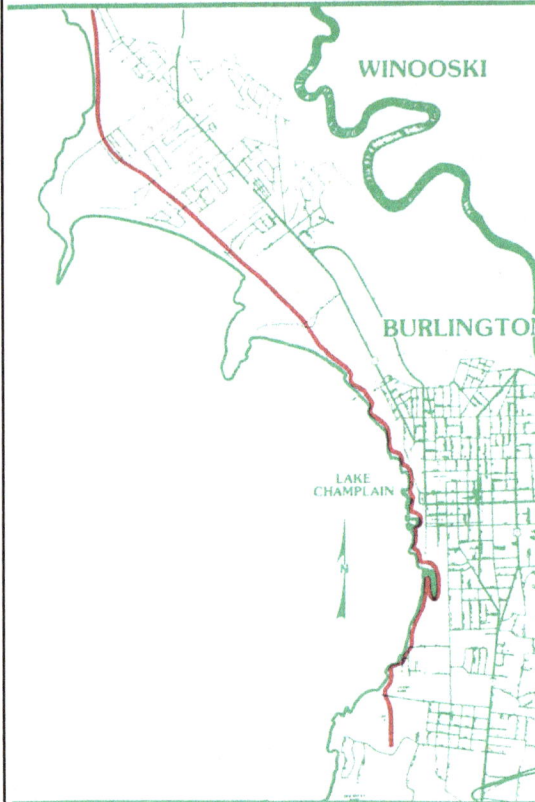

SUPPORT PUBLIC ACCESS
TO THE BURLINGTON WATERFRONT

WINOOSKI

BURLINGTON

LAKE CHAMPLAIN

VOTE YES
ON QUESTIONS 10 AND 11

THE STRUGGLE FOR PUBLIC ACCESS

● 1980 - Pomerleau Agency plan for luxury hotel and 18 story condominium towers on the waterfront are announced.

● 1980 - Rick Sharp, Howard Dean and Tom Hudspeth join with other citizens concerned about public access to the Burlington waterfront to form the Citizen's Waterfront Group (CWG), a non-profit public interest group dedicated to preserving public access to the Burlington waterfront.

● 1980 - CWG formulates plan for bicycle path from Oakledge Park to the mouth of the Winooski River along the lake shore as means of achieving maximum public access similar to coastline protection laws in the West.

● 1980 - Public referendum for waterfront park and bicycle path receives support of over 75% of City voters.

● 1980 - Lawsuit by landowners adjoining former railroad right-of-way in new north end is filed claiming right-of-way is private property. CWG opposes action.

● 1980-1981 - Public support for bicycle path is raised with clearing projects on railroad right-of-way and at the foot of College Street sponsored by CWG.

● 1981 - State law on railroad abandonment is changed to preserve former railroad rights-of-way for public use forever.

● 1981 - Mayor Bernard Sanders is elected partly on campaign promise of "no enclaves for the rich" on Burlington waterfront.

● 1982 - Pomerleau plan is withdrawn due to public opposition, zoning uncertainties and the "public trust" problem.

● 1982 - Federal grant money is obtained to pave 1.5 miles of railroad right-of-way between Starr Farm Road and the mouth of the Winooski River. CWG is instrumental in obtaining funds.

● 1983 - Alden plan for luxury hotel and high priced condominiums within 25 feet of the lake's edge is announced.

● March 1984 - $2 million bond for creation of waterfront park and bicycle path proposed by CWG receives support of 55% of City voters, but fails to receive necessary 66.7%.

● October 1984 - Lawsuit over public trust doctrine is filed.

● November 1984 - $750,000 bond is approved by over 67% of City voters for construction of bicycle path.

● June 1985 - CWG proposal for 80 foot set back for hotels and condominiums receives support of 45% of City voters.

● July 1985 - State and City win lawsuit over railroad right-of-way in new north end. Clearing for construction of bicycle path is begun.

● December 1985 - Alden waterfront plan is defeated due to insufficient public space and the public trust doctrine.

● June 1986 - Eight out of nine miles of bicycle path are completed with bond funds.

● November 1986 - Public trust and 100 foot recreation, conservation zone are placed on the City ballot through petitioning of CWG.

Sanders, who acknowledged he used the public trust doctrine as negotiating leverage with Alden said he doubted Sharp's idea would work.

So even though he had no other viable alternative, Sanders just couldn't bring himself to support our position. The sniping went on for a while thereafter. I can remember hearing snickers from some people in restaurants downtown when I walked by. But I pressed on. I met with several legislators who were interested in pursuing the Public Trust Doctrine in the legislature. Notable among those were Barbara Hockert and Ben Truman from the center city's Ward 2 and Ward 3 districts. Howard Dean led the legislative initiative.

And in order to firmly establish the concept of the Public Trust Doctrine among Burlington voters and ensure more public space on the waterfront for our bike path and waterfront park, we proposed putting both the Public Trust Doctrine and a 100-

SUPPORT PUBLIC ACCESS
TO THE BURLINGTON WATERFRONT

VOTE YES ON
QUESTIONS 10 AND 11

On November 4, 1986 Burlington voters will have an opportunity to voice their opinion on the two most important issues affecting the future of the Burlington waterfront: zoning and the public trust doctrine.

The exact wording of these two ballot items appears below:

Question 10

Shall our elected representatives in the Vermont Legislature and on the City Council be advised to jointly pursue the public trust doctrine as applied to filled lands in the Burlington harbor in order to obtain maximum public access and recreation and conservation space?

Question 11

Should the City of Burlington rezone a strip of land at least 100 feet wide along the waterfront as recreation conservation space and establish a waterfront park and bicycle path extending from Oakledge Park to the mouth of the Winooski River?

These are advisory ballot items. They do not commit our elected representatives to anything. They merely inform our representatives of your opinion on these two critical issues. Our collective answers to these questions will set a tone for development of new zoning rules and resolution of the public trust issue.

Question 10

Question 10 advises our elected officials to actively pursue the public trust doctrine to retain our rights to the so-called "filled land" in the Burlington harbor.

Over the past 200 years, 55 to 60 acres have been created in the downtown area by filling in the lake. The State of Vermont owns the bed of Lake Champlain which it holds in trust for all Vermont residents.

The railroads were given the right to use this filled land for a public transportation purpose in 1874. The railroad is no longer using this land for this public purpose and is now attempting to sell it to developers for $400,000 an acre.

The railroad did not pay for this land, and it has not paid taxes on it for 112 years. The public trust doctrine would allow us to reclaim this land and put it to new public uses (set forth below) which are consistent with public needs in the 20th and 21st century.

The City of Chicago reclaimed its waterfront from the Illinois Central Railroad in 1892, and today the Chicago waterfront is open to the public with private structures set back from the lake's edge hundreds of feet.

Pursuit of the public trust doctrine does not mean we should refuse to negotiate a fair settlement of this issue however. If adequate public space is preserved and the public participates in the decision-making process, certainly a negotiated settlement is in order.

foot setback on the March 1986 city ballot. Once again we collected petition signatures and got both initiatives on the city ballot. A copy of the flyer we distributed to city voters in support of these ballot items appears here. It provides a good chronological summary up to this point.

Both advisory items received the support of more than 76% of city voters. The directive to the Sanders Administration was unmistakable.

Without the six million dollars from the city, the Alden plan was dead on arrival. Paul Flinn announced that Alden would not proceed without public money. To his credit, Bernie Sanders unleashed John Franco to aggressively pursue the Public Trust Doctrine in the previously filed lawsuit, which suddenly turned adversarial, as it should have been from the start. As Sandy Baird later remarked, the Sanders Administration were "good losers." They got the message, changed their approach to the waterfront and pursued the will of the people of Burlington for more public space.

That ultimately saved the waterfront for public uses, but it also allowed Bernie Sanders to revise the history of the waterfront struggle and take full credit for the subsequent incredible metamorphosis there, even though he had fought us tooth and nail on behalf of the Alden plan from 1983 through 1985. In his recent book, *Our Towns* (2018), James

Fallows captured Sanders' revised historical account as follows:

> As Sanders has not been shy in pointing out...he directly fought back [against developers], and overcame rather than compromised with his main opponents. His city attorney and the state attorney general sued the Central Vermont Railway for control of waterfront property then used for petroleum storage and a rail siding. They won, and now the land is the site of an aquarium and science center, bike paths, and other public facilities. 'We put together a grassroots coalition and made the city as open as we could,' Sanders told me.

In fact it was the Citizens Waterfront Group and Citizens for a BETTER Waterfront that were the true grass roots coalitions that saved the Burlington waterfront from the developers Sanders had so ardently supported. And the Sanders Administration had actually done its best to thwart an open conversation about Alden. If Bernie Sanders had his way in 1985, he would have been standing on top of a luxury condominium on the waterfront when he announced his campaign for President in the summer of 2015.

The minority of 46.6% of the voters that opposed the Alden plan saved the majority from what would have been a big mistake. Looking back on it now, most agree that we came out of this process with a much better waterfront. Sanders came around in the end, after his administration tried everything else first. And of course, one of the biggest lessons to be learned here is to respect the views and opinions of the minority. Sometimes the minority is right.

Franco and the Attorney General's office did their best in pursuit of the Public Trust Doctrine in the Chittenden Superior Court. But the decision of the trial court was far less than any of us attorneys were hoping for, with the Court finding fee simple title in the railroad, meaning that the trial court reaffirmed the railroad's ownership of the property, subject to the Public Trust Doctrine. The state of Vermont and the city appealed to the Vermont Supreme Court.

In 1989 the Vermont Supreme Court reversed the Superior Court and issued a sweeping decision by one of the most conservative justices on the court at the time, confirming the application of the Public Trust Doctrine to the filled land in Burlington harbor and insisting that such lands must be devoted to public uses. In essence, the 1989 decision put an end to any possibility of developing hotels and condominiums on the filled land in Burlington harbor. *State v. Central Vermont Railway.*[22]

With that kind of development off the table, the filled land was greatly devalued. Acreage which had previously been valued as high as $400,000 by some estimates, the most valuable acreage in Vermont at the time, was suddenly rendered almost worthless. When you can't build hotels and condominiums all over the land, it loses most of its value.

By 1990, Bernie Sanders was off to greener pastures as a member of Congress in Washington, D.C. and Peter Clavelle had taken the helm as mayor.

Clavelle negotiated the purchase of 8.5 acres of the Alden property from Central Vermont Railway for half a million dollars. After voters approved a $1 million bond to buy an additional 45 acres of filled land from the railroad to set aside as an "urban reserve" in March 1991, Clavelle negotiated a "fire sale" purchase of the railroad's remaining interest in Burlington harbor for $1.8 million, one tenth of its value unencumbered by the Public Trust Doctrine. In his book, *Burlington A History of Vermont's Queen City* (2015), Vincent E. Feeney calls this purchase the "sale of the century." It allowed the city to set aside the filled land for park space, the bicycle path and other public uses forever.

The Vermont legislature took up the Public Trust Doctrine and enacted legislation authorizing the city to develop the filled land while carefully specifying allowed public uses and prohibiting private uses. Under this arrangement, the state still holds the filled land in trust for all the people of Vermont, but administrative authority over this land is delegated to the city.

In 1987, city voters approved funds for the waterfront boathouse that Bernie Sanders had insisted on in negotiations with Alden, but failed to secure. Local architect, Marcel Beaudin, designed a building on a floating barge that was anchored at the end of the spit of land protruding into the lake at the foot of College Street that the CWG had converted into the first "pocket park" along the pathway in the early 1980s. *(See Chapter Four.)* Beaudin's design mimicked the roofline of the old Lake Champlain Yacht Club from the 1880s. *See the photo on page 13* of the dilapidated wreckage on the same spot in Burlington harbor in 1935.

The Sanders Administration initially considered a site off Roundhouse Point for the boathouse and that site was recommended in *A Study of Public Access and Improvements for the Burlington Water-*

---

22. *State v. Central Vermont Railway, 153 Vt. 337 (1989).*

front, September 1986. But the sewer outflow pipe did not extend beyond the breakwater at that time, so there was a fear of foul odors there, at least until the pipe was extended. That's why the Boathouse was built on a barge. The Sanders Administration wasn't sure the Boathouse would remain at its location at the foot of College Street permanently. Clearly, College Street is the correct location for the Boathouse. Together with the ECHO museum and the boardwalk, it provides a focus for visitors where one of the only "through streets" in the city meets the water.

U.S. Senator Patrick Leahy was instrumental in getting the Naval Reserve facility just south of College Street on the waterfront to relocate, thus making that parcel available for redevelopment. Funds were secured for a museum and lake science center focused on educating children about the ecology and geology of the Lake Champlain Basin. ECHO is an acronym for Ecology, Culture, History and Opportunity. ECHO is always high on the list of Burlington Attractions on Trip Advisor. It also provides a great venue for weddings, for watching the 3rd of July fireworks and private events like the *Seven Days* "Daisies" Party each year.

By the early 1990s the Bike Path was complete thanks to the funds provided by the 1984 bond. South of Perkins Pier the Bike Path was routed along the shoreline west of the sewage treatment plant out onto Roundhouse Point. A bridge was built across the Barge Canal and the Bike Path was then squeezed into a narrow strip of land between the railroad tracks and the lake. Although there are great views of the lake from this portion of the path, its aesthetics leave a lot to be desired, with a narrow pathway hugging a chain link fence for almost a mile.

The best solution to this problem is to fill in a shallow portion of the lake between the Barge Canal and the former Blodgett Oven property to create a linear park with a sandy beach. The Bike Path could then be rerouted through this filled in parcel and then over Blodgett Beach for a much more appealing approach to the Lakeside neighborhood. *(See the path of the dotted line on the map on page 81.)* The Blodgett property was recently purchased by Russ Scully. He runs a kayak, windsurfing and paddleboard operation on the property called the Burlington Surf Club. He has also developed a business incubator space called Hula on the property. Hopefully he will eventually understand the value of running the Bike Path along the lakeshore of his property instead.

At the Lakeside neighborhood, it was necessary to run the Bike Path along the side of existing streets past the main park there. This is an acceptable route but not the best solution. It was a compromise. The better route through Lakeside would begin at the south end of the Blodgett Beach extension of the path and reconnect to the existing path just north of the bridge across Englesby Brook. *(See*

page 81.) That still leaves the Harbor Watch condominiums west of the Bike Path, but that's the best that can be done without extensive filling of the lake that would probably be prohibited by the Army Corps of Engineers.

Harbor Watch and the development of two condominiums on the west side of the Bike Path just south of the Preseault condominiums north of Rock Point were the only two lakefront projects in Burlington approved after the initiation of the campaign for the Burlington Bike Path. These two lakefront projects are typical of what would have happened all along the Burlington shore were it not for the Bike Path. Just imagine a shoreline crowded with lakefront units like that.

Harbor Watch condominiums in 2019. Aerial photo by *A. Patterson.*

This is an aerial photo of the two additional lakeside units Preseault built in 1982. *A. Patterson.*

Another bridge was necessary to cross Englesby Brook. From there south, the path was constructed over a grassy strip separating an oil tank farm from the lake. Oakledge Park then provides ample space for the pathway all the way to Austin Drive just north of the South Burlington line.

Through the downtown area, the pathway was snaked in between the parking lot just north of Perkins Pier and the railroad tracks. The path was then routed across the tracks at King Street and run down the east side of the tracks to College Street. It was much cheaper to paint a bike path on existing pavement through that area than it would have been to build it correctly along the west side of the railroad tracks. *More on that in Chapter Twenty.*

At College Street the pathway was routed back across the tracks and continued north on the west side of the tracks in the newly created Waterfront Park. This was the route we had insisted on all through the Alden debate, but instead of 80 feet of park space, the city ended up with over 200 feet. Thanks to city Arborist, Warren Spinner, linden trees were planted along the pathway that have now matured into a wonderful canopy of fragrant buds in early July each year and welcome shade from the sun all summer long. A boardwalk was constructed along the shoreline with swinging chairs. People often play with Frisbees or play volleyball or soccer on the grass between the Bike Path and the boardwalk. This is indeed the most appealing waterfront imaginable. We have succeeded beyond my wildest dreams.

A little north of College Street the filled land juts out into the lake a bit further. This is the area where the Pomerleau Agency had proposed two 18-story luxury condominium towers in 1980 — a project Tom Hudspeth had labeled a "mini-Acapulco." The berms surrounding the old Shell oil storage tanks in this area were flattened. Contaminated soil was removed and clean top soil applied. Grass and trees were planted and this area was magically transformed into Burlington's "event space" — the area where festivals are conducted all summer long.

From there the path was run northward along an access road to the old Texaco oil storage tanks north of downtown, by painting a line on the existing pavement through the so-called "north 40 urban reserve" that the city had acquired in the "Sale of the Century." From the end of that road the path was routed northward on the old rail bed to the mouth of the Winooski River.

So by the early 1990s, when the Bike Path was complete, families could finally take their children on a ride from Oakledge Park to the old railroad bridge abutment at the Winooski River without having to fight car traffic. People immediately took to the pathway and it quickly became the most popular attraction in the city. People living in nearby towns now take their families to Burlington to pedal down the Burlington Bike Path, just as my wife and I did when our children were young. I sometimes wonder how many lives have been saved by the Burlington Bike Path because people took their children there rather than risk a bike ride along a busy street with cars and trucks that can easily kill you.

People in the New North End often build pathways from their back yards to the Bike Path. The fear of crime is long gone, and homes along the Bike Path fetch a higher price at sale.

The Burlington Bicycle Path has changed the culture of the city by making it a mecca for bicyclists. When I arrived in Burlington in 1978, very few people rode bicycles. I found a great apartment on Buell Street, sold my car and got around exclusively by bicycle for over a year, but that was fairly uncommon at that time. Current City Councilor, Max Tracy, is an avid bicycle advocate who doesn't own a car. He gets about exclusively by bicycle. That is probably much more common today with carshare vehicles available by the hour or the day. Terry Precision Cycling moved to Burlington from Manchester, NY in 2009 and Budnitz Bicycles moved here in 2014 to be part of the biking scene in the Queen City.

Local Motion picked up the torch in 1999 and has become the most active and effective bicycle advocacy group in the U.S. today. *More on Local Motion in Chapter Fifteen.*

The Vermont City Marathon is another concrete consequence of the Bike Path. It brings over four million dollars of business to Burlington in May each year, packing hotels and restaurants downtown during a period of time when they would otherwise be virtually empty. Views of the lake and the Adirondacks along the Bike Path, as well as the vigorous crowds of outdoor enthusiasts greeting and cheering on racers each year, make the Vermont City Marathon a favorite on the marathon circuit, now a qualifying event for the Boston Marathon. Would the marathon have come into existence or be as popular without the Bike Path? What will bicycling and other alternate forms of urban transportation mean to the city in the future? Read on.

THE BURLINGTON BIKE PATH & WATERFRONT PARK

Colchester
Bike Bridge

The Intervale

Overlook at
Northshore

Winooski River

Appletree
Point

Burlington Bike Path

Leddy
Park

Burlington

Rock
Point

North
Beach

Waterfront Park

Battery
Park

Lake Champlain

Boathouse

Perkins Pier

Barge Canal

Blodgett Beach

Lakeside

Oakledge Park

N
W · E
S

Bike Path
Park Space

Maps on these five pages by Marie Letourneau.

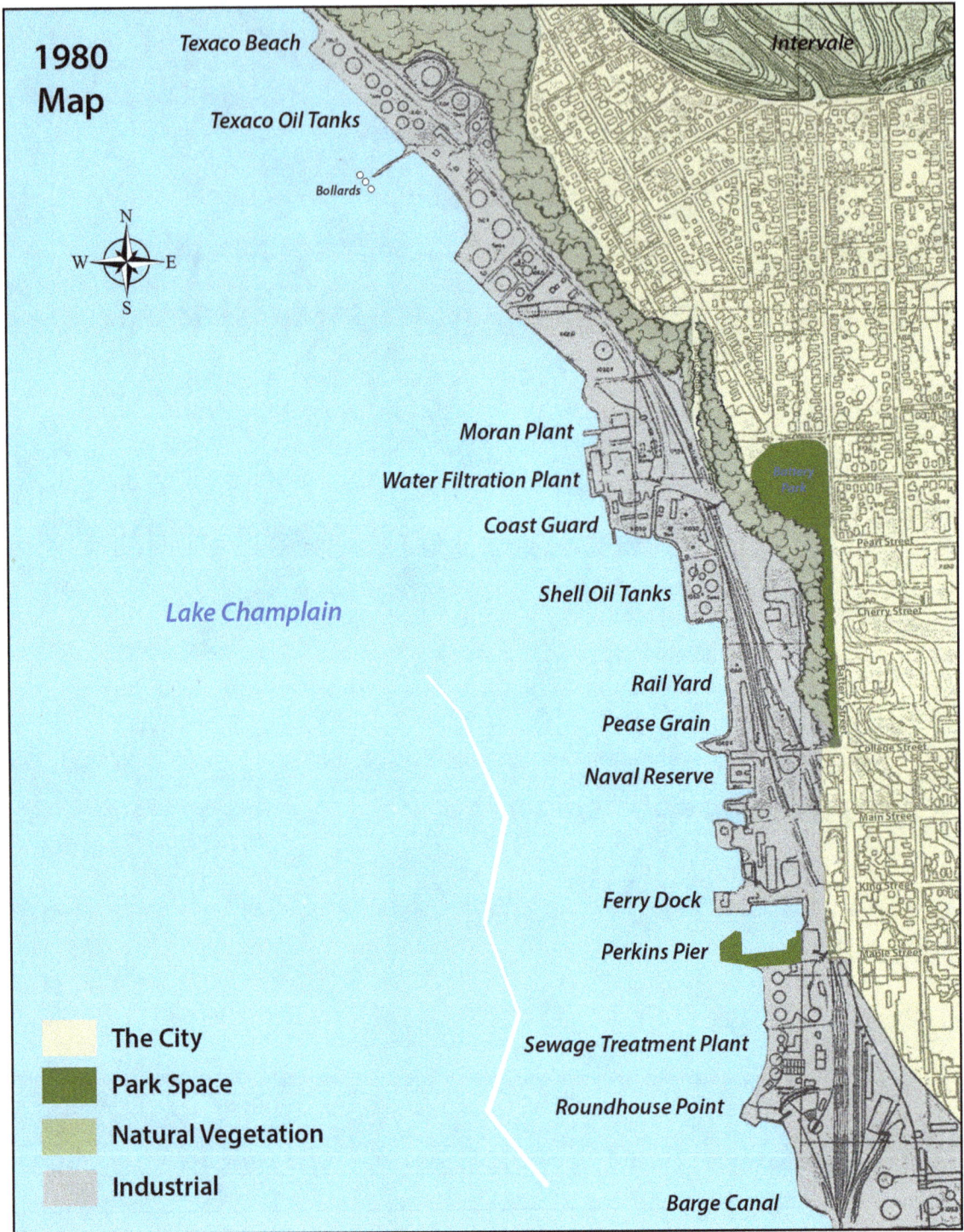

1980
Map

Texaco Beach

Texaco Oil Tanks

Bollards

Intervale

N
W   E
S

Moran Plant

Water Filtration Plant

Coast Guard

Shell Oil Tanks

Lake Champlain

Rail Yard

Pease Grain

Naval Reserve

Ferry Dock

Perkins Pier

Sewage Treatment Plant

Roundhouse Point

Barge Canal

The City

Park Space

Natural Vegetation

Industrial

2019 Map

Texaco Beach

Intervale

Bollards

Community Sailing Center

Skate Park

Moran Plant

Water Treatment Plant

Coast Guard

Waterfront Event Space

Lake Champlain

Boardwalk

Waterfront Park

Boathouse

ECHO

Ferry Dock

Perkins Pier

Sewage Treatment Plant

Roundhouse Point

Barge Canal

Pearl Street

Cherry Street

College Street

Main Street

King Street

— Bike Path

The City

Park Space

Natural Vegetation

Industrial

1980 Map

Barge Canal

Lake Champlain

Coal Tar Superfund Site

N
W   E
S

Blodgett Beach

The City
Park Space
Industrial
Superfund Site

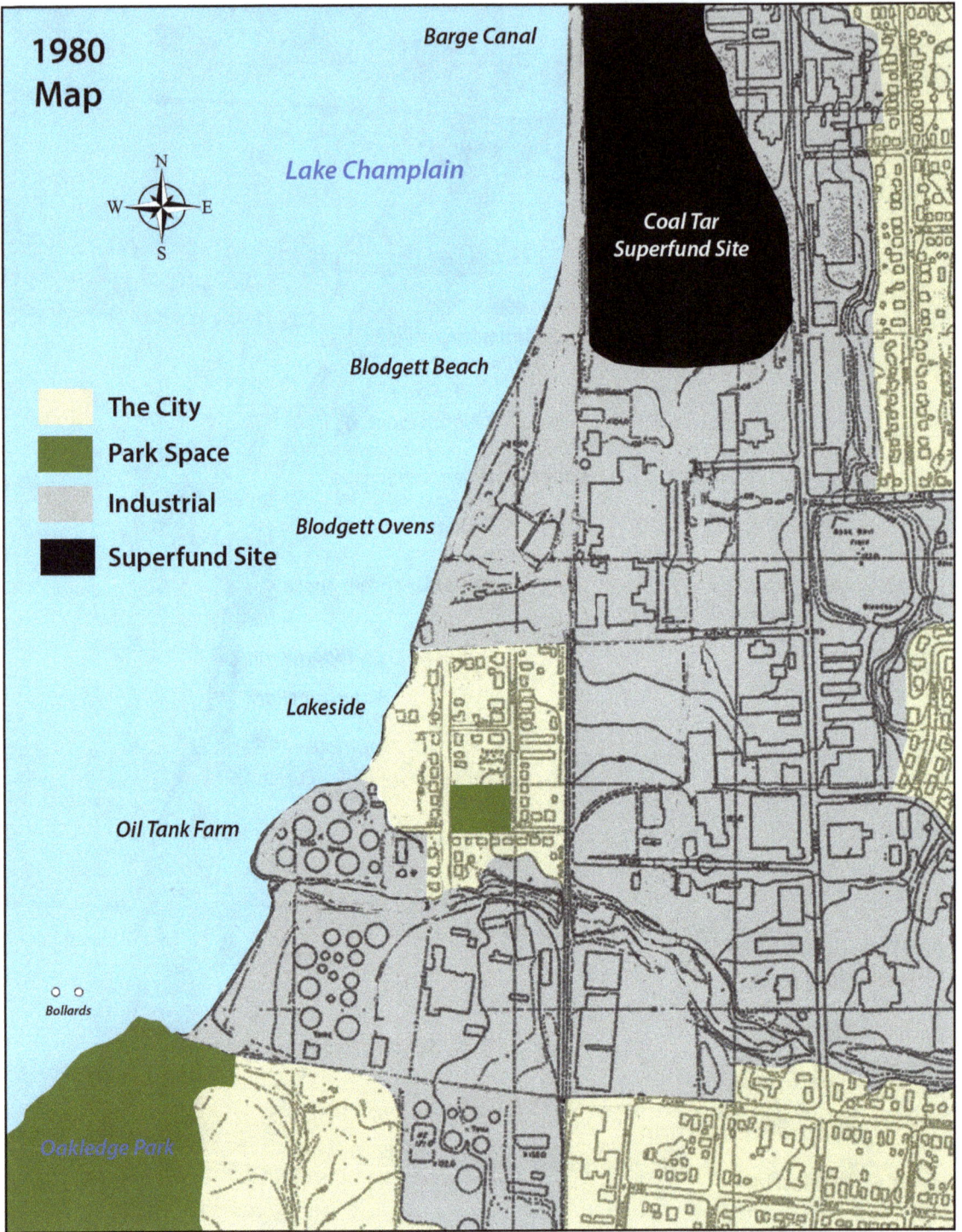

Blodgett Ovens

Lakeside

Oil Tank Farm

○ ○
Bollards

Oakledge Park

2019 Map

Legend:
- ━━━ Bike Path
- ▪▪▪▪ Proposed Pathway
- ▢ The City
- ▢ Park Space
- ▢ Industrial
- ▢ Superfund Site

Barge Canal

Lake Champlain

Coal Tar Superfund Site

South End Arts District

Blodgett Beach

Proposed Pathway

Burlington Bike Path

Burlington Surf Club

Hula

Lakeside Ave

Lakeside

Harbor Watch

Bollards

Oakledge Park

CHAPTER FOURTEEN
The Landmark Decision

The 1986 decision of the ICC approving rail-banking and interim trail use of the railbed through the New North End allowed the city to complete the Bike Path past the Preseault property and the others who had joined the litigation. But as long as Preseault's court appeals were pending, there was still a question as to whether the Rails-to-Trails Act was Constitutional. The landmark decision of the U.S. Supreme Court in *Preseault v. ICC*[23] in 1990 answered that question. The issue before the Court was the Constitutionality of the Rails-to-Trails Act, which allows municipalities and other qualified trail sponsors to purchase or lease railroad rights-of-way over which operations have ceased and convert them to interim trail use.

As you will recall from Chapter Four, Paul Preseault started in the Vermont state courts arguing that the railroad right-of-way automatically reverted to him under state property law when the tracks were taken up in the 1970s. Unfortunately for him, the state of Vermont and VTR never applied for an abandonment certificate from the ICC when they removed the rails for critical repairs to the tracks south of Burlington. After Preseault was thrown out of state court due to the lack of an abandonment certificate, he petitioned the ICC to recognize a "de facto" abandonment. The ICC would have none of that, instead granting the competing application of the state of Vermont and VTR to allow conversion of the rail line to a bike path under the provisions of the Rails-to-Trails Act. Preseault then petitioned for judicial review in the federal courts challenging this conversion. After a torturous path, this case ended up at the U.S. Supreme Court in 1990. This case was the first to attempt to apply the Rails-to-Trails Act since its enactment in 1983 to reach the U.S. Supreme Court — the "case of first impression."

Preseault's attorneys argued that under Vermont law, upon abandonment the rail bed reverted back to the original owner and then through a legal chain of title down to Preseault. Thus, Preseault claimed what is known in legal jargon as a "springing reversionary interest."

His attorneys contended that the Rails-to-Trails Act was an unconstitutional taking of private property (Preseault's springing reversionary interest). The Fifth Amendment prohibits taking private property without due compensation. By allowing the state or the city to convert the old railroad right-of-way to a whole new use — a bicycle path — instead, they pointed out that their client would never get the property back.

The Rails-to-Trails Act of 1983 made it clear that it is the intention of Congress to "railbank" old rail beds throughout the U.S. for possible future transportation purposes even if there is no foreseeable reuse for rail transportation. That is a very wise public policy. Once these rail corridors are abandoned they are almost impossible to reassemble. *See Chapter Fifteen*. But of course, this policy was in direct conflict with Preseault's springing reversionary interest.

---

23. *Preseault v. ICC, 494 US 1 (1990).*

By the time the case got to the U.S. Supreme Court it had over two hundred *amicus curiae* briefs filed in support of the conversion of abandoned rail beds to bike paths from other bicycle advocacy groups across the country who wanted to convert similar railroad rights-of-way to bike paths under the Rails-to-Trails Act.

In a landmark decision affecting all railroad rights-of-way throughout the United States, the U.S. Supreme Court ruled that Congress had the power under the Commerce Clause to authorize rail banking upon abandonment of rail lines nationwide, clearing the way for the conversion of rail beds throughout the country to multi-use recreation paths.

But Preseault still wasn't done. After the Supreme Court decision, he filed a complaint with the U.S. Court of Claims under the Tucker Act, seeking compensation from the federal government for a taking of his reversionary interest. Preseault lost the first two rounds, in the Court of Claims and before a three-judge panel of the U.S. Court of Appeals. But he went on to a suc-

Rick Sharp and John Dunleavy in 2018. *R. Masters.*

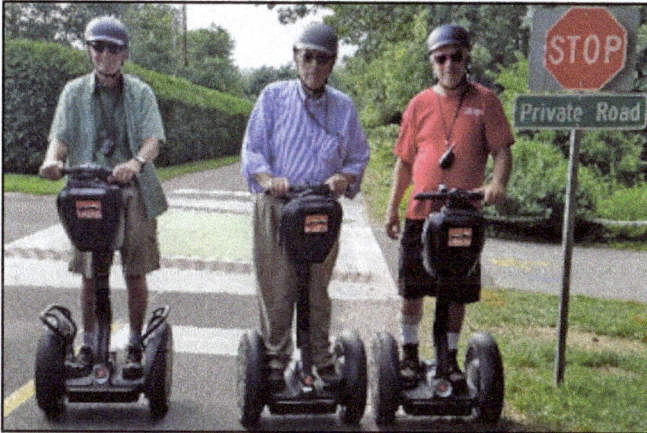

John Leddy, John Dunleavy and Rick Sharp on Segway PTs on the new 12 foot wide pathway as it intersects with Preseault's driveway. *2018 R. Masters.*

cessful conclusion on the taking issue in an opinion from the Circuit Court sitting *en banc.*

This decision raised a lot of eyebrows at the Rails-to-Trails Conservancy and in the environmental community due to the fact that a number of the judges on the *en banc* court were alleged to have recently attended an "educational conference" on property rights sponsored and fully paid for by a conservative property rights group called the Foundation for Research on Economics and the Environment (FREE), at a posh resort in Montana. Judges and their spouses attending the conference also enjoyed time for "cycling, fishing, golfing, hiking and horseback riding" on what was described as a "traditional dude ranch."

Although this decision was widely criticized as an aberration, it had very limited applicability beyond the Preseault case. So it was not appealed. However, even though the *en banc* court found this conversion to be a taking, Preseault was not entitled to possession of the property. Instead he ended up with an award of $234,000 for his "springing reversionary interest" and almost $895,000 for attorney's fees.

No one else along the rail bed received compensation for the extinguishment of their "springing reversionary interest" in the old rail bed. They didn't complain. But we can thank Paul Preseault for pursuing this case to the landmark set of decisions that allow the conversion of rail beds throughout the United States to recreation paths under the Rails-to-Trails Act.

Attorney John Leddy represented the city of Burlington in this litigation. Attorney John Dunleavy represented the state of Vermont and argued the case in the State Courts, before the ICC, the Second Circuit, the U.S. Supreme Court, the Court of Claims, and the Federal Circuit Court. They did a great job. We were all proud of the role we played in setting the nationwide precedent that would lead to the conversion of thousands of miles of old abandoned railroad beds to multi-use recreation paths. The final result of that lawsuit is far beyond my wildest dreams when we started.

With the Preseault decision and the Public Trust case completed, the last major obstacles to completion of the Bike Path were behind us. The city could proceed with setting a course through the downtown area. To save money and to get the pathway completed from one end of the city to the other with only $750,000, compromises were made. Once the pathway left the rail bed north of downtown it was diverted to an old industrial road through the so-called "north forty" urban reserve. This road had too many potholes to count that often filled with rain water. When the city finally rebuilt the Bike Path through the downtown area in 2016 (Bike Path 2.0), it relocated the pathway closer to the water with multiple viewing spots and exercise stations provided by the UVM Medical Center. The cost to completely rebuild the Bike Path in 2016-2020 was more than $15 million, with the local share of the project financed with a bond proposed by the Weinberger Administration.

But the rest of the pathway through the downtown area was now surrounded by park space, just as we had insisted all along. It wasn't Russia or Nazi Germany. It was old Roman and English law that had prevailed after all.

That left only a two-block section of the path between College and King Street that still needs to be realigned to eliminate two railroad crossings and produce a truly world class bike path. *See Chapter Twenty.*

The Preseault decision opened the flood gates on the conversion of old abandoned railroad beds across the country to recreation trails in all fifty states. According to the Rails-to-Trails Conservancy, by 2019 there were 2,130 open rail trails totaling 24,000 miles nationwide. But not only have those trails provided precious recreation space in urban environments, they have also preserved that right of way for future uses as a transportation corridor. It's amazing how once a good idea catches on it can be repeated time after time with the support and drive of the local community.

Thirty years later this nationwide movement to reclaim abandoned railroad beds for recreational uses is still a work in progress. Each year miles of old rail beds are added to the nationwide network of rail trails criss-crossing the nation. If such a great resource like an abandoned railbed exists in your community, by all means form a group and get into converting it to a multiuse path. Don't let a resource like that go to waste. For assistance in this process contact the Rails-to-Trails Conservancy. They are the experts in rail conversions with a wealth of information on the process involved.

CHAPTER FIFTEEN
Across the Winooski
The dream of the String of Pearls becomes the reality of the Island Line Trail

I still remember the first time I rode my bicycle northward all the way to the end of the railroad right-of-way at the south bank of the Winooski River. It was 1980. I wanted to actually see the rail bed that we were proposing to convert to a bicycle path. It was very rough in places and very wet in others. Some of the bed still had railroad ties in place. A lot of brush was encroaching from the sides. Roots were growing into the rail bed in places and there were landslides and erosion. But the rail bed itself had a fairly decent cinder bed throughout its course.

At the south edge of the Winooski River there was a huge cement bridge abutment. The railroad bridge itself had been removed years before in the 1970s after the rail line had been abandoned. The cinder bed ended at the edge of the abutment. Teenage daredevils sometimes jumped from the concrete slab into the river below in the summertime.

I stared across the river as it joined the lake, too wide to throw a rock across, and thought to myself, "So this is it. This is as far as the Burlington Bike Path will ever go." I just couldn't even imagine a new bridge across that expanse of the Winooski River — a bridge devoted only to pedestrian and bicycle traffic.

We were all intrigued by a proposal by UVM Professor Fred Sargent during the Hoff Administration in 1965 called the String of Pearls. The focus of Sargent's study was what to do with the old rail line built from Burlington through the Lake Champlain Islands that the state had acquired for $20,000 in a fire sale from the Rutland Railroad in 1963.

The String of Pearls was a brilliant plan way ahead of its time. It embraced the future of Lake Champlain for its recreational assets rather than as an industrial seaway that had been proposed at about that time to allow supertankers passage

The old railroad bridge during demolition in the early 1970s. Only the main span remains in this photo. *Courtesy of Local Motion.*

Swimming at the railroad bridge abutment. Note the bicyclist at the end of the pathway above. *Caroline Bates. Courtesy of Local Motion.*

from Albany to Montreal via Lake Champlain. That ill-fated plan was killed in the cradle by the Lake Champlain Committee along with a 1967 proposal to build a nuclear power plant in Charlotte. Clearly the value of Lake Champlain is far greater for its recreational resources than it ever would have been for petroleum transportation and industrial uses.

The String of Pearls identified eleven "pocket parks", or pearls, strung along a 37 mile stretch of the old rail line north of Burlington. It would have connected two state parks in the Islands with other special areas of interest renowned for their stunning views and/ or wildlife habitat in a linear park inspired by famous landscape architect, Frederick Law Olmsted. Olmsted designed a world-renowned park along the Charles River in Boston called the Emerald Necklace in 1878. He also designed the landscape for Shelburne Farm for Dr. William Seward and Lila Vanderbilt Webb in 1888.

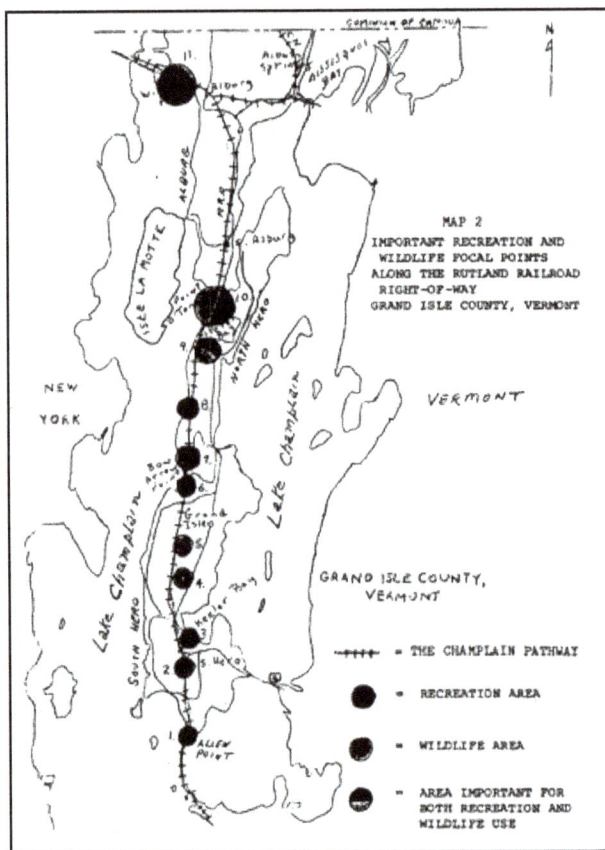

Map of the String of Pearls by Professor Fred Sargent 1965.

We became aware of the String of Pearls shortly after forming the Citizens Waterfront Group in 1980. But as a small public interest group focused on the Burlington waterfront, the String of Pearls was far too ambitious for us to bite off. We dreamed of the String of Pearls, but focused on a path from Oakledge Park to the Winooski River.

And as it turned out, we would have been too late anyway. The State Commissioner of Forests and Parks in the early 1960s was Perry Merrill. Merrill is perhaps best known for his promotion of leases of state forest land to ski areas largely responsible for Vermont's winter ski industry today. Unfortunately, as a forester, Merrill's emphasis was on forests, not parks. He didn't see the value of the String of Pearls proposal. He couldn't see how recreation in the Islands could be monetized like stumpage or ski areas on state forest land.

Property owners in the Islands did not take kindly to the String of Pearls proposal. They wanted the railroad right-of-way to revert to them. And that was the law in Vermont at that time. Merrill exploited their short-sightedness and got the legislature to deed the railroad right-of-way back to adjoining landowners in the Islands for $50 an acre! Augh!

A section of the railroad bed north of the Winooski River in Colchester and south of Airport Park was lost to a housing subdivision in the late 1960s, long before the rail banking provisions of the Rails-to-

Trails Act that might have saved that section of track. The rest of the old rail bed north of Airport Park out to the Causeway was still there, but it continued to deteriorate and became more overgrown with brush and trees throughout the 1980s. People buried the rail bed with trash in places. Things didn't look good for a revival of the String of Pearls proposal.

But then the Burlington Bicycle Path was completed to the Winooski River and suddenly there was renewed interest in extending the path across the river into Colchester. Good ideas like the Burlington Bicycle Path and the String of Pearls are like snowballs rolling downhill. They have a tendency to pick up momentum. That's exactly what's happened with bicycle paths and bicycling in general in the greater Burlington area.

In Colchester the effort to extend the Bike Path north across the Winooski River was largely driven by Colchester Selectboard Chairman Bill MacLeay. MacLeay was a tireless bicycle advocate who regularly used his bicycle as his primary means of transportation about Colchester. He wanted to connect Airport Park to the Burlington Bike Path. Together with others he also championed the idea of turning the railbed out to the Causeway into a bike path. MacLeay got an advisory item onto the March 1992 ballot asking Colchester voters if they supported an effort to build a new bridge across the Winooski River to connect the Burlington Bike Path to Colchester.

That's when all hell broke loose. Doug Wolinski was a well-known bankruptcy attorney who happened to live in Colchester just north of Delta Park in the Biscayne Heights subdivision that had been built on top of the old rail line. He was adamantly opposed to building a bridge across the Winooski River.

Because the rail bed had been obliterated in the late 1960s, replaced by the homes of the Biscayne Heights subdivision, bicyclists coming across a bridge over the river through Delta Park would then

Map by M. Letourneau.

have to be routed northward through the subdivision to connect to Airport Park. From Airport Park north the rail bed was still intact in various states of decay all the way out to the Causeway. *See map.*

Colchester Parks and Recreation Director, Betsy Orselet (now Terry), and Parks and Recreation Board Chairman, Buzz Hoerr, strongly supported the connection to Burlington. So when MacLeay put the bridge item on the 1992 ballot he didn't expect a lot of opposition. It was only advisory and there was no money attached, so the ballot item wouldn't cost taxpayers anything. It should have been a no-brainer.

What town planners didn't foresee, of course, was the NIMBY factor — Not In My Back Yard. As an attorney, Doug Wolinski was fairly well spoken, and he knew many of the people living in the subdivision. He battled the bridge through hearing after hearing. There were reports that some of the residents of the Biscayne Heights subdivision believed that a bridge across the river would bring an undesirable element living in a low-income housing project in Burlington's New North End on the Bike Path right into their neighborhood. This highly vocal group preferred to use the Winooski River as a moat.

By the time the voting took place, the NIMBYs outnumbered those with an eye on the old String of Pearls proposal and the vote on the bridge was a surprising NO.

That didn't stop MacLeay and a growing group of Colchester bicycle advocates. They argued that development of a recreation path out onto the Causeway would be an economic benefit to the town as well as a great improvement to the quality of life of residents of Colchester. Undeterred by the vote, they turned their attention to converting the old rail bed north of Airport Park into a bike path out to the Causeway. The Parks and Recreation Department was firmly behind this reclamation. They actively recruited volunteers to clear the right-of-way north of Airport Park of trash and brush.

Brian Costello moved to Colchester in 1986. He could see the Causeway from his living room. Betsy Terry recruited him to join the clearing parties. On Green Up Day, Costello joined other volunteers who removed trash from the rail bed out to the Causeway. Together with Lew Wetzel, Costello joined work parties that replaced the boards over the only remaining railroad bridge on the Causeway near Law Island to allow bicyclists to proceed all the way out to the "Cut," or gap, in the fill that

The Causeway after it was abandoned as a railroad but before it was reclaimed as a recreation trail. *Circa 1990. Courtesy of Joe Frank*

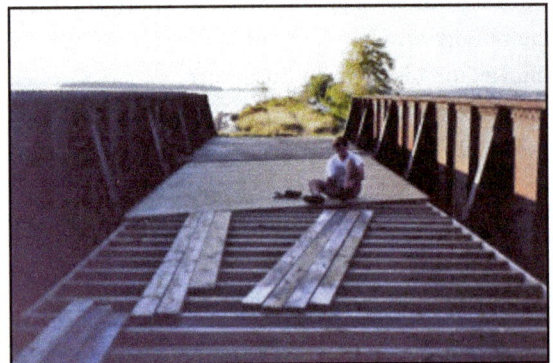

Replacing the decking on the Law Island bridge. *Circa 1992. Courtesy of Brian Costello.*

THE BURLINGTON BIKE PATH & WATERFRONT PARK

allows sailboats to pass between Malletts Bay and the open lake.

Costello did research into the history of the old rail bed and soon uncovered Fred Sargent's String of Pearls proposal from 1965. It didn't take him long to dust off that proposal; making it a reality would be a bit more challenging.

After several years of hard work, the pathway out to the Causeway was restored to bike-passable condition on a gravel and cinder bed. It was time to celebrate. Betsy Terry organized a ribbon cutting for the new Causeway bike trail for December 1994. By that time Howard Dean had become governor. He was the featured speaker at the event. The moment wasn't lost on Governor Dean. The fulfillment of a dream first hatched in 1980 at the inception of the Burlington Bike Path — a large chunk of the String of Pearls — had in fact become a reality!

Of course, the bridge proposal had been defeated by Colchester voters only two years before this event. But that didn't deter Governor Dean. He heard that Costello was a boat captain. There was talk of a ferry to transport bicyclists across the Winooski River. Dean turned to Costello and said, "I hear you have a plan to operate a bike ferry across the river. Get it on my desk by Monday and I'll get you some money out of the Transportation budget."

Costello had no plan. He spent the weekend typing one up for the Governor and had it on his desk by the following Monday. With the assistance of Dick Mazza, who just happened to be Chairman of the Vermont Senate Transportation Committee and a State Senator representing Colchester and Grand Isle, $20,000 was appropriated for the bike ferry in the 1995 state budget. The problem was that this special appropriation had to be kept under

Aerial photo of the Causeway from Colchester Point. *A. Patterson.*

It's Ba-a-a-ck!

MAY 6 1996

LIBRARY

BURLINGTON

BICYCLE FERRY

Colchester cartoonist Chuck Newsham penned this cartoon over a year ago, the last time the Colchester bike path ferry became a public issue. Here he spoofs one of the concerns expressed about connecting the Burlington and Colchester bike paths: criminal elements from North Burlington using the bike path to enter Colchester.

Criminals on the river. *Colchester Chronicle, May 2, 1996.*

wraps until the budget was set and it was locked in. In the meantime, despite the efforts of this group of bicycle enthusiasts and a lot of others with a larger vision, there was still a lot of opposition to bringing bicyclists into Colchester across the river.

When the new chairman of the Colchester Selectboard, Bill Stafford, a staunch opponent of the bridge, got wind of the $20,000 grant for the bike ferry, he was furious. Stafford accused Costello of engineering an end-run around the Selectboard. Costello never intended to usurp the power of the Selectboard. But Stafford got the Selectboard to turn down the $20,000.

Costello asked if the funds could simply be dispersed to him directly. The math was simple: $16,000 for a bike-equipped ferry and $4,000 for staff and gas for the summer. That wasn't possible. The funds had to go to a municipality or a non-profit corporation. With Colchester out, Burlington was a possibility.

But that smacked of Burlington shipping low-income criminals into Colchester neighborhoods.

That wouldn't work. The only solution was a non-profit. Burlington Bikeways, Inc. was born. The name was changed to Local Motion in 2003 to avoid the appearance of a group of bike advocates from Burlington imposing their will on Colchester.

Costello is a great boat captain, but he lacks the organizational skills to operate a successful non-profit by himself. That's where Chapin Spencer came in. Spencer is a lifelong bicyclist. He rides bikes as a primary means of transportation around Burlington. Rain, snow, ice, day or night, you'll find Spencer getting about town on his bicycle. Spencer also has great organizational skills and he was an outstanding spokesman and tireless fundraiser for Local Motion. The combination of these two men is one more example of what can be accomplished with a lot of hard work

THE BURLINGTON BIKE PATH & WATERFRONT PARK

The original 4 bike river ferry in 1999. *Courtesy of Local Motion.*

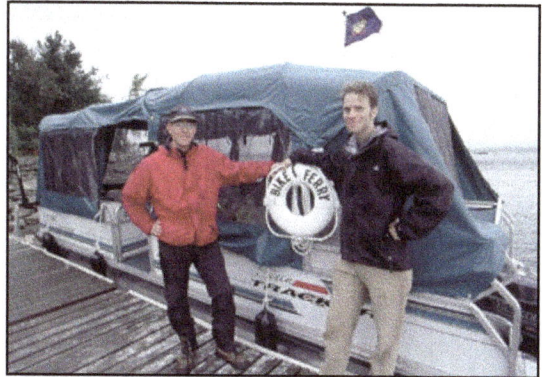

Brian Costello and Chapin Spencer in front of the 3rd version of the river bike ferry in 2003. *Courtesy of Local Motion.*

by two determined individuals and the support of an enthusiastic community.

A major battle with the NIMBY community then raged on for several years through the Environmental Court. Burlington Bikeways operated a very small four bike ferry across the Winooski River in a trial run in 1999. A permanent permit for operation of a bike ferry across the Winooski River was finally secured by Burlington Bikeways for the 2001 summer season.

Joe and Cathy Frank were early supporters of the bike ferry project. Joe Frank had gone to grade school with Charlie Auer who ran a small mom-and-pop fishing operation at the mouth of the Winooski River on the Burlington side. Frank convinced Auer to allow them to run the ferry from his boathouse. Cathy Frank later became chairperson of the Local Motion Board of Directors and was instrumental in fundraising activities coordinated by Spencer as Executive Director.

The landings on each side of the river weren't the best. They were slippery when wet and the ferry was fairly unstable, which forced it to close down in bad weather. Boards had to be laid down in the rail bed north of the river through Delta Park to keep bicyclists out of the mud. The boards had to be taken up each fall and replaced each spring. This was a very labor-intensive exercise.

Bicyclists on the boardwalk through Delta Park in dry conditions. © *Paul Broudy. Courtesy of Local Motion.*

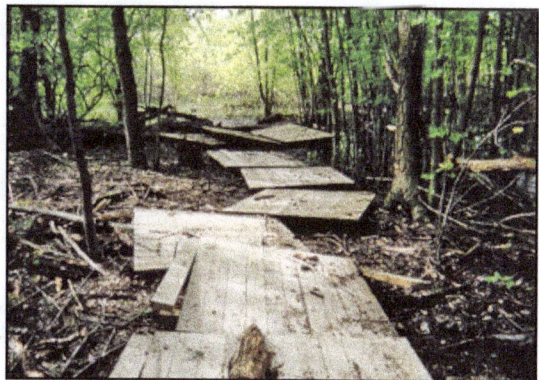

The problem is that the boardwalk floats when it floods. *Courtesy of Local Motion.*

The bike ferry across the river was a big success with over 40,000 people paying a donation of a dollar a head over the three years the ferry operated. The bike ferry galvanized the biking community in Burlington and Colchester and seemed to get them focused on getting a bridge built. And the NIMBY crowd seemed to be appeased by the lack of criminal activity in the Biscayne Heights neighborhood during the three years the river ferry was operated.

Governor Howard Dean directed his Secretary of Transportation, Brian Searles, to put a top priority on getting funding to build the bridge into the state transportation budget. A plan for rebuilding the bridge had already been developed by the Agency at the Governor's direction in the 1990s. But of course, the NIMBYs had been in control up to that point.

With the opposition effectively silenced by the bike ferry, Brian Searles put together a plan with an estimated price tag of $1.4 million for a new steel bridge across the Winooski River to replace the old railroad bridge, using the same cement abutments, at about 12 feet above the water. An elevated path through Delta Park would be constructed

The main span of the bike bridge being floated into place on a barge. *Winter, 2004. Courtesy of Local Motion.*

with pressure treated wood to address annual flooding and to reduce the impact on wildlife. With the help of State Senator Dick Mazza, Governor Dean got the appropriation through the legislature during the 2002 session, his last at the State House.

A problem soon emerged in the form of a demand from the Coast Guard for 18 feet of clearance under the bridge so that Coast Guard vessels could be taken up river to a boat landing. Environmentalists also objected to using pressure treated wood in the Delta Park wetland because of the toxins released as the wood slowly disintegrates. Wood is usually very slippery in a wetland like Delta Park. The town of Colchester worried about having to spend a lot of money on maintenance of a wooden elevated path.

The new plan, with 18 feet of clearance 567 feet across the Winooski with a 1,651 foot elevated cement walkway, had ballooned to $2.9 million. The elevated walkway through Delta Park added another $800,000. Viewing spaces for fishing and viewing the river out of the path of pedestrians and bicycles added an additional $80,000.

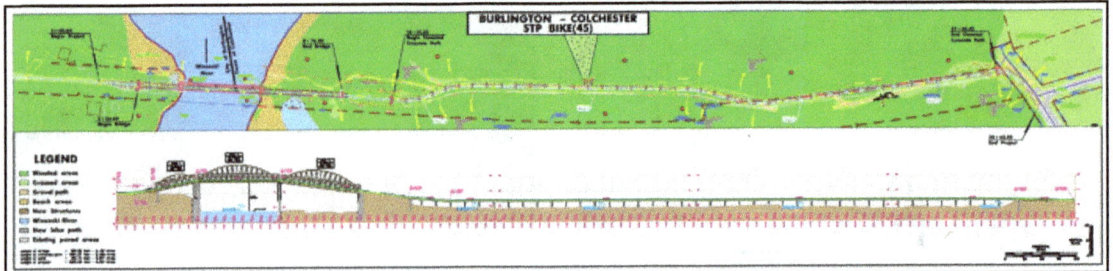

VTrans diagram of the Bike Path Bridge and Causeway through Delta Park. *Courtesy of Local Motion.*

THE BURLINGTON BIKE PATH & WATERFRONT PARK

Aerial photo of the bridge at the dedication in August, 2004 looking up the Winooski River with bike ferry and kayaks joining the celebration. © *Paul Boisvert. Courtesy of Local Motion.*

The rest of the additional cost was due to raising the bridge. Brian Searles later noted that in the spring of 2011, when the lake got to an all-time record high of 103.2 feet above sea level, the concrete walkway was underwater. Being concrete, however, it stayed put. A wooden walkway would have washed away.

Since the legislature was out of session at that point, the increased cost had to be approved by the Vermont Transportation Board, an obscure committee of legislators charged with scrutinizing cost overruns of approved transportation capital projects. Howard Dean's term as Governor

Governor Howard Dean at the dedication with Peter Freyne in the background. *Courtesy of Local Motion.*

was ending in January 2003. Governor-elect, Jim Douglas, was opposed to spending that kind of money on a bike bridge. The race was on to get the additional funds approved and start construction.

In December 2002, the Transportation Board, led by long-time bike advocate John Ewing, with strong support from "a parade" of supporters, including Colchester Town Manager Al Voegele and Burlington Parks and Recreation Director Wayne Gross, voted 6-1 to approve the $2.9 million revised project. Brian Searles had the contract ready and he signed it the following day. By the time a group of disgruntled legislators filed a lawsuit to halt the project in its tracks, the contractor had already begun work that could only be completed during the winter in the sensitive wetland of Delta Park. Douglas took office in January 2003, too late to kill the bridge project.

BIKERS RULE!

Inside Track

August 4, 2004

By Peter Freyne

Howard Dean, in sweat-soaked shirt and shorts, was the star Sunday-morning attraction as the $3.5 million triple-spanned bridge and causeway across the mouth of the mighty Winooski River officially opened. It was a wee bit of a ride down memory lane, too.

The dream of a bikepath along Burlington's lakeshore, a bikepath that would one day connect to Colchester, Grand Isle and Mont-real, first surfaced almost 25 years ago with the formation of a tiny do-gooder group called the Citizens' Waterfront Group.

A young doctor who had recently completed his residency at the Mary Fletcher Hospital teamed up with a young lawyer who had be-gun practicing in the Queen City.

Dr. Dean has since gone on to become an American household word, while Rick Sharp has faded from the spotlight.

Few people still remember Sharp's role. In fact, his name was glaringly absent from Sunday's program.

Mr. Sharp was in the big crowd, though, and Ho-Ho graciously gave credit where credit was due.

"This would not have happened without Rick Sharp," said Gov. Dean, pointing out Rick in the crowd for a generous round of applause.

"I was the doctor, but he was the lawyer," said Dean. "He could figure out how to make all this stuff work."

Dean also highlighted the contributions of his former secretary of transportation, Brian Searles, and State Sen. Dick Mazza of Colchester, the long-time powerful chairman of the Senate Transportation Committee.

Ho-Ho called Mazza "my best friend in the Senate for the entire time I served."

Our once-favorite presidential hopeful also recalled a lesson he learned years ago from North Carolina Gov. Jim Hunt.

"Jim Hunt once told me," said Dean, "that 90 percent of what we do is urgent. The other 10 percent is important."

"This is important," said Ho-Ho, "because it will last long, long after people have no idea who put this together. They will be incredibly grateful," he predicted, "that we were willing to go to the mat and spend $3.5 million — less than one-tenth of 1 percent of our budget — to make sure this happened. I am so grateful to the people of the state of Vermont who were willing to push this through!"

One unheralded hero of the bike-bridge project was unable to attend, but was fondly remembered nonetheless. Former Colchester Selectboard Chairman Bill MacLeay was out for a bike ride along Colchester's Lakeshore Drive one Sunday morning two years ago this month when he was struck and killed by a drunk driver with her small kids in the back seat.

The current Selectboard chair, Dick Paquette of Shadow Cross Farms fame, told the crowd, "Bill MacLeay would have been so pleased to see this. It was one of his top priorities."

Local Motion Director Chapin Spencer echoed the Egg Man's tribute to MacLeay. "Bill was a tireless advocate for this project," said Spencer. A memorial bench in MacLeay's honor, he noted, has been installed on the Colchester side of the bridge.

Ah, sometimes life's not fair, is it?

If anything, the grand opening of the beautiful bridge and causeway is proof that good things take time. Persistence is the key.

Dick the Egg Man waxed philosophically: "This was not an easy project to move forward. However, nothing that is worthwhile is easy to accomplish."

Amen.

© Paul Boisvert. Courtesy of Local Motion.

Everyone involved in construction of the bridge agrees that it would never have happened without Howard Dean's dogged insistence. "It should be named the Howard Dean bridge" says Brian Costello. Unfortunately, Bill MacLeay didn't live long enough to see the fruits of his labor. He was killed by a drunk driver on his bicycle in August 2002.

The new bridge over the Winooski River was dedicated in August 2004. The final cost with road widening, cross walks and other expenses was $3.5 million. Peter Freyne's "Inside Track" column in *Seven Days* on August 4, 2004 is perhaps the best record of the dedication. *See previous page.*

Freyne went on to note that Douglas had a lot of "balls" to show up at the dedication of a bike bridge he had opposed and take credit for it. The irony of Governor Douglas, or Governor Scissorhands as Freyne labeled him, cutting the ribbon on the bridge was not lost on the crowd. They were all veterans of the fight for bike paths.

As Freyne noted, "Since taking office, Douglas has not exactly championed the pedal projects. In fact, Gov. Douglas was so miffed at his predecessor's spending on two-wheeled travel routes while letting the potholes grow, the new governor quickly instituted a moratorium on bicycle projects last year."

This is a clear example of the difference between a chief executive who understands the importance of safe bicycle transportation and one who only pays lip service to it. Governor Dean had directed a small portion of the state transportation budget to an essential connection for a visionary bike path network built around an old rail bed. In 2010 that trail was named to the Rails-to-Trails Conservancy's Rail-Trail Hall of Fame as the Island Line. Check out the other 30 at their web site. At least a portion of the String of Pearls had become a reality. And indeed, the Causeway is the most spectacular bike path I have seen anywhere in the world.

Former Governor Howard Dean, left, Governor Jim Douglas and former Burlington Mayor Peter Clavelle cut the ribbon at the bridge dedication. *R. Masters.*

Bicycling was great on the Island Line for seven years thereafter. The fears of the NIMBYs never materialized. Doug Wolinski moved away and the people in the Biscayne Heights development now welcome bicyclists on the streets through their subdivision. Local Motion was able to relocate the bike ferry five miles north to the "Cut" in the Causeway that allows sailboats passage between Malletts Bay and the open lake. The new bike ferry now allows bicyclists to get out to South Hero to access bike routes throughout the Islands. With access to a world class recreation path all the way to the Lake Champlain Islands, Burlington and the Islands attract more tourists every year, benefitting economically from a wise investment that will return dividends for generations to come.

In 2007 Local Motion kicked off an ambitious campaign to upgrade the ferry service to the Islands with a new larger boat and floating docks with wave attenuators that would enable the ferry to operate safely during strong winds. The total for the project would be more than a million dollars. Local Motion received a $300,000 grant from VTrans to install a turnaround on each side of the Cut for maintenance and emergency vehicles. The rest had to be raised from private contributions. The campaign was very successful and they had almost reached their goal.

Then the spring flood of 2011 almost washed the Causeway away. The lake got to 103.2 feet above sea level that year, a foot higher than ever recorded before and seven feet higher than normal. It remained at flood stage for 67 days. The winter snowpack was deeper than usual and early spring rains resulted in a rapid snow melt. The resulting erosion on the Causeway was severe to catastrophic. The large slabs of marble and granite were still there, but a lot of the gravel and ballast of the rail bed had been washed away.

Local Motion, VTrans and the town of Colchester stepped up to the plate. Local Motion raised over $1.5 million dollars from over 500 local people and businesses for the "Big Fix" in an enthusiastic campaign to rebuild the Causeway bike path and finally install the new docks and wave attenuators.

The cost of reconstruction of the Causeway exceeded $550,000. FEMA ended up funding 80 percent of that cost and the state picked up 10 percent. Local Motion supplied the town of Colchester's 10 percent. The rest of the funds were used to buy a new larger boat and install the docks and wave attenuators. That process was long and arduous. The Causeway did not reopen to bicycle traffic until October 2012.

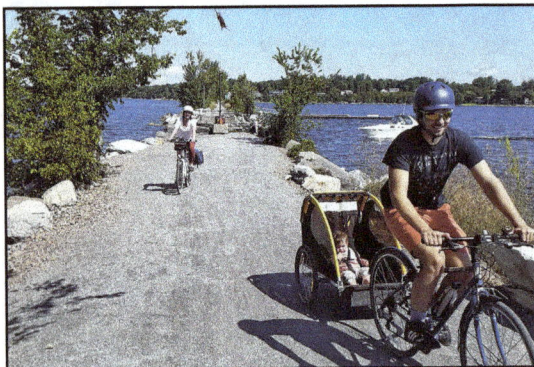

Mom, dad, and baby Annabella in trailer on her first ride on the Causeway, summer 2019. *R. Masters.*

Aerial photo of the Causeway from South Hero. *A. Patterson.*

THE BURLINGTON BIKE PATH & WATERFRONT PARK

William (Bill) MacLeay was a life long bicycle advocate. His primary mode of transportation about town in Colchester was his bicycle. He tirelessly promoted a system of separated bike paths throughout the Town during his 13 years on the Colchester Selectboard, nine of which he served as chairman. That's why it is so ironic that he was hit by a drunk driver on his bicycle on West Lakeshore Drive in Colchester just before noon on August 4, 2002. He died two days later at the age of 54, two years before the bike path bridge was constructed. Fortunately, he knew the funds had been approved for the bridge before he died.

MacLeay was an education consultant and a professor at Johnson State College. He followed the progress of the Burlington Bike Path closely during the 1980s and became the leading advocate for extending the Bike Path across the Winooski River into Colchester in the early 1990s. In 1992 MacLeay got an advisory item onto the Town ballot asking voters if they supported the construction of a new bridge across the Winooski River just for pedestrians and bicyclists.

That's when the NIMBY (Not In My Back Yard) crowd emerged in force with a disinformation campaign to stop the proposed reconnection to Burlington. Calling themselves the "Colchester Bike Path Coalition" this group distributed flyers and put up signs about town misinforming voters that the bridge would cost them $811,000 and lead to an increase in noise and crime in the Biscayne Heights neighborhood.

MacLeay called the opponents out on their disinformation, but the NIMBYs prevailed and voters turned down the proposal. MacLeay wrote an editorial in the Colchester Chronicle deploring the tactics employed by this group and pointing out that the real issue at stake was the use of public roads through the Biscayne Heights subdivision:

"As it happens, the public is the largest landowner along the controversial leg of the project. The public owns Delta Park and the Windemere Way and Biscayne Heights streets. So as a community, we have to decide whether the special concerns of the residents in the neighborhood are so great that public activities ought to be curtailed on public property there."

Obviously, MacLeay felt that the inconvenience to local residents due to bicyclists utilizing public streets in the Biscayne Heights subdivision should not be the determinative factor keeping Colchester out of a regionwide bicycle network. He ended his editorial with this prophetic observation:

"As the connection of the Burlington Bike Path has been a matter of discussion for many years it is likely that we will visit this topic again at some point in the future."

The new Causeway path is much improved, with a packed gravel travel surface twice as wide as the former pathway. In a lot of ways the new rebuilt Causeway is a big improvement over the old pathway. Thank goodness that the flooding of 2011 occurred over a decade after the railroad causeway had been reclaimed as a recreation path. That made it town infrastructure, which entitled the town to FEMA money when that infrastructure was destroyed by the flood, but the FEMA money wasn't enough. The town would have to chip in funds and private money needed to be raised as well. The popularity of the path by 2011 guaranteed that it would be saved despite the devastation of the flood. If that damage had been done before the Causeway had become so popular, it is likely that the railroad bed would have been abandoned forever.

Once again, in May 2018, an elevated lake level due to spring snow melt and 80 mile an hour winds over an extended period led to extensive damage to the Causeway. Brian Costello initially canceled bike ferry service across the Cut for the summer, believing it would take years to raise the money necessary to restore the Causeway, just as it had in 2011. Fortunately, VTrans put a priority on getting the Causeway open for the 2018 summer season. They came up with $350,000 in emergency funding to temporarily repair the Causeway, making it bike passable all the way out to the Cut, by the July 4 weekend in 2018. That rapid response clearly demonstrates how important the recreational infrastructure of the Causeway has become to summer tourism in our area in the early part of the 21st century. In April 2019 FEMA awarded the town of Colchester $1.1 million to complete more extensive permanent repairs to the Causeway over the winter months of 2019-2020.

Today Local Motion is an advocate for biking throughout the state. Brian Searles calls them the most effective bicycle advocacy organization in the United States today. With an annual budget of over $1 million, they rent bicycles at their Trailside Center on the Bike Path downtown, they advocate for safe streets in Burlington and throughout the state, and they run a range of safe bicycle programs for kids. Their army of volunteers provide a free bike valet service at many Burlington events to reduce the use of cars downtown. About a third of the Local Motion budget comes from bike rentals, one third from their membership of over 1,200 and one third from programs, grants and donations. Over 16,000 people took the ferry across the Cut in 2017. Although ridership increases every year, the ferry still loses money. Nonetheless, with generous

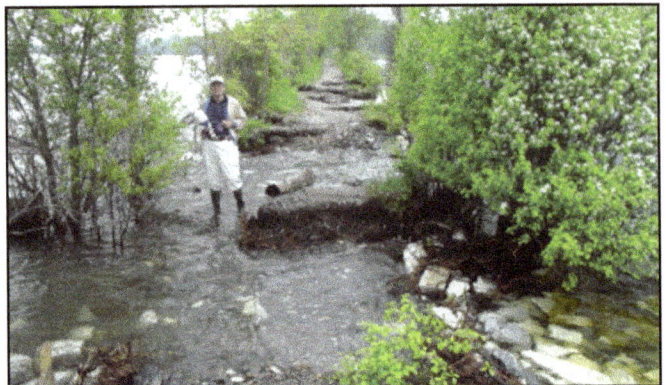

What remained of the Causeway after the 2011 flood, before the Big Fix. *Both photos © Cathy Frank.*

THE BURLINGTON BIKE PATH & WATERFRONT PARK

riders and grants, Local Motion will continue to provide this service indefinitely. It's what they do.

Looking back on it all now, Brian Costello thinks that if the original vote on the bridge in 1992 had been in the affirmative there would have been no need for a bike ferry across the Winooski River. Perhaps Local Motion would never have been formed and the bike ferry service at the Cut never initiated. Sometimes overcoming adversity to creating separate bike paths actually furthers the cause because bike path proponents have to work that much harder to overcome that adversity.

As of this writing in 2018, Brian Costello still operates the bike ferry across the Cut in the Causeway during the summer months. In early July 2018, Costello responded to a Coast Guard report of a capsized catamaran nearby in Malletts Bay. Before the incident was over, the bike ferry had plucked seven girls from a nearby camp on the catamaran and three kayaks from the angry waters of a storm on Lake Champlain. So this unlikely project may have saved seven young lives.

After serving as Executive Director of Local Motion for 14 years, Chapin Spencer was appointed Director of Public Works in Burlington by Mayor Miro Weinberger. He has championed the effort to make Burlington a more walkable/bikeable city his entire adult life. Betsy Terry is now the Executive Director of the Vermont Recreation and Parks Association. They should all be commended for their contributions to the biking cause in Vermont.

One final word on the String of Pearls. For years Brian Costello and others on the Local Motion staff have attempted to put Humpty Dumpty back together again by reassembling the railroad bed through the Islands. This task involves almost 100 private parcels, 80% of the 37-mile rail line. The other 20% of the line is in causeways and parcels owned or controlled by the towns along the way. After contacting property owners involved, Brian Costello and his staff have gotten a "no and don't call me again" from only two owners.

To date, two small sections of the old railbed have been recovered and deeded to the town in which they are located. Local Motion is always interested in talking to property owners in the Islands about the railbed. As biking becomes even more popular and the Islands benefit even more from bike tourism, it is hoped that more parcels or easements can be acquired.

More than one hundred years after Frederick Law Olmsted first envisioned the Emerald Necklace along the Charles River in Boston, it is still an incomplete work in progress. And so it is with the String of Pearls. Like the Emerald Necklace, maybe someday it will be completed. As Bill MacLeay noted in his 1992 editorial, "…it is likely that we will visit this topic again at some point in the future." Stay tuned.

The bike bridge at sunset over the frozen Winooski River. *Courtesy of Local Motion.*

CHAPTER SIXTEEN
The flourishing

Flash forward to 2019. Burlington is truly flourishing, with ample green space in a waterfront park with a bike path meandering through it. Trees shade the pathway. Children are playing with Frisbees on the grass lawn north of College Street. Others are jogging or riding bicycles or skateboards on the 7.9-mile bike path that provides public access to Lake Champlain from Oakledge Park at the city's southern border to the mouth of the Winooski River at the northern boundary.

People are lined up for creemees at Ice Cream Bob's stand on the side of the Bike Path just south of College Street across from the ECHO Lake Aquarium and Science Center. At the Community Boathouse, people are enjoying lunch at Splash, the restaurant on the floating platforms attached to the west side of the Boathouse. It's a beautiful day and people are strolling the boardwalk along the lake's edge just north of College Street. Others are resting on swinging chairs along the boardwalk. Children and dogs are playing in the water just off a sandy beach.

Each year the city hosts the Burlington Marathon in the third week of May, utilizing Waterfront Park as the finish line and the Burlington Bike Path for much of the course. Two recent national triathlons were held in Burlington because of the facilities it can offer. Each of these events brings millions of dollars in commerce to the Burlington area. The Marathon is especially important because it fills hotels and restaurants at a time of the year when they would be mostly empty otherwise.

The Burlington Bike Path has put Burlington on the map as a bike-friendly community. It has encouraged the use of bicycles as a primary means of transportation for many. And it's always great to see 200 bicycles at the free secure bike parking services provided by Local Motion at the Grace Potter Grand Point North Concert on the waterfront. Grace Potter is a nationally known singer who grew up in the nearby Warren/Waitsfield valley. Her three-day concert each September draws some of the largest crowds to the waterfront in the early part

Waterfront boardwalk, summer 2018. *R. Masters.*

Kids and dogs in the water at College Street, summer 2018. *R. Masters.*

Ice Cream Bob's stand, summer 2019. R. *Masters*.

July 3, 2019 crowd at Waterfront Park. R. *Masters*.

of the 21st century. Perhaps as much as one quarter to one third of the crowd at her concerts get there by foot or by bicycle.

Specialty bicycle manufacturers like Budnitz and Terry Bicycles have moved their operations from other communities to what is now described as the "cycling hub of Burlington, Vermont" by biking magazines. And the Director of Public Works, Chapin Spencer, is the former Executive Director of Local Motion.

In addition to the marathon and triathlons, Waterfront Park is the preferred venue for events ranging from the Jazz Festival to the brew fest to wine and food festivals all summer long. Rarely a week goes by during the summertime without some kind of celebration happening on the water-

front. And Waterfront Park is the most used park in the center city on a nice day. Battery Park has better views of the lake and the Adirondacks beyond, but you will find more people enjoying Waterfront Park, drawn by the water's edge. Add in the throngs of people who flood Waterfront Park for the fireworks on the third of July, New Year's celebrations, and the Penguin Plunge and you have a well-used public facility.

Uptown, the Church Street Marketplace is buzzing with activity. Church Street was closed to automobile traffic and converted into a pedestrian mall over a period of time, starting in 1971, in the face of intense competition from Interstate exit shopping malls in South Burlington and Williston. The Marketplace is largely attributed to local archi-

The Vermont City Marathon, 2019. R. *Masters*.

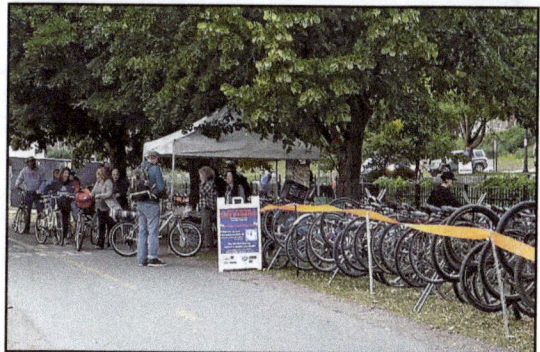

Free bike parking provided by Local Motion at the Grace Potter Concert, 2019. R. *Masters*.

tect, Bill Truex, who had seen a street converted to a pedestrian mall in Copenhagen in the 1960s called the Strøget. Bill thought the concept would work for Church Street in Burlington. With the help of a leading local businessman named Pat Robbins, Church Street was first partially closed to traffic in 1971. Over the years this closure proved so successful that two blocks were permanently closed to auto traffic in 1981 and it became a pedestrian mall. By 2005 all four blocks of Church Street downtown were permanently closed to motor vehicles. Senator Patrick Leahy secured funding for the conversion, and his former chief of staff, Paul Bruhn, deserves credit for his work on the Marketplace as well.

With Church Street closed to car traffic, there was space for open-air seating for cafes and restaurants. The newly bricked-over pedestrian way soon filled in with a wide range of eatable options, to the delight of locals and tourists alike. On warm summer nights, it's hard to get a table at popular restaurants on Church Street, with waiting lines at most establishments. Merchants along the Marketplace are thriving. The Church Street Marketplace rarely has a vacancy. It always amazes me how many people are still congregating on the Marketplace at 10 or 11 p.m. on a nice summer evening. There is an electric atmosphere downtown that just doesn't exist at the Interstate exit malls. But the success of the Church Street Marketplace is not just due to brick and mortar. Much credit goes to Ron Redmond and the Marketplace management team he supervises that keeps the place clear of trash, snow and ice, maintains the bricks, takes care of graffiti quickly and markets the marketplace.

As the railroads declined in importance in the 1950s, Burlington was fortunate to have an IBM manufacturing plant locate in nearby Essex Junction, eventually turning into the largest employer in the state. The University of Vermont and the hospital complex, as well as three other local colleges, also fueled the Burlington economy during this period. More recently high tech employers like Husky in Milton and Dealer.com downtown have taken up the slack in employment at the old IBM plant in Essex which was sold to Global Foundries a short time ago.

A host of social activities and a thriving arts community have made Burlington a great place to live for fairly well-educated people who love the arts and festivals. First Night, the non-alcoholic New Year's celebration attracting thousands annually, started as a grass roots effort in 1982.

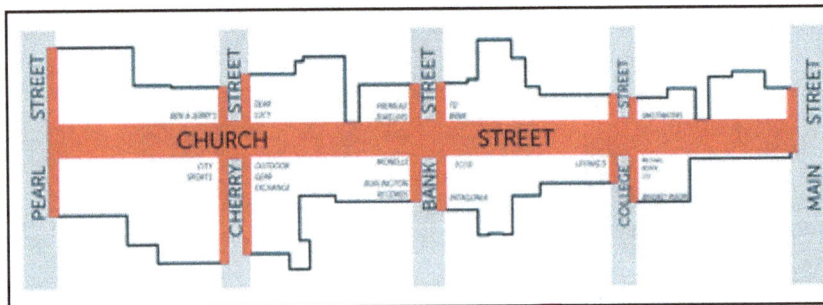

The Church Street Marketplace 2018. R. *Masters. Graphic courtesy of the Marketplace.*

The Bike Path at the Skate Park, 2019. *R. Masters.*

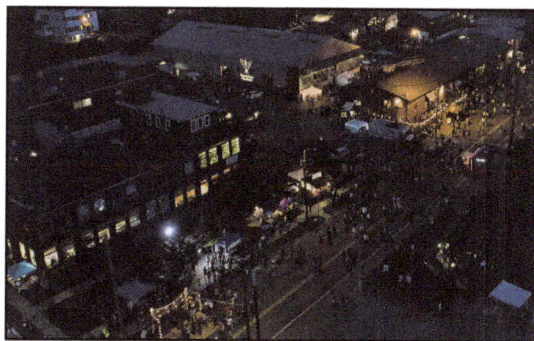

Aerial photo of Pine Street closed to car traffic Friday night of the 2019 Art Hop. *A. Patterson.*

It packs hotel rooms and restaurants downtown on New Years Eve. Unfortunately, it was suspended in 2018. Hopefully it will be revived again in the near future. The Jazz Festival, begun by a local group of jazz enthusiasts in 1983, brings some of the best jazz musicians in the world to Burlington. It attracts thousands to Burlington in early June each year. The Lane Series and the Mozart Festival bring fine music and world class performances to Burlington. The Festival of Fools and the Dragon Boat races are more recent additions to the offerings downtown during the summertime. The long derelict Flynn Theater was restored to its former glory in 1982 and now brings world class acts to the Burlington stage and smaller performances to the Flynn Space next door. And the Art Hop each September is still another home-grown, not-to-be missed, uniquely Burlington celebration of the Arts.

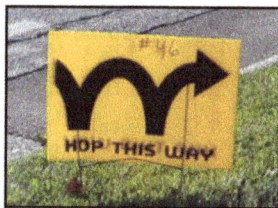

Although the population of Burlington has been stagnant over the past 35 years, except for the increase in Burlington's student population, the general atmosphere in the Queen City today is almost that of a Renaissance. Burlington continually gets named as one of the best cities in the U.S. today to live, recreate and raise a family. Whether it

is sailing in the summer, skiing or snowboarding in the winter or enjoying an afternoon on cross-country skis or a bicycle on the waterfront Bike Path, Burlington has it all for the well-educated, active outdoors type of people it attracts.

Recently Burlington is enjoying a flourishing economic boom as well. For almost forty-five years the Radisson Hotel (now the Hilton) was the only hotel downtown. The Courtyard by Marriott was constructed in 2007 and Hotel Vermont opened in 2013 right behind it on Cherry Street. The Hilton Garden Inn on Main Street opened in 2015. The two-story Burlington Town Center enclosed shopping mall is in the process of demolition, to be replaced by a new downtown development with much needed housing and with towers up to 14 stories tall, called City Place.

So a very remarkable development is unfolding in Burlington. The city went from one hotel to four downtown in the space of less than eight years. Recently a fifth hotel was proposed on Pearl Street between Church and Battery Streets. What is to account for this explosion in hotel rooms downtown? The answer: Hotels are full on weekends in the summer, and marketing surveys have led builders to locate new hotels downtown. Certainly the

Marathon, triathlons and other events on the waterfront and downtown account for a portion of this healthy demand for hotel rooms. This is concrete evidence of a flourishing or renaissance economy.

One could argue that all this has happened by chance or happenstance, that there is no rational reason for this flourishing. On the contrary, I would argue that much of the renaissance Burlington is experiencing today is because of the wise public investments it made over the past 35 years.

The number one attraction for Burlington on Trip Advisor today is the Burlington Bike Path. Waterfront Park is number two. The Church Street Marketplace is number three. Thousands of people are drawn to Waterfront Park and the Bike Path on a daily basis throughout the summer. The Church Street Marketplace is packed with people from early in the morning until well after midnight. Certainly these amenities have had a tremendous economic impact on Burlington. But perhaps even more important is the impact of these facilities on the quality of life in the city and the image and identity of the city itself.

Burlington now has an identity as an active outdoor city. Certainly much of that is due to its location on Lake Champlain, close to skiing, sailing and other outdoor activities. That hasn't changed in the past forty years. But what has changed dramatically is the Burlington waterfront and Church Street. Over this period of time the waterfront has witnessed an incredible metamorphosis from a desolate wasteland of ugly industrial uses to a spacious park that draws people to the water's edge downtown. *See maps on pages 78-81 for a before and after comparison.* And closing off Church Street has created a Marketplace with open air cafes that can't be duplicated at Interstate exits.

We'll never know what Burlington would be like today without the Bike Path, or if the Alden plan had been approved in 1985 and Waterfront Park had been covered with hotels and condominiums *(See Chapter Seven)*, but it's fair to say that there would be far fewer activities on the waterfront today. Would the marathon have become as popular as it is today without the Bike Path or Waterfront Park? It's almost certain that the last two national triathlons would not have been held in Burlington.

Ample park space on the waterfront has also preserved some great views that have resulted in private investment in condominiums on the east side of Lake Street and the Main Street Landing complex. Thanks to the Weinberger Administration, in the past two years the Bike Path has been almost completely rebuilt downtown (Bike Path 2.0). A whole new pathway was constructed between downtown and North Beach through the old "north forty reserve," reclaiming forty acres of land filled into the harbor and effectively tripling the size of Waterfront Park. The new world-class skate park and the Community Sailing Center will serve the city well for years to come. Now Burlington has attracted a developer who is poised to make a huge investment in the central "urban renewal" district where a failed shopping mall will give way to storefronts oriented toward a reestablished street grid and much needed housing downtown.

Much of the flourishing economy Burlington is experiencing in the early decades of the 21st century can be traced back to Ira Allen and his foresight in establishing the University of Vermont in Burlington. Champlain College certainly has contributed to Burlington's image as a college town as well. But much credit needs to be attributed to the investment the city made in the waterfront and the Church Street Marketplace over the past 35 years for its flourishing success in the early days of the 21st century.

CHAPTER SEVENTEEN
Rails-to-Trails 2.0

The lawsuit over the Burlington Bike Path cleared the way for the conversion of thousands of miles of old rail beds to recreation trails across the country. The railbanking provisions of the Rails-to-Trails Act have preserved these rail beds and allowed some interesting redevelopment of elevated rail lines in cities across the U.S. In this chapter I will explore the reclamation of several elevated rail lines in the U.S, and around the world.

THE HIGH LINE IN NEW YORK CITY

In June 2009, the first leg of the much-acclaimed High Line on the east side of lower Manhattan just above Greenwich Village in New York City opened to the public with great fanfare. Crowds lined up for hours to access elevators and stairways to the old elevated rail line. There were arts festivals with music from every genre. There were children with flags and parents with strollers. The mayor cut a ribbon and crowds thronged onto the former elevated rail line that had magically been converted into a linear park with fantastic views of the Hudson River and the New York skyline. *National Geographic* labeled the High Line the "Miracle Above Manhattan."

Just like our Bike Path in Burlington, the High Line is a product of the Rails-to-Trails Act — abandoned railroads 2.0. Who would have ever thought that a peaceful linear park could be created from an elevated steel industrial relic out of a bygone day,

The view of the High Line from the Standard Hotel. R. *Masters.*

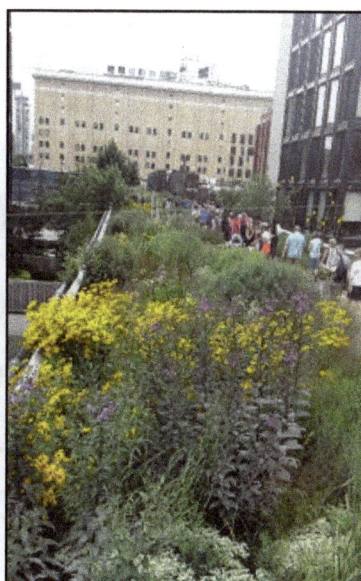

A few dozen of the 7 million people that visit the High Line each year. R. *Masters.*

The Empire State Building from the High Line. R. *Masters.*

thirty feet above the automobile-clogged streets and avenues of New York City? That's the miracle of creative thinking in an urban environment.

In 2011 the second section of the High Line was opened to the public, followed by a final leg around the Hudson Yards development project in 2014, with a termination on 34th Street, 1.45 miles or almost two kilometers from end to end. The total cost of this conversion was more than $187 million.

Initial projections were for 300,000 to a half million visitors a year. As of 2017, when my wife, my daughter and I visited it, the High Line had become the busiest tourist attraction in New York City, drawing over seven million visitors a year. But in many respects, the High Line is a victim of its own overwhelming success. It has contributed to gentrification in the Chelsea neighborhood. On nice days, it is sometimes packed from end to end with tourists from early in the morning until late in the evening. We stayed at the Standard Hotel which straddles the High Line near its southern termina-tion point. We had a great view of the High Line at all hours of the day right from our hotel room. We can certainly attest to its popularity.

The old elevated rail line was built in 1934 to transport goods from docks about one block west along the Hudson River to various industrial buildings and warehouses, mostly involved in food processing and particularly meat packing, on the west side of lower Manhattan. The elevated railway replaced a street level track that had resulted in multiple deaths over the years. But rather than run-ning the rail line over streets in the area, as is tra-ditional in New York City, the rail line was routed right through industrial buildings and warehouses along its path.

This rail line was only in service for 46 years. By 1980 the rail line had been abandoned, as trucks replaced rail transportation for moving freight in the city. The slowly decaying rail line lay fallow for almost twenty years, an all-but-forgotten relic of a long-gone era. Weeds, brush and even small trees

Steps cut into the elevated structure form an amphitheater to view the street below. *R. Masters.*

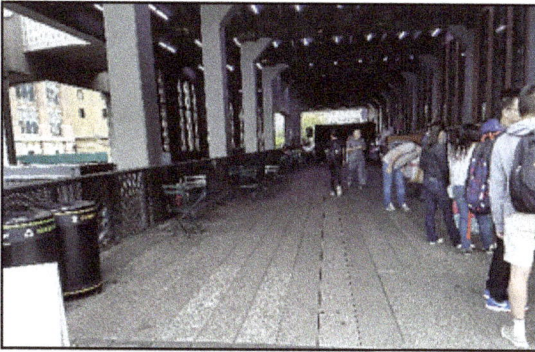
The pathway through an old industrial building. *R. Masters.*

Preserved rails with trees growing from the bed. *R. Masters.*

took over the former railroad tracks, creating a green ribbon through the old meat-packing district thirty feet above street level. In time, some locals began to think of the old rail line as a possible respite from the hustle and bustle of the city streets below.

In 1999 a group of local residents led by Joshua David and Robert Hammond formed Friends of the High Line. They tirelessly pursued a plan to convert the old elevated rail line into a linear park, using many of the wild plants that had taken root on the elevated rail over the years as natural landscaping.

The steel structure itself was in good condition. Having been built to transport freight trains, it was certainly strong enough to accommodate a throng of people. But it had to be completely sand blasted to remove lead paint at a cost of over sixteen million dollars. The entire line had to be cleared of

debris, rails, soil, everything, so that proper drainage could be restored and repairs to the structure completed. Elevators, stairways and sanitary facilities had to be incorporated into the structure at considerable expense.

New York Mayor Rudolph Giuliani was opposed to reclaiming the line as a city park. Most property owners in the area favored demolition. The race was on. Giuliani actually obtained a demolition permit in the closing days of his administration. But he didn't have time to actually begin demolition. Fortunately, his successor in the mayor's office, Michael Bloomberg, saw the value of converting the rail line to a linear park. He called it a "no brainer" and supported the idea enthusiastically.

Once again it took the dedication and persistence of two leaders to turn a pie-in-the-sky idea

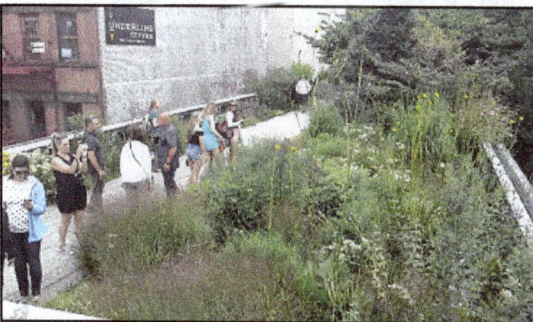
Tourists snapping photos on the High Line. *R. Masters.*

Bikeway along the Hudson River one block west of the High Line (visible in background). *R. Masters.*

(literally) into reality. (Check out their book: *High Line — The Inside Story of New York City's Park in the Sky*, (2011)). Over time, what at first seemed like a very improbable reuse of the old rail line began to pick up momentum. It didn't hurt that members of the Friends were politically astute and they were able to enlist some influential designers in the Chelsea neighborhood to raise some serious funds to design the new park, advocate for its implementation, and then actually construct it.

The abandoned rail line's owner, CSX, was amenable to the transfer for public use. Just like the Burlington Bike Path, the Rails-to-Trails Act played a key part in the preservation of the High Line. It encouraged the railbanking and reuse of the old rail line as a park in the meantime.

Although the elevated rail line is wide enough to accommodate a bike trail, the Friends decided against bicycle use. They say they listened to local comments that people didn't want to see bicycles on the High Line. And of course devoting so much of the rail line to bicycles would have left little space for landscaping and an escape from the hustle and bustle of the city below. And as it turned out, the throngs of people the High Line attracted would have overwhelmed any attempt to use the line as a bicycle corridor anyway. There is a very well-used bike path separated from automobile traffic along the Hudson River one block to the west of the High Line. So, in my opinion, the decision to make the High Line a walking trail with an emphasis on landscaping was the right one for this location. Obviously, a lot of other people agree. The High Line has become a huge tourist attraction for New York City.

The best article on the High Line is a piece written by Phillip Lopate from Columbia University entitled *"Above Grade: On the High Line,"* published in *Places Journal* in November 2011. In addition to recounting the history of the Line and how it came

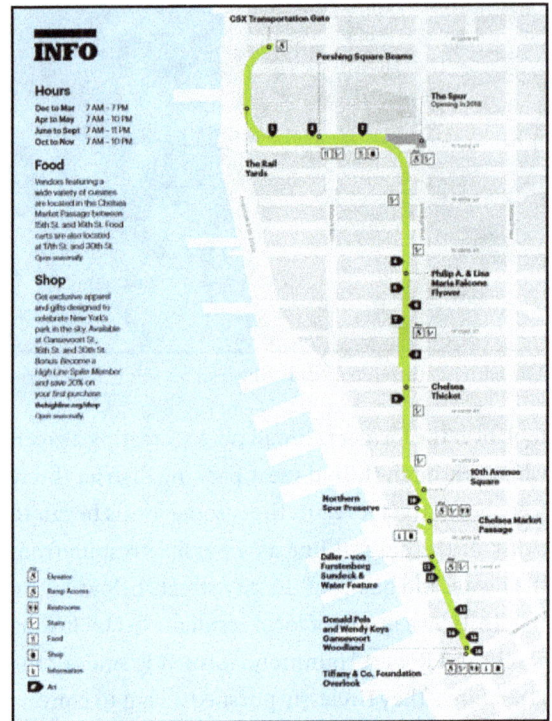

to be transformed into a linear park in the heart of Manhattan, Lopate describes the metamorphosis of the area from a grimy industrial zone, once known as the meat-packing district, to the new center of hip night life in lower Manhattan.

The High Line passes through West Chelsea, a "neighborhood in transition" — usually the euphemism for blight but, in this case, the opposite. What began as a ragtag assemblage of warehouses, factory buildings and four-story tenements has been transformed, in the last decade, through Manhattan real estate mania, into a high-end art district: the large floors of unbroken space, formerly given over to industry, have proven perfect for chic austere galleries displaying large sculpture or multimedia installations. Meanwhile, restaurants, watering holes, Japanese tearooms and ancillary cultural offices have taken root near the galleries. The new Chelsea, which has supplanted Soho as New York's premiere art district, flaunts a spacious interior aesthetic that makes the most of its industrial origins (exposed timbers, tin ceilings, concrete columns), embracing plain, functional warehouse architecture as the new purity.

Some say the Chelsea district was already in transition to replace Greenwich Village as the arts center of lower Manhattan prior to the arrival of the High Line, but the success of the High Line has certainly accelerated gentrification in the area. Luxury condominium developers can pay far more for precious acreage in the area than the meat packers can. So as of 2017, all but one of the meat packers have vacated the area and a building boom is now in progress. The prices of properties along the High Line have literally doubled in less than a decade.

The High Line may be an extreme example of what happens to property values close to newly created urban amenities like a bike path, park space or a public trolley. There is no doubt that residences along the Bike Path in Burlington fetch $5,000 to $10,000 more than similar properties in the same neighborhood not located close to the Bike Path. An increase in property values similar to those along the High Line accompanied the conversion of the old elevated rail line along Chicago's Bloomingdale Avenue into a linear park and bike path called the 606 in 2015. I'm sure studies of properties along old rail lines converted to bike paths under the Rails-to-Trails Act in other American cities would reveal similar results.

THE 606 IN CHICAGO

The 606 in Chicago took a different approach to the rehabilitation of an elevated rail line, going with a bicycle/pedestrian path instead of just a walking

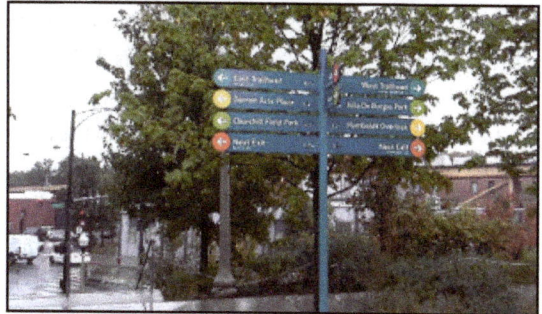

The newly opened elevated bike path in north Chicago called The 606. *R. Masters.*

Access ramps to The 606 are landscaped and fit into the urban landscape. *R. Masters.*

path with landscaping. It is 2.7 miles long running east from the Humboldt Park neighborhood to a termination at Walsh Park. It uses an old elevated abandoned rail line running along Bloomingdale Avenue in Chicago's north side as a great get-away from the congestion of city streets below. It is a well-manicured cement pathway separated from car traffic woven into the fabric of Chicago's urban environment.

The 606 uses an ingenious system of ramps allowing access from key intersections below to the pathway. These ramps are nice and wide, having been designed for wheelchair access, so they are perfect for bicycle access as well. We were impressed by the way they were carefully fitted in between buildings in this urban Chicago neighborhood.

Like the High Line, the 606 has spurred a lot of new development close by. Property values adjacent to the 606 have nearly doubled. Once again, housing located close to a public amenity like an elevated rail line converted to a multi-use pathway is in great demand. The building heights are nowhere near what we witnessed along the High Line, but it is apparent that many formerly vacant lots and derelict buildings along the 606 are being redeveloped as of 2017.

The 606 is another fine example of the reuse of an abandoned rail line under the

The 606 has clearly spurred private development along the path. *R. Masters.*

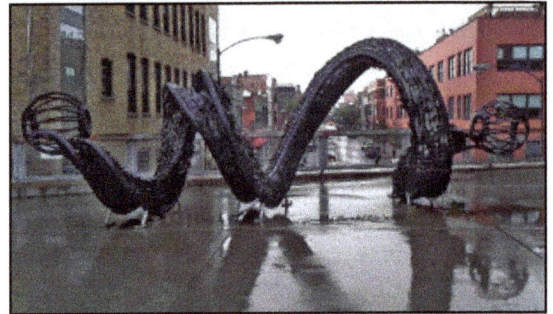

Artistic touches add to the fun. *R. Masters.*

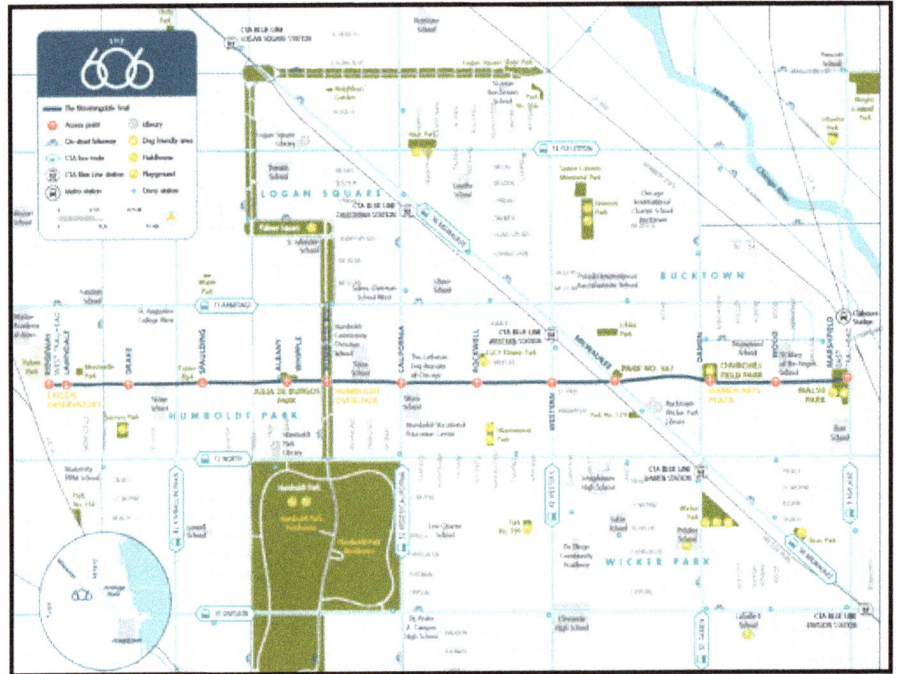

THE BURLINGTON BIKE PATH & WATERFRONT PARK

Rails-to-Trails Act. The rail line was originally constructed in 1873 along Bloomingdale Avenue. It was elevated twenty feet above grade in 1910 in order to eliminate pedestrian fatalities at grade crossings. It was constructed with steel-reinforced concrete embankment walls with 38 viaducts to accommodate at-grade traffic.

The city of Chicago first investigated converting the rail line to a bikepath in a 1997 bicycle facilities plan. At that time the rail line still carried some freight. The idea was revived in 2002 as part of the Logan Open Space Plan. A grass roots non-profit called Friends of the Bloomingdale Trail focused public support for the project, and it received strong support from Mayor Rahm Emmanuel.

At a cost of $95 million, the final design included a ten-foot-wide concrete pathway for bicycles and pedestrians with a two-foot soft shoulder on either side.

This old rail line now forms the backbone of a network of bicycle paths, parks and trails in Chicago's north side called The 606. Zip codes in this area of the city all begin with 606, so this number was selected as a means of symbolizing the cooperation of the neighborhoods it links together.

It doesn't take a lot of imagination to envision an extension of the 606 all the way into downtown Chicago. Across a wide boulevard at the eastern termination of the path at Walsh Park is a tangle of elevated roadways leading into downtown. A separated elevated multiuse path through this tangle of an automobile sewer would probably allow a bicyclist to regularly beat traffic on the highways into downtown. The 606 extended into downtown could thus become a major artery for thousands of bicyclists commuting into the heart of Chicago each day from the north end. Such a bicycle superhighway into downtown Chicago could relieve traffic on the highways into downtown at a small fraction of the cost of adding another lane to the highway, which wouldn't work anyway (See Janette Sadik-Khan's book: *Streetfight*).

THE PROMENADE PLANTÉE IN PARIS

Restored 19th Century railroad colonnade with boutiques and shops under the path on top. *R. Masters.*

The conversions of the High Line and the 606 were preceded and inspired by the Promenade Plantée, also known as the Coulée Verte, in Paris, the very first abandoned elevated railway in the world to be rehabilitated into a linear park and bike path, opening in 1993. Joshua David and Robert Hammond visited the Promenade Plantée early in the planning process for the High Line and then modeled much of the elevated rail line through lower Manhattan after this Paris trail.

This elevated parkway, 33 feet above the busy streets and avenues in the heart of Paris, begins at the Bastille Opera House, on a plaza marking the famous "storming of the Bastille" prison that ignited the French Revolution. The first half mile of the path is located on top of a beautiful red brick viaduct constructed as a rail line alongside Avenue Daumesnil in 1858. It ceased operation as a railroad in 1969. The viaduct fell into disrepair and remained a derelict structure for years thereafter.

In 1979 urban planners started considering options for reuse of the viaduct, drafting a formal plan in 1983. Construction began in 1988 and was completed in 1993. Many local Parisians initially thought the garden path on top of the viaduct was a colossal waste of money, but over time these locals have come to regard the Promenade Plantée as a hidden gem right in their backyard. The 25 brick archways of the viaduct were transformed into artisan showrooms ranging from a bike shop to a jeweler to a tapestry restorer, to hand bag shops and cafes in 2000 as the Viaduc des Arts.

The end of the Promenade Plantée abutting the Bastille Opera House is accessed by ascending a set of stairs that climb 33 feet to a lovely linear garden above the viaduct between the Avenue Daumesnil and a row of residential structures several stories taller than the viaduct on the opposite side. Stairways and lifts provide access to the streets below. Full grown trees and benches line the pathway with interesting plantings, including a bamboo forest and other fast-growing species along the way. It is a pleasant respite from the hustle and bustle of the streets below, hard for tourists to find, but enjoyed by locals on a regular basis for walking their pets or an evening stroll.

The most memorable aspect of the Promenade Plantée is the lush gardens overgrowing the pathway in places with arches and flower beds that burst to life in the spring. It is 2.8 miles from end to end, starting as a foot path over the viaduct, weaving between apartment buildings, under balconies, over city streets to a sunken park with an interesting wooden arch bridge spanning expansive playing fields and playgrounds below.

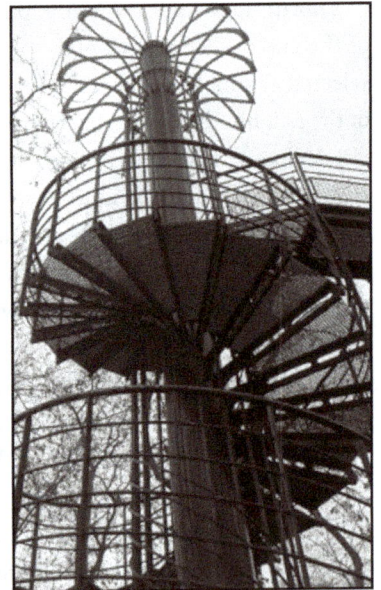

A portion of the bike/pedestrian trail through a trench and an old railroad tunnel to a spiral staircase in downtown Paris. *R. Masters.*

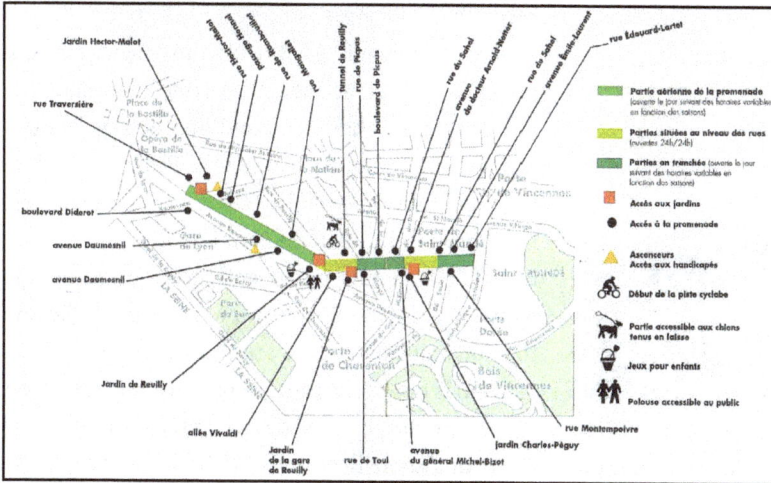

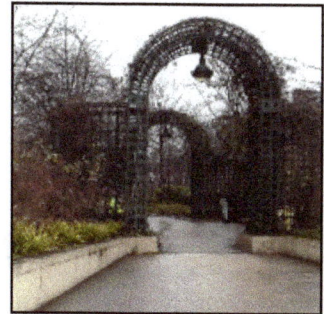

unmarked, or barely marked, and very hard to find, even when you ask locals. They are not depicted on most maps.

We were able to find three of them by locating lifts and stairways from intersections with surface streets we identified on Google Maps as likely candidates based upon our understanding of a ring railroad that once encircled the city called La Petite Ceinture. This rail line was abandoned in 1934. The first section of this abandoned railway to be reclaimed as a walking and biking path opened to the public in 2007 in the 16th arrondissement between the Porte d'Auteuil and the Gare de la Muette. It is 1,500 meters in length. A 200-meter nature trail and shared garden is accessible at Rue Rottembourg. In 2013 a 1.5 kilometer section of the rail line between the Place Balard and the Rue Olivier de Serres was opened for public use. The last section of the old Petite Ceinture line to be converted to a trail before publication of this book

Once the pathway reaches ground level on the opposite side of the park, it becomes bicycle accessible as well. The pathway then descends into the trench that used to bring trains into downtown Paris and continues on through two well-lit tunnels to a two-story circular staircase that takes you back to street level. It's a refreshing stroll through the heart of the French Capital.

The Promenade Plantée reuses a small portion of the old railroad lines that provided public transit in downtown Paris before the subway system was constructed late in the 19th century. Most of those rail lines have been abandoned now. A few of them have been converted into walking and biking paths for short stretches at odd locations throughout the city. Most of these short trails are is a short section between the Charles Trenet garden and the Moulin de la Pointe garden.

It may be possible to link some of these trail segments together at some later time to create more usable separated pathways connecting downtown neighborhoods, but many of these abandoned rail lines are now lost forever. Paris has done a great job of installing bike lanes throughout the city. It's too bad they didn't get to these abandoned rail lines sooner.

THE TRESTLE IN ST. LOUIS

The so-called "Iron Horse Trestle" in St. Louis is an iron elevated rail line, slated to be converted to a bicycle path at some future date if the $60 million necessary to complete the project can be raised. This rail line runs approximately two miles from the McKinley Bridge over the Mississippi River in "Old North" St. Louis through a derelict section of the city north of downtown to a termination just west of Interstate 70. It was built in the 1920s as an electric commuter train bringing passengers into downtown St. Louis across the Mississippi River from Illinois. Passenger service was terminated in 1958. The rehabilitated Trestle would connect with the McKinley Bridge Bikeway, a recently completed $12 million bike project, at its northern end and could easily be extended into downtown St. Louis at its southern end at grade with little additional expense.

The problem is that the old rail line trestle runs through a decrepit industrial zone dominated by mountains of scrap metal and boarded-up old factories and warehouses. Unlike the Promenade Plantée, the High Line or the 606, which run through neighborhoods full of potential path users, this area of north St. Louis is currently an ugly industrial wasteland. It contains very few residences. Most of the housing stock in the area was abandoned years ago and is now falling into ruin with collapsed roofs and walls that cannot be easily repaired. Most of those houses will have to be demolished to make way for new housing if this project eventually gets off the ground (literally).

My wife and I visited St. Louis in September 2017 to check out the Trestle. We were able to gain access to it by hiking through some abandoned lots filled with rubble and overgrown brush at its south-

Derelict buildings populate most of North St. Louis. *R. Masters.*

The end of the rail bed just north of downtown St. Louis. *R. Masters.*

ern terminus just north of Cole Street. The photo on the preceding page captures the end of the overgrown rail bed just after it crosses Interstate 70. The photo below was taken from the railroad bridge over Interstate 70 looking toward downtown St. Louis.

The other photos below depict the bridge over Interstate 70 and portions of the elevated railway extending northward to the McKinley Bridge.

Redevelopment of the Trestle into an elevated pedestrian/bikeway is estimated to cost over $60 million. The structure itself is sound, and as a former rail line it is certainly sturdy enough to handle

plenty of foot traffic. In a lot of ways, it's a majestic metal relic of a bygone era of life on the Mississippi River in Old North St. Louis. It's worth saving. But the structure itself will have to be sandblasted like the High Line. Lifts and ramps to make the Trestle accessible to all, including the handicapped, will have to be added at considerable cost, and sanitary facilities, lighting and security will add still more to the final price tag.

The city of St. Louis also has a very limited budget for the development of an ambitious system of bikeways called the Great Rivers Greenway that will one day provide residents with over 600 miles of separated bicycle/pedestrian paths that would service the entire St. Louis region. Over 113 miles of the Greenway have been opened to the public to date. At this point funding for rehabilitating the Trestle is on the back burner. Other projects have a higher priority, according to city planners, because other projects are less expensive and produce more of a bang for the buck.

It may very well turn out that it will take a major facelift of the entire Old North St. Louis

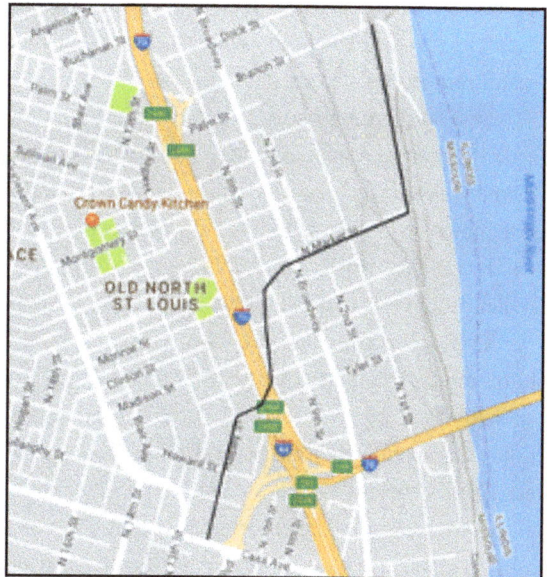

neighborhood to make the Trestle a viable project. With a little imagination, the Trestle could become the majestic central pedestrian artery high above the city streets of a newly revitalized, much more walkable/bikeable, north St. Louis.

Like most American cities, downtown St. Louis suffered from suburban flight, as people and businesses fled the center city in the later decades of the 20th century. A lot of other American cities are witnessing a rebirth of their downtown areas as the millennial generation, tired of traveling to school, soccer practice and everywhere else in a car growing up in the suburbs, have decided to shun automobiles in favor of a more healthy urban existence. Unfortunately, that trend has not taken root in St. Louis yet.

When we visited St. Louis in the early fall of 2017, we stayed in a hotel downtown the first night, shortly after a white police officer fatally shot a black man in the center city. There were very few people on the sidewalks and boarded-up windows downtown. At first we thought downtown St. Louis was really down and out, but it turned out the boarded-up windows had been smashed in protests over the incident the night before. We ate dinner at a nice restaurant in the city center.

Several days before we traveled to St. Louis, we attempted to arrange a Segway PT tour of downtown. We were told they didn't do Segway PT tours downtown in St. Louis as they do everywhere else we travel. The tour operator told us we would need bullet-proof vests to do a Segway PT tour downtown.

Our second night in St. Louis we stayed in a hotel off an Interstate exit near Forest Park in the suburbs west of downtown St. Louis so we could take a Segway PT tour of the Park the next day. Forest Park is the site of the St. Louis World's Fair in 1904, the centennial celebration of the 1803 Louisiana Purchase. It's a great ride. We ate at a restaurant in a shopping mall/office park that had become the center of that suburban area, with a band playing outside into the evening, a suburban entertainment center with plenty of free parking. That's why the crowds aren't downtown, yet. It will take a major change in thinking among those living mid-continent in where they wish to live before there will be any hope for the Trestle in St. Louis.

THE BELTLINE IN ATLANTA

The BeltLine in Atlanta is the mother of rail rehabilitation projects in the United States and the world as a whole. The scope of this Atlanta project is far beyond anything I have discussed in this book

Before: The Sears Roebuck building in Atlanta in the early 1950s. *Special Collections Department, Pullen Library, Georgia State University.*

After: The same building after its amazing transformation in 2013. *M. Pendergrast.*

THE BURLINGTON BIKE PATH & WATERFRONT PARK

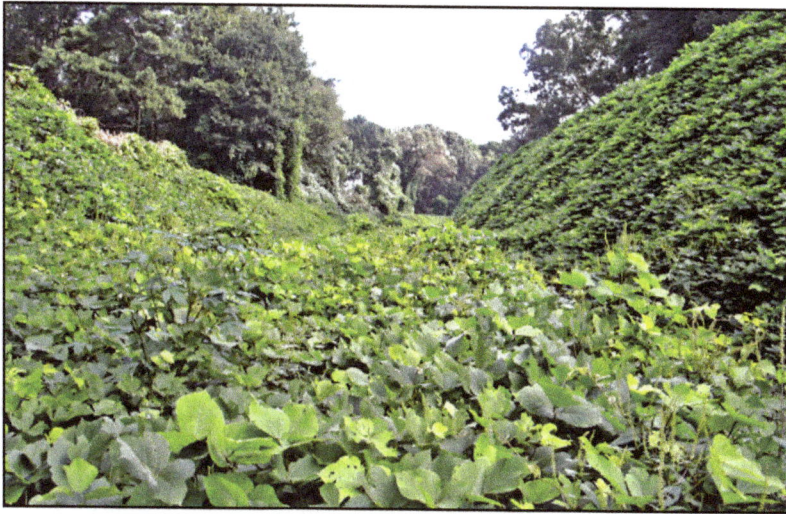

The future Atlanta BeltLine rail corridor, covered in Kudzu. *M. Pendergrast.*

Ryan Gravel — His 1999 graduate architecture thesis at Georgia Tech has the potential to completely transform downtown Atlanta into a series of interconnected walkable/bikeable communities in the early decades of the 21st century. *M. Pendergrast.*

to this point. It was inspired by the 1999 thesis of a Georgia Tech graduate architecture student named Ryan Gravel, who proposed the reuse of four separate railroad lines, built in Atlanta in the late 19th and early 20th centuries as "belt lines" to circumvent the railroad-congested downtown area. They were then mostly abandoned as trucks took over freight hauling and businesses moved further away from the city center. Over time the former railroad beds were taken over by wild kudzu and homeless encampments.

Perhaps the most notable victim of this business flight was the gigantic Sears Roebuck building, built in 1926 with a siding right on one of the belt line rails. For decades, it was mostly abandoned, other than use by a few city offices.

Gravel, who had lived in France as an exchange student, was inspired by the multi-layered Parisian transportation system. In his master's thesis, he proposed that the four former Atlanta railroads be linked into a 22-mile loop around the center city with streetcars rather than automobiles providing local transportation within this loop. This plan was

soon modified to include a pedestrian/bike trail to run parallel to the streetcars around the loop.

Gravel's thesis lay dormant and forgotten for several years, but his co-workers encouraged him to brush it off and promote it. It was finally taken up by city council member Cathy Woolard, who championed the idea. She and Gravel held grassroots meetings throughout the city to promote the idea. It met an enthusiastic response from nearly everyone: new urbanists, environmentalists, neighborhood activists, developers, and philanthropists. The Trust for Public Land hired famed city planner Alexander Garvin to produce his *Emerald Necklace* proposal for the BeltLine, published in December 2004, and the following year Mayor Shirley Franklin finally adopted the BeltLine and set up a semi-autonomous city bureaucracy to plan, fund, and build it.

As Mark Pendergrast details in his extensively researched book, *City on the Verge: Atlanta and the Fight for America's Urban Future* (2017), construction of the BeltLine is far from finished and has encountered bitter criticism of various aspects, including plans for two residential towers, 38 and 39 floors in height, somewhat reminiscent of the Pomerleau twin tower plans on the Burlington waterfront. Fortunately that plan, like the Pomerleau plan, never materialized.

The 2.25-mile Eastside Trail was the first segment of the trail to open in 2012, next to the newly developed Historic Fourth Ward Park and the future Ponce City Market (the former Sears Roebuck building), which is now a wonderful and very successful mixed-use development of small businesses, restaurants, and apartments. This trail, in the heart of a racially mixed area that was already rebounding from suburban flight, proved to be wildly popular. It did not yet include the planned streetcars, but its 14-foot width was jammed with bicyclists and strollers instead. An annual Lantern Day parade lit up the trail that fall. New apartment buildings, restaurants, and bars sprang up along the trail like wildflowers.

And of course, rents went through the roof. As we have seen before, the popularity of these trails soon boosts property values along the way. The Belt-Line planners anticipated this problem and set aside 15% of bond proceeds for affordable housing along the route by forming a TAD (Tax Allocation District) similar to the Tax Incremental Financing eventually used very successfully in Burlington as well. But after

The popularity of the Eastside Trail is very evident in this recent photo. *M. Pendergrast.*

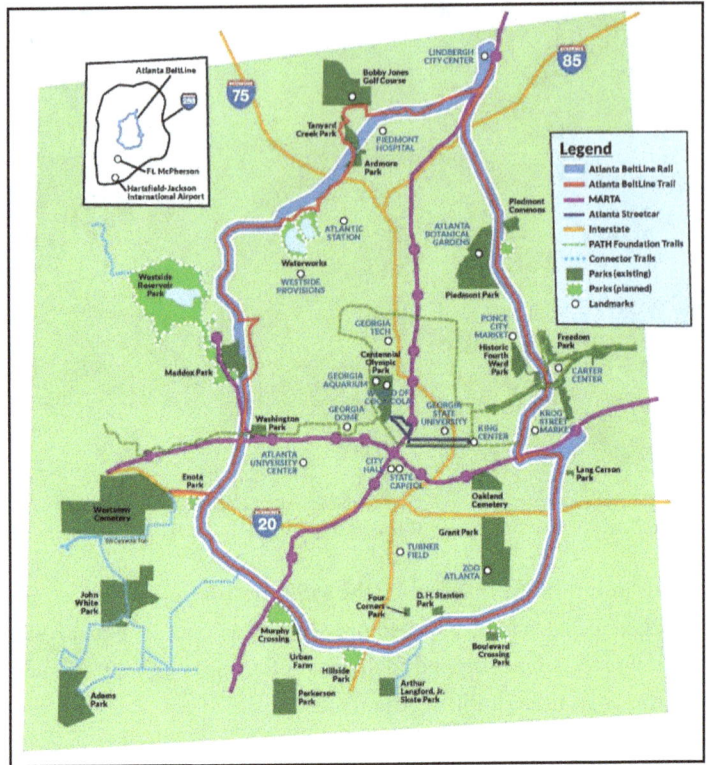

The Atlanta Belt Line, Westside Trail. *M. Pendergrast.*

THE BURLINGTON BIKE PATH & WATERFRONT PARK

the initial bonds were issued, funding was slowed by the 2008 recession, and these bonds weren't enough to complete this ambitious project. Affordable housing and inclusionary zoning have been hot topics in Atlanta over the past several years. Like the High Line and The 606, the BeltLine is a victim of its own success, pushing out the very residents it was built to help connect throughout its 45 neighborhoods.

There is a large racial component to everything that happens in Atlanta, although it often remains unspoken. The BeltLine offers hope that mixed income, mixed used, and racially integrated neighborhoods will thrive. But it is mostly lower income African Americans who are being pushed out of their homes and apartments by higher prices. The city is struggling to cope with these problems along with homeless issues.

Other sections of the Atlanta BeltLine, such as the Northside Trail, were built through a park in a primarily white residential neighborhood separate from the planned streetcars. The next major section of the BeltLine trail, the 3-mile Westside Trail, was built at the expense of $43 million with a large dose of federal funding. It was expensive to build because, like the Eastside Trail, it was built streetcar-ready, which required a parallel path with all the electronics and retaining walls capable of supporting a light rail line installed and ready for the addition of the streetcars at a later date. With a course through a much more economically challenged, primarily African-American side of town, the Westside Trail was not immediately jammed when it opened late in 2017. The recent addition of Monday Night Brewing and other adjacent businesses seems to be attracting more bicyclists and pedestrians all the time.

The city recently purchased the southern-most section of the abandoned rail line that will link the Eastside and Westside Trails. Hopefully the entire 22-mile loop will be finished before the deadline for project completion in 2030, overcoming current areas of discontinuity, competition with active rail lines in the northwest section, problems of gentrification, and challenges of putting a streetcar on the BeltLine, along with bikes and pedestrians. Various new parks are being built along the new trail as well, including the massive Westside Reservoir Park, which will feature a lake built in a former quarry.

In his 2016 book, *Where We Want to Live: Reclaiming Infrastructure for a New Generation of Cities*, Ryan Gravel not only discusses the Atlanta BeltLine, but he also explores other "catalytic infrastructure" projects, among them New York's High Line and prospective East River Blueway, Miami's Underline, Philadelphia's Rail Park, Detroit's Dequindre Cut Greenway, the Los Angeles River restoration, the Iron Horse Trestle in St. Louis, the Harismus Stem Embankment in Jersey City, the Midtown Greenway in Minneapolis, Lafitte Greenway in New Orleans, Buffalo Bayou Park in Houston, the S-Line in Salt Lake City, Singapore's Rail Corridor, Vancouver's Arbutus Corridor, Buffalo's Belt Line, and Paris's Promenade Plantée and Petite Ceinture. I have covered a few of these in this book, but even this extensive list is not exhaustive. Unfortunately, Gravel did not learn of our efforts to create the Burlington Bike Path with its crucial Supreme Court decision that preserved the BeltLine railroads under the Rails-to-Trails Act that his plan utilizes. All of these projects are reinventing old infrastructure (mostly abandoned rail lines).

The Atlanta BeltLine is among the earliest and most ambitious of these projects, which constitute a new movement to help answer Gravel's essential questions: *What kind of place do we want to live in? And how can we start to build that vision?* His book provides inspiring examples.

As Gravel notes, the BeltLine is "emphatically simple and unbearably complex…a thing and also a place; a project and also a movement." It is indeed a simple idea — a city loop of trail and transit, linking parks and inspiring development. It is also incredibly challenging to execute. It's a much larger project than our efforts in Burlington with much greater challenges. I wish them the best.

THE LONDON SKYCYCLE

Finally, let's take a quick look at a very interesting futurist approach to whisking bicyclists into downtown London, somewhat reminiscent of L.A. freeways, called the "SkyCycle." Like the Atlanta BeltLine, this idea originated with a student paper — this one a dissertation — by Oli Clark, who proposed an elevated bikeway through a portion of south London. Like Ryan Gravel, Clark never thought his idea would come to fruition, but when he joined Exterior Architecture, a London firm, his boss, Sam Martin, collaborated with him to produce a much larger plan, first proposed in 2011, calling for an elevated bike path above existing rail lines. It would be 15 meters wide (about 50 feet) and would serve as a kind of bicycle interstate, with 200 on and off ramps to key intersections at street level. A projected 136 miles in length, this "superbikeway" would easily accommodate 12,000 cyclists an hour and would allow for much easier and safer urban commuting in the crowded heart of London. This superbikeway would also be much faster than fighting traffic on the streets below.

The problem is this project would cost billions. Although endorsed by Network Rail, which owns the trains and plans to charge a one pound bike toll to help defray expenses, it would require funding to be diverted from automobile-centric infrastructure. Nonetheless, by taking advantage of existing rail corridors, it could revolutionize travel in the city, providing a much healthier alternative to sitting in traffic or descending into a cramped Tube station. How much more pleasant to ride a bike over the tracks with tremendous views of the city as you speed along to work.

Some critics worry that this superbikeway may be too windy or rainy aloft for pleasant bicycling, that the ramps would be too steep, or that the money would be better spent on bike trails at ground level. "We certainly don't want to take money away from making cycling safe on the roads," says Sam Martin. "That should remain the priority. But our ambition is to redirect some of the money spent by central government on rail and road expenditure. Those billions can be used much more efficiently."

As always, it is a matter of priorities. Most governments around the world routinely spend billions on superhighways for cars without a second thought. They just can't seem to understand that diverting only a small portion of the car highway budget to a superbikeway is a much better investment of public funds in the long run. So far, the SkyCycle remains a grand idea on paper only. As more and more cyclists take to the streets of London, far too many cyclists have been killed in collisions with cars. The SkyCycle would save not only time, but even more importantly, lives. Let's hope this "pie-in-the-sky" adventure someday becomes a reality.

CHAPTER EIGHTEEN
The Post-Auto Era

I am a student of Burlington history and very much enjoy understanding how it became the city it is today. For a long time, I wondered why Burlington, the largest city on Lake Champlain, was built on a shallow unprotected bay with no natural harbor? Shelburne Bay and Malletts Bay offer much more protection from the wild weather that can cross the twelve miles of Lake Champlain in the wink of an eye, wreaking havoc on boats tied up at docks in Burlington. To answer that question, you have to understand how our transportation systems over the years have shaped the development of Burlington.

The lake was the superhighway of that early era in Burlington from its founding in 1783 until the railroads arrived in town in the 1850s. In the early years the frozen lake provided easy access to Burlington from points south during the winter months. And in the summer, the lake was a great way to transport goods and people cheaply. Everything that came into Burlington or left it did so by water. When the Champlain Canal opened in 1823, connecting Lake Champlain to the Hudson River, that was like extending that water superhighway all the way to New York City. Goods could then be loaded into a boat in New York harbor and unloaded at a dock in Burlington. That greatly reduced the cost of manufactured goods in northern Vermont.

The Erie Canal opened two years later in 1825. The growth of New York City into the largest city in the United States is largely due to the Erie Canal and commerce on the Hudson River. Clearly, waterways were the primary means of moving goods and people in America during the first half of the 19th century.

A safe harbor was essential to protect boats on Lake Champlain when they docked at Burlington. That's why the U.S. Congress appropriated more than half a million dollars over a period stretching from 1836 to 1890 to build an expensive breakwater offshore at Burlington. So why would the largest harbor on the lake during that period of lake dominance in commerce turn out to be located in an unprotected shallow sandy crescent called Burlington?

You have to remember that Ira Allen's target in 1772, when he first surveyed the north end of the lake, wasn't Burlington bay. There was nothing remarkable about another sandy crescent on Lake Champlain. It was the Onion River valley (now known as Winooski) that caught his attention. Ira wasn't just looking for good farm land. He immediately recognized the falls on the Winooski River as a source of industrial power for saw mills and grist mills. And of course, the falls provided ample power for woolen mills years later. When the early settlers built the first road to this area from Middlebury, it didn't go to Burlington bay. It went to the falls on the Winooski River.

According to Vincent E. Feeney in *Burlington, A History of Vermont's Queen City* (2015), Burlington bay became the most important port on Lake Champlain because it was located just over the hill from the great falls on the Winooski River. The bay in Burlington was the closest location on the lake where goods could be loaded and unloaded from boats using the lake. A small footpath from the bay to the settlement at the falls soon became a rutted wagon trail. We now know that pathway as Pearl Street and Colchester Avenue.

The point to all this is that Burlington grew up on lake commerce in the early years, and that's why it exists where it does. It's interesting to trace the different eras of public transportation in Burlington and examine the effect of each on the development of the Queen City. First it was lake commerce that dominated transportation in and out of Burlington from its establishment in 1783, immediately after the Revolutionary War, until the arrival of the railroads in the 1850s. Lake transportation slowly declined thereafter, giving way to the steel rails.

Even after automobiles arrived in the early part of the 20th century, roads in Vermont were little more than cow paths. The railroads dominated for an entire century, from the 1850s until the 1950s in Vermont. The overhead electric street car made a brief appearance in Burlington in the early years of the 20th century but, like the railroads, it passed into history in the headlong rush to automobiles after the Second World War.

The Interstate Highway System proposed by President Eisenhower in 1956 represents the apex of automobile mania. It was finally extended all the way to Burlington in the late 1960s. Suburbs and shopping malls sprang up, often around Interstate exits across the country. National Landmarks like the C & O Canal became targets for the development of highways. (*See Chapter Three*). With almost all our transportation turned over to automobiles, big problems like smog and traffic sewers began to choke urban living across the country. Perhaps the best example of the automobile's influence on Burlington are photos of Church Street before it was converted to a pedestrian mall in 1981, below.

As Jeff Speck notes in his masterpiece on the principles of "new urbanism," *Walkable City, How Downtown Can Save America, One Step at a Time* (2012), "...since midcentury, whether intentionally or by accident, most American cities have effectively become no-walking zones. In the absence of any larger vision or mandate, city engineers — worshiping the twin gods of Smooth Traffic and Ample Parking — have turned our downtowns into places that are easy to get to but not worth arriving at."

By the 1970s the Burlington downtown commercial shopping district known as Church Street was in serious trouble, facing stiff competition from suburban shopping malls located at exits of Interstate 89 in South Burlington and Williston. The auto dominant era was at its zenith in Burlington.

The brilliant solution to anywhere USA choked by car traffic, of course, (it's so obvious now, but it

Church Street in the late 1970s. *Courtesy of The Church Street Marketplace.*

THE BURLINGTON BIKE PATH & WATERFRONT PARK

The Church Street Marketplace, 2018. R. *Masters*.

Church Street at night, 2017. R. *Masters*.

wasn't back in the 1970s) was to close Church Street to automobile traffic and replace the street with a pedestrian mall. As *noted earlier in Chapter Sixteen,* this was the brainchild of architect, Bill Truex, who had seen the first European example of a successful street closing in Copenhagen called the Strøget in the 1960s. What's now called walkability came to Burlington early in the "New Urbanism" movement before it was even called that.

By 1981 Church Street was closed to automobile traffic. That allowed the restaurants and cafes along the street to bring their seating out into what had formerly been car space. Although it's somewhat counter-intuitive that open air cafes would work in a northern climate like Burlington, the brief season we have for that activity is embraced by locals and tourists alike. It's hard to find an empty seat at a café on Church Street on a warm summer evening. The success of these open-air cafes quickly led to even more successful restaurants and cafes on Church Street and an almost electric atmosphere in the heart of Burlington that can't be matched at sterile food courts at Interstate exit malls.

It's interesting to note that the conversion of Church Street to a pedestrian mall is perhaps the poster child for success for closing streets across the country. Speck notes that of over 200 street closings

like Church Street in the U.S. over the past 40 years, only 30 remain as of 2012. Only a handful of them are considered successful.

Burlington and Boulder lead the pack. Aspen and Miami, the Third Street Promenade in Santa Monica and Denver's 16th Street "show that successful pedestrianization is possible. It's just very, very unlikely," according to Speck. Charlottesville, Virginia also features a long, successful street closed to automobiles for strolling and shopping.

The unusual success of Church Street is really attributable to the fact that it has become the beating heart of the entire city, the focus of festivals and parades all year long, from the Jazz Festival to the Christmas tree lighting to the Mardi Gras parade and the marathon. It also has its own management district that keeps it clean and thriving.

Although Church Street caters to tourists, its greatest strength is that the majority of its business is local. That assures high quality in restaurants on Church Street. If quality is not up to the taste of locals, the restaurant won't survive.

The success of walkability for Burlington is certainly stunning. Over 130 shops, restaurants and cafes make up the Church Street Marketplace today, and there is rarely a vacancy. Compare that to the failing shopping malls at Interstate exits across the country today as shopping trends turn to online purchases.

The pedestrian mall of the Church Street Marketplace was the first step for Burlington toward what I call the Post Auto Era. Others, like Jeff Speck and Philip Langdon, have labeled it New Urbanism — the concept of designing urban living space with a focus on walkability instead of automobiles. The Post Auto Era is the fifth major stage of evolution of public transportation in the Queen City. Check out the chart below:

Water Transportation Era	1772-1860
Railroad Era	1850-1950
Electric Trolley Era	1920-1950
Auto Dominant Era	1950-2000
Post Auto Era	2000-present

Each of these eras has had a profound effect on the evolution of Burlington. The same or similar patterns are apparent in cities across the country and around the world, of course.

Like many other cities around the world today, Burlington appears poised to move into the Post Auto Era. The Church Street Marketplace was the first step into this era for Burlington. The Burlington Bike Path is another important step. Local Motion, with its success implementing safe bicycling practices and in extending the Burlington Bike Path out to the Lake Champlain Islands, is yet another step in that direction. In fact, I have dated the boundary of the Post Auto Era in Burlington to the year 2000, one year after the founding of Local Motion.

Some progress has been made recently with the installation of inexpensive, temporary and experimental fixes — painted crosswalks, bump outs at intersections, painted-on bike lanes, the "wiggle" and flashing lights at crosswalks on Pine Street. With the help of Local Motion, the city recently installed plastic bollards to create a separated bike lane on Union Street. And there is a plan to revitalize lower Main Street, converting it to a "complete street" to make it much more pedestrian and bicycle friendly.

Local Motion is now a state-wide bicycle advocacy organization. Some say it's the most effective bicycle advocacy organization in the U.S. today. Over the past several years, members of Local Motion and other bicycle advocates have worked with the Weinberger Administration to come up with a comprehensive plan to convert Burlington into a truly walkable/bikeable city. The *BTV Walk/Bike Plan* is a blueprint for Burlington to lead the way into the Post Auto Era and establish itself as a leading bicycle-friendly city. That doesn't mean abolishing the automobile from downtown. What it does mean is spending significant resources on an infrastructure of pathways for pedestrians, bicycles and light electric vehicles like ebikes, electric scooters and devices like Segway® Personal Transporters (PTs), separated from automobile traffic.

In 2013 my wife, Ruth, and I opened Burlington Segways to offer Segway PT tours of the Queen City, mainly for tourists, but also to introduce the local community to these machines. Invented by Dean Kamen in Manchester, New Hampshire in 2001, the Segway PT was initially promoted as a machine that would revolutionize urban transportation throughout the world. The idea of replacing 2,000-pound automobiles propelled by internal combustion engines with a much more efficient and pollution free 100-pound electric Segway PT as a means of local urban transportation is indeed tempting.

But that promise never materialized, mainly because the infrastructure to operate these vehicles in an urban environment does not exist in most cities. Some cities, like New York, completely banned Segway PTs for this reason. Others, like Boston and

San Francisco, banned Segway PTs from sidewalks. Segway PTs are also very expensive compared to a bicycle or an electric bike. So far their primary use is to allow tourists to see much more of a city than they could on foot and in specialized locations such as warehouses, parking lots, etc.

In order for bicycles, Segway PTs, electric bikes, electric scooters and other light electrically propelled vehicles to live up to their potential to replace a significant number of automobiles in urban environments, city streets must be redesigned to accommodate at least ten-foot-wide pathways for these alternate forms of urban transportation separated from cars. Curbs, parking, trees, green belts and streets all need to be realigned and rearranged throughout the city to accommodate these pathways in this new Post Auto Era city.

Five-foot-wide sidewalks are just too narrow to get bikes, electric scooters, Segway PTs and ebikes off the street. These new urban pathways must be wide enough to allow these devices, as well as wheelchairs, to pass safely without forcing anyone off the pathway or out into the street to compete with cars.

These changes are expensive. Fortunately, they don't have to be accomplished overnight. They can be implemented over time, with less cost if they are planned out intelligently. It always burns me up when a sidewalk on a main thoroughfare like Main Street, where there is plenty of room to widen the sidewalk into a much more useable ten-foot-wide pathway, is installed with only five feet of concrete. The master plan for the city needs to dictate a ten foot wide pathway separated from car traffic the length of Main Street, and then make sure that when sidewalks are replaced they conform to desired width standards that will actually be used by bicyclists and light weight electric vehicles.

Much of this expensive infrastructure can be paid for with fees generated by more dense and taller housing structures downtown. Burlington has also taken the first steps in that direction as well with the redevelopment of the Burlington Town Center property as City Place. Although there was considerable opposition to the density and height of some of the buildings in the City Place project, everyone seems to agree that "infill development" should lead to greater density of housing downtown. Dense residential development downtown will lead to a whole new community in the center city that will demand local services that do not require automobile transportation.

That's the definition of New Urbanism. Create a critical mass of housing downtown to make walkable/bikeable doable. People living in these new urban cities won't need cars to get about from cul-de-sac to shopping to restaurants to hardware stores and dry cleaners. They can walk to all that and take Uber or Lyft, or, in the near future, an autonomous vehicle, to get where they want to go outside downtown.

When groceries, movies, shops, the best restaurants in Vermont, world class entertainment, festivals and parades are only an elevator button away, young professionals from the millennial generation can't be far away. This generation appears drawn to the ease, convenience and fun of urban living that is not tethered to the automobile. Many of them don't own cars or even have driver's licenses.

Cities all over the world are now beginning to limit automobiles in the center city. Copenhagen was probably the first to close an entire street to automobile traffic to create a successful pedestrian mall in the early 1960s. Many cities around the world have followed suit, closing streets in center cities to automobile traffic, from Sydney, Australia to Prague to London to Paris. The center of Madrid is almost entirely closed to auto traffic. Most of downtown Barcelona is narrow streets and alleys closed to auto traffic. Florence, Italy only allows commercial vehicles into the center city. And some cities like London and Mexico City have adopted "congestion pricing" utilizing fees for automobiles designed to reduce auto traffic in order to reduce congestion and pollution. The Mayor of London says the city will completely ban diesel cars by 2020.

Burlington currently has a deficit in affordable housing downtown. For years Progressive administrations and zoning rules have unreasonably restricted the construction of more living units downtown. Economist Art Woolf notes that Burlington's population has remained stagnant since 1980, except for the influx of college students.

This deficit in housing has led to higher and higher rents as students outbid everyone else for housing downtown, particularly between UVM and Church Street. Burlington has suffered from a very unhealthy low vacancy rate for at least 40 years. The Progressive solution in the 1980s was rent control. Obviously, the real solution is to build more housing downtown. Once the supply of housing is brought into balance with demand, rents will stabilize. Under the leadership of the Weinberger Administration, several thousand new housing units are now being built downtown or within walking/biking distance of downtown. The 2020 census will reveal a substantial increase in the population of the city — the first real increase in decades.

Every new unit of housing built downtown means one less house built in Underhill or Charlotte. That means less farmland being gobbled up by subdivisions, fewer high speed separated highways (traffic sewers), less pollution and less of a carbon footprint. A person living in a residential tower in downtown Burlington without a car, who can use an elevator and her own feet to get about, will have a carbon footprint that is a quarter of someone living in Milton tethered to a car for transportation.

According to Janette Sadik-Kahn in *Streetfight: Handbook for an Urban Revolution*, (2017), New York City residents have a carbon footprint that is 25% of a person living in a suburb on Long Island. *(See Chapter Nineteen)*.

It should be the policy of the state of Vermont to concentrate development into already existing urban centers like Burlington, Rutland, Barre, Bennington and Brattleboro. Unlike Burlington, where there is rarely an abandoned building, Barre and Rutland have a problem with derelict properties. The situation is ripe for reuse of these structures by concentrating any increase in population into those existing communities rather than sprawl.

For Burlington, that means more infill development and it also means taller, denser buildings. It takes a critical mass of residents living downtown to attract the services necessary to live without an automobile. Redevelopment of the former Burlington Town Center property into City Place is a start. Much more housing needs to be built downtown to create the Post Auto Era city I'm talking about here.

Living without an automobile and getting around only on foot, by bicycle, light electric vehicle or public transportation is much easier today than it has ever been, with ride share services like Uber and Lyft and inexpensive rental zip cars. And fortunately the millennial generation seems to enjoy urban living without the expense and the carbon footprint of an automobile.

That means fewer resources need to be devoted to creating parking spaces downtown. Perhaps some of these resources, which would have been spent on providing parking spaces, could instead be diverted to redesigning the city into a Post Auto Era community with a system of separated multiuse pathways.

How can Burlington evolve into a Post Auto Era city? Obviously, it starts with planning. The

THE BURLINGTON BIKE PATH & WATERFRONT PARK

city is now well underway toward adopting a bold and detailed master infrastructure plan for sharing streets now devoted almost exclusively to automobiles with bicycles and light electric vehicles. Fortunately, Burlington has a very active biking community now. That will only grow as these safer pathways are installed, and no doubt over time, these pathways will be as cherished as the Burlington Bike Path is today. Amsterdam didn't become the biking mecca it is today without the conscious decision in the later decades of the 20th century to turn away from the automobile in favor of preserving the quaint canals that make Amsterdam so special today. In the 1960s there was a plan to drain the canals to make way for wider streets and boulevards. Amsterdam residents wisely resisted the headlong rush to automobiles that most cities around the world succumbed to in the 20th century.

When the gasoline crisis hit the Netherlands in the early 1970s, area residents parked their cars outside the city and took bicycles into the center city. Parking lots were built outside the city with a metro stop that whisks passengers to the Centraal Train Station where they can retrieve their bicycles for local transportation downtown. Curiously, another quaint custom in Amsterdam is that almost no one wears a helmet. We were told that drivers are very cautious because they are generally assigned the blame in the event of a collision with a bicyclist. Personally, I would never ride a bicycle or Segway PT without a helmet.

The sea of bicycles parked at the Centraal Train Station in Amsterdam in 2018. Our hotel manager insists they can all find their bikes.

The photo of the sea of bikes at the train station below was sent to us by the hotel we stayed at in Amsterdam.

Likewise, Vancouver, British Columbia, was indistinguishable from a typical American city until the 1950s. City planners then turned away from auto-centric development in favor of high-rise housing, public transportation and generous green space with abundant bike paths. A major avenue, called Granville Street, was converted to a pedestrian mall in the 1970s and an expanded bike lane network was installed in 2008. According to *Business insider.com*, the result is that walking and biking doubled, with over half of all trips in the city now completed by foot, bike, bus or subway as of 2015, considerably better than any U.S. city.

I would suggest that an appropriate way to fund this infrastructure in Burlington is to collect a fee for all new housing units built downtown in exchange for not being required to build parking spaces. Fees collected by the city for commercial use of the Bike Path by Segway PTs and escooters should also flow into such a fund for building these separated pathways. But the most important source of funding for the construction of Post Auto Era cities nationwide would be a federal source. A couple of pennies on the national gasoline tax could be used to establish a fund that grants municipalities nationwide the funds necessary to build the infrastructure of separated pathways that Congress neglected to provide for along with the Interstate Highway System starting in 1956.

CHAPTER NINETEEN
New Urbanism

New Urbanism has its roots in Jane Jacobs' epic struggle to save Manhattan from being overrun with automobiles over a half century ago in the 1960s. Jacobs fought New York City's "tyrannical masterbuilder," Robert Moses, for decades as he proposed roadways and even a federally funded superhighway that would criss-cross downtown Manhattan and take out most of Washington Square Park and Greenwich Village. Her groundbreaking masterpiece, *The Death and Life of Great American Cities*, (1961), was the first flickering hope against the automania that consumed America after the Second World War.

Rather than yielding to the automobile, Jacobs advocated for walkable cities with neighborhood stores and shops where people could live fulfilling lives interacting with their urban neighbors in a living, breathing, evolving city that renews itself as the tastes, desires and needs of its inhabitants change over time. That's the description of current-day Greenwich Village, SoHo and now the Chelsea district in lower Manhattan, with perhaps the most extravagant example of modern walkability — The High Line. Jane Jacobs was the pioneer in walkability that saved Manhattan from the auto-centric traffic sewers of Moses' plans and dreams. You can thank her for the streets of lower Manhattan cherished by so many today.

In his recent book, *Walkable City Rules: 101 Steps to Making Better Places* (2018), Jeff Speck describes the evolution of thinking among city planners over the years, recalling a lecture by Andres Duany called "The Story of Planning."

In it, he would recount the formative victory of the planning profession. It happened in the 19th century, when people were choking on the soot from what poet William Blake called Europe's "dark, satanic mills." The planners, who were not yet called planners, said, "Hey, why don't we move the housing away from the factories?" They did it, and lifespans increased immediately and dramatically.

The planners were hailed as heroes, and, as we like to say, they have been trying to repeat that experience ever since. This story is admittedly an oversimplification, but at its heart it is true. Modern city planning began with the intention of separating incompatible uses from each other, and evolved somewhat mindlessly into separating all uses from each other.

By the mid-20th century, planners seemed to have gone berserk. Having witnessed the life-changing benefits of zoning, they became zone-happy, introducing more and more categories and more and more rules about what should be separated from what else, until the city of neighborhoods was replaced by the city of zones.

Superimpose the utter dominance of the automobile in America by the middle of the 20th century and its effect on zoning, allowing all those separate zones to be connected to one another at high speed with automobiles, and you have the recipe for sprawl. Once walkable downtowns turned into auto-dominated streets and avenues, boulevards and separated highways all across America. Almost the exact opposite of walkable became the norm downtown, as short-sighted zoning rules and economics built suburb after suburb, farther and farther out, completely dependent on automobiles to get anywhere. Ryan Gravel's book, *Where We Want To Live*, describes this sprawl taken to eleven on a scale of ten in the metropolitan Atlanta area. The same process is at work in Los Angeles, Houston, Dallas, Chicago, New York and most major cities of America today.

This all started early in the 20th century when Henry Ford introduced the first mass-produced automobile for the common man — the Model T. Ford wanted to make the automobile affordable to ordinary working people. So he came up with a simple-to-build, sturdy vehicle produced on an assembly line, and cranked out over 15 million identical copies over a decade and a half.

You have to remember that up until the railroad train was invented in the 19th century, the fastest a human could travel about was by horseback. The freedom and mobility of the masses ushered in by the automobile quickly led to a love affair with the car that completely reshaped life in the 20th century. It started in the U.S. and spread throughout the world.

In 1919 General Motors introduced an irresistible alternative to the Ford in the form of the Chevrolet. This GM offering was sleeker and sexier than the Model T, and Ford soon saw sales slipping. GM changed their design every year. The automobile became a status symbol and people soon clamored for the latest model with the newest and freshest features. The race was on for market share. Ford responded with the Model A. People seeking to claw their way up the social status ladder traded up

from a Chevrolet to a Pontiac to a Buick and finally, when they had arrived at the top, a Cadillac.

More and more roads were paved, allowing automobiles to travel faster and faster and cover far greater distances than ever imagined. Separated highways for automobiles, called turnpikes, autobahns or freeways, whisked cars along even faster. In 1956, President Eisenhower shepherded the Interstate Highway System into existence as a massive military project. The car completely changed the American economy and the way we live.

The walkable city that had become the hallmark of American life, so well described by Philip Langdon in *Within Walking Distance, Creating Livable Communities for All,* (2017), was abandoned in favor of the suburb. Levittown on Long Island became one of the first of thousands of suburbs to pop up across the country after the Second World War in the early 1950s. My father moved us there when I was a toddler.

As millions and millions more cars were produced each year to satisfy an almost insatiable demand, existing roads simply couldn't handle the ever-increasing volumes. Traffic jams clogged highways in major cities like New York and Chicago and particularly Los Angeles, where GM actually bought out public transportation systems and closed them down simply to eliminate the competition and drive car sales higher.

More lanes were added to existing freeways, and a road construction frenzy resulted in more and more superhighways clogged with more and more cars. An unending feedback loop had developed. More cars led to more roads. More roads led to more cars. That led to still more congestion, smog, pollution, and sprawl.

Los Angeles has certainly gotten completely out of control. I went to school there as an undergraduate in the early 1970s. It was bad then, but it was so much worse in 2018 when I visited my daughter there. All the freeways have been expanded to the max, with even the former breakdown lanes converted to carry traffic. Almost no curbside parking is available city-wide. L.A. has even installed traffic signals to limit access to freeways. Commute times of two hours to go fifteen miles are common.

It has finally become apparent that it is impossible to build our way out of congestion. Janette Sadik-Khan describes the addition of a lane to the 405 freeway in Los Angeles in her recent book, *Streetfight*, concluding that the additional lane did not reduce congestion. It just encouraged more drivers to fill the new lane, resulting in no improvement in traffic or congestion at all. Jeff Speck calls this induced demand in *Walkable City* "increasing the supply of roadways lowers the time cost of driving, causing more people to drive and obliterating any reductions in congestion."

There have been hiccups along the way. The oil embargo in the early 1970s gave us pause as we began to realize the effect that the car was having on geopolitical events worldwide. Military tensions reached a boiling point and multiple wars broke out over the fuel we now depend on for the American way of life. Pollution from internal combustion engines produced so much smog that the government was forced to react. California implemented some of the most restrictive antipollution laws in the world. The federal government enacted fuel economy standards. Then we became aware of climate change and global warming due to all the carbon dioxide we are spewing into the atmosphere.

Predictions emerged that we would run out of oil as some experts claimed "peak oil" production worldwide would occur early in the 21st century, followed by a long decline in production and ever-increasing prices for oil. Fractural hydraulics, commonly known as fracking, saved us from that fate and extended the oil supply for at least a few more decades anyway. Fracking has produced environmental degradation for those living nearby, including water and air pollution and earthquakes, and it has exacerbated the global warming problem by contributing megatons of carbon dioxide to the atmosphere over the next several decades. But as noted in various accounts throughout this book, the love affair with the car that Americans had enjoyed for almost a century was finally beginning to falter.

As Jeff Speck notes in *Walkable City*, "Long gone are the days when automobiles expanded possibility and choice for the majority of Americans. Now, thanks to its ever-increasing demands for space, speed, and time, the car has reshaped our landscape and lifestyles around its own needs. It is an instrument of freedom that has enslaved us."

Some cities began to search for alternatives to the automobile by consciously promoting the use of bicycles instead. Amsterdam and Copenhagen led the vanguard in the early 1970s in response to the oil embargo. Helsinki, Finland, was early to install bike lanes, together with Oslo, Norway and Stockholm, Sweden. A lot of other cities around the world joined the two-wheel revolution as the 20th century came to a close. Hamburg, Germany, closed streets downtown to car traffic and installed miles and miles of bike lanes and separated bike paths. Paris has done a great job of installing separated bike lanes. Even London got into the act with Mayor Boris Johnson and the "Boris bike" rental fleet he brought to the city.

In Spain, Madrid and Barcelona have closed most of their old town areas to automobiles, creating pedestrian ways like La Rambla and other shopping districts and plazas instead. In 2007, Seville, a major city in southern Spain, choked by four rush hours a day due to siestas, closed the main boulevard through the old town section of

THE BURLINGTON BIKE PATH & WATERFRONT PARK

the city to automobile traffic and installed an electric street car. They also built over 80 kilometers of completely separated bike paths. The result was an eleven fold increase in bike trips, from less than 0.5% of trips to over 6%, in just a few years. Thus, Seville became the unlikely poster city for sustainable bicycle transportation in southern Spain. "It is, proponents say, living proof that more or less any urban area can get lots of people on bikes by the relatively straightforward means of building enough connected, safe lanes on which they can ride," concludes an article in *The Guardian* in 2015 by Peter Walker entitled *How Seville Transformed Itself Into the Cycling Capital of Southern Europe*. Cities and towns throughout the world have repeated this process over and over again, installing bike lanes and taking at least the center city back from exclusive automobile dominance.

In the United States, cities like Portland, Oregon, and Boulder, Colorado, led the effort to install bike lanes and take the street back from cars for bikes and pedestrian use. Sadik-Khan describes the effort to take back the streets of New York City from the car under the Bloomberg Administration in her book, *Streetfight*, by installing bike lanes and creating plazas for those on foot out of space formerly devoted to automobiles. Closing off portions of Times Square to automobiles to make more space for pedestrians led to fewer injuries in the square. Chicago, Atlanta, St. Louis and a host of other American cities have followed suit.

Finally, during the last few decades of the 20th century, it dawned on some urban planners that the natural progression, or evolution, of this auto-centric society is to continue to build suburbs until there is no space left to expand, or congestion on highways finally makes further development impossible. As Jeff Speck notes, "Were it not for congestion, we would drive enough additional miles to make congestion." Urban planners finally realized that in the end you can't build your way out of highway congestion. They began to see the wisdom of Jacobs' ideas of walkable cities instead. That was the birth of what is now known as New Urbanism — what I have labeled the Post Auto Era — from a transportation perspective.

Jeff Speck is just one of many advocates for this New Urbanism. Philip Langdon speaks of this new walkable urbanism in his recent book, *Within Walking Distance* (2017). "In these pages, I show that places where the best of life is within walking distance ought to be our goal." Langdon then goes on to describe the New Urbanism movement as "composed of designers, builders, developers and citizens who wanted to create or live in compact communities where a person could get somewhere useful on foot."

As an example, Langdon describes Philadelphia at the end of the eighteenth century, the second largest city in the U.S. at the time, as the quintessential walkable city, 2.7 miles from end to end, walkable in about an hour.

> Building a city or town at the scale of the pedestrian meant that any able-bodied person could navigate the full range of local businesses, homes, institutions, and attractions without relying on anything more than his or her own power. Philadelphia, according to urban historian Sam Bass Warner Jr., 'functioned as a single community'. It was not necessary to own a horse or an ox cart — or, later, a motor vehicle — to participate in the life of the town. The built environment and the human body were in accord.

Langdon names several new large-scale developments in New York, Denver, Gaithersburg, Maryland, and Portland, Oregon, that pioneered this new concept in urban planning. He devotes the remainder of the book to the description of six locations in the U.S. that "relate well to the human eye, human size, and human gait." One of those locations is Brattleboro, Vermont.

In *Where We Want To Live*, Ryan Gravel compares his life in auto-centric suburban Atlanta, where he would spend over an hour by himself in an automobile to get to college classes each morning in bumper to bumper traffic, with his life commuting to graduate school in Paris, interacting with scores of French men and women on the same morning commute in a neighborhood instead of alone on a ten-lane highway in Atlanta.

I will briefly recount the most obvious advantages of living in a walkable urban environment versus living in the suburbs here. For a full explanation of these advantages, read Jeff Speck's *Walkable City*. The first of these is the central thesis of Ryan Gravel's book. How would you rather live, spending two hours or more in a car by yourself on a highway commuting each day, or interacting with neighbors on a short walk to work in the morning and a pleasant stroll home in the evening?

The car dependent life style we mindlessly rely on now is also the primary cause of the obesity epidemic we are experiencing today. People just don't get the exercise they do in a walkable community. This is also one of the major causes of the increase in diabetes, heart disease and some cancers in the United States today. Add to that pollution, congestion, frustration and the planet-killing carbon dioxide generated by automobiles, and it's easy to see the advantages of a walkable/bikeable community.

And don't forget about the economics of having to maintain an automobile: buying a car, repairing it, feeding it gasoline and oil, tires and air filters, insurance, parking, etc. According to Ellen Dunham-Jones and June Williamson in *Ret-*rofitting Suburbia, Urban Design Solutions for Redesigning Suburbs* (2011), household transportation costs range from 14 percent of income in walkable neighborhoods to over 30 percent in suburbs. For a significant number of American families, their car is more expensive than their housing. Economist David Stiff concludes that the longer the commute, the steeper the drop in home resale prices.

The advantages of evolving once again, leaving behind the car-dependent lifestyle we have become accustomed to during the 20th century, are obvious. In fact, the future of the planet depends on it. We can no longer squander the resources it takes to live in suburbia today. According to David Owen in *Green Metropolis: What the City Can Teach the Country About True Sustainability* (2009), a person living in New York City without a car will have a carbon footprint that is a quarter of the person living in a Dallas suburb driving everywhere. These numbers are even better for European and Asian cities. Even if we transition to electric vehicles, the electric power necessary to service these suburbs must be generated somehow. Right now that means a lot of coal, oil, gas and nuclear generation and very little renewable power.

What does all that mean for Burlington and its surrounding communities? First and foremost: STOP BUILDING SUBURBAN SUBDIVISIONS. If you really want to reduce your carbon footprint, move out of your suburban subdivision, give up your car, and live downtown instead. We didn't build the Circumferential Highway in Chittenden County. Our roads are already at capacity now in 2019, maybe a bit beyond at rush hour. We can't build our way out of congestion. That has become obvious in communities from Atlanta to Los Angeles. If we keep on adding more and more subdivisions farther and farther out, paving over the cornfields of Addison and Franklin counties and sacrificing all those dairy farms to sprawl, the resulting congestion will make Chittenden County look like rush hour in L.A. almost all day long, to say nothing about the waste of resources and the carbon footprint that would entail forever. Remember, once those suburbs are built, they will be there forever. If the gasoline runs out and we can't service these subdivisions, we still have to deal with that inefficient buildout.

Even Los Angeles has seen the light recently and begun to embrace New Urbanism. I have reprinted below two sections of a recent article about the reinvention of L.A that appeared in the magazine of my Alma Mater, USC, for fall 2018:

RIDING' ON THE FREEWAY OF LOVE?

As postwar L.A. benefited from a boom economy, thanks largely to the aerospace industry, the city enjoyed seemingly endless space for affordable housing as it sprawled further into the surrounding landscape. The American Dream, it seemed, was within everyone's reach — thanks in large part to L.A.'s futuristic freeways.

"You could live in an affordable suburb and commute because we had these beautiful highways," [USC Professor of History and Political Science, Philip] Ethington said.

Indeed, the freeways were once the glory of L.A., considered one of the city's most fascinating and attractive features, he noted.

That started to wane in the 1970s with increasingly severe pollution and congestion.

"People came to hate the freeways," Ethington said. "People aren't fascinated by them anymore. Nobody goes to a city now because they think it's fun to drive on the freeway."

AN IRONIC REVERSAL

As the imprint of the city reaches its maximum potential and population pressures make it impossible to build enough freeways to relieve the resulting congestion, public fascination has shifted to the nodes created by the new public transit lines and stations. When a transit line station opens, Ethington notes, land value nearby skyrockets. That, he says, is driving momentum toward the smart urbanism that is now increasingly directed toward public transit and vertical living, instead of the old model of private automobiles, freeways and single-family homes.

"It's quite revolutionary, a completely different way of envisioning L.A. and a function of the fact it used up all the available suburban space," he said.

"Those factors really just forced this new urbanism. But it's definitely a sea change. It's a reversal of a century of the way L.A. developed."

After the Watts riots in downtown L.A. in the 1960s, USC seriously considered relocating to a safer suburb — a kind of university suburban flight. Pepperdine University uprooted its entire campus to Malibu from the center city in response to the riots. USC stayed downtown and now has a vested interest in revitalizing the City of Angels from the inside out. USC is now a champion of New Urbanism, and it has taken a role in the revival of the Los Angeles River — a project mentioned earlier as "catalytic infrastructure" by Ryan Gravel.

Some city planners forecast a future where at least some suburbs, lacking public transit lines, will fall into desolation. In this darker version of the future, some suburbs may become slums. Some may be abandoned altogether. Jeff Speck already has documentation of falling values of homes dependent on automobiles versus similar properties in walkable communities. See *Walkable City*.

In Vermont, we need to take note of what has transpired in L.A. and Atlanta and most American cities and avoid building outward, helter-skelter, until we use up all the available space between Rutland and the Canadian border. We need to discourage sprawl and instead build walkable communities. That means infill development, greater density and taller buildings in Burlington, Winooski and other Vermont communities. We must reverse the trend during the latter part of the 20th century in Chittenden County of population increases in suburbs rather than in downtown Burlington driven (literally) by auto-centric development.

The chart at right displays the population of Burlington relative to the rest of the county since the first census in 1791. As you can see, the highest percentage of the population living in Burlington relative to the rest of the county occurred between 1920 and 1950, when Burlington housed over half the population of the county. It's interesting that this is the same time period in which Burlington was a much more walkable community with electric street cars for public transportation about town and out to Winooski and Essex. Since then, the automobile, cheap gasoline, cheap land outside the city, favorable zoning rules and the American propensity toward sprawl has led to a lower and lower percentage of county residents living in Burlington. As of the last census in 2010 only 27% of Chittenden County residents called Burlington home. This trend must be reversed.

Some interesting observations apparent from the chart on this page are, first, that only a small percentage of the population of the county resided in Burlington in the early years from 1783 to at least 1840, when most of the population was engaged in agriculture. Charlotte was the most populous town in Chittenden County until about 1808. Burlington gained population faster than surrounding agricultural communities as industry employed more people downtown. Incredibly, the population of Burlington almost doubled between 1860 and 1870, as Burlington became the third largest lumber port in the world. A majority of the population of the county lived in Burlington by 1920.

Right now, Vermont appears to be losing population. Chittenden County is experiencing anemic

	Burlington	Chittenden County	Percentage of County Population in Burlington
1791	332	3,866	8.6%
1800	816	9,396	8.7%
1810	1,690	14,499	11.6%
1820	2,111	17,167	12.3%
1830	3,526	21,502	16.4%
1840	4,271	22,969	18.6%
1850	7,585	28,981	26.2%
1860	7,713	28,169	27.4%
1870	14,387	36,480	39.4%
1880	11,365	32,791	34.7%
1890	14,590	35,668	40.9%
1900	18,640	39,690	47%
1910	20,468	42,447	48.2%
1920	22,779	43,694	52.1%
1930	24,789	47,291	52.4%
1940	27,686	52,094	53.1%
1950	33,155	62,567	53%
1960	35,531	74,425	47.7%
1970	38,633	99,131	39%
1980	37,712	115,534	32.6%
1990	39,127	131,761	29.7%
2000	38,889	146,571	26.5%
2010	42,417	156,545	27%

THE BURLINGTON BIKE PATH & WATERFRONT PARK

growth with little increase in population, but that is likely to change. Burlington is a very attractive place to live in the early decades of the 21st century. It is consistently named as one of the best places to live in one magazine article after the next. It should become a target for millennials. Speck contends that the brightest minds of this generation decide where they want to live first and then look for a job in that city. That's much different than previous generations that simply moved to where they found a job. The message to city planners is clear — build it and they will come. If you build the walkable city the younger generations now want to live in, they will come.

If we project the longer term rate of growth in Chittenden County over the next 200 years based upon the past 200, we should expect an increase of at least 1.5 million residents county-wide by 2219. That is a staggering number. It is important to house most of that increase in population in walkable communities instead of automobile-dependent, traffic-choked suburbs.

And don't think those numbers are impossible. According to that article in the *USC Alumni Magazine*, in half that time — the 100 years between 1910 and 2010 — Los Angeles grew from 319,000 residents to ten million.

It's tempting to end this chapter with that. Unfortunately, we still have to deal with the bedroom community suburbs that have already been built in a semi-circle around Burlington. Almost three quarters of all the people in Chittenden County today live in those auto-centric communities. And as of 2019 we are still building more cul-de-sac subdivisions throughout the county, like lemmings rushing toward a cliff.

So we have to assume that roughly 75% of the population in the county prefers to live in these auto-centric suburbs, or at least they don't have or can't imagine or understand a viable alternative —

a walkable community instead. It is important to educate the masses and change attitudes before the natural progression of pollution and congestion turn Chittenden County into L.A. or Atlanta over the next 200 years.

This is not impossible. Sprawl is not inevitable. The millennial generation has already registered its preference for living in walkable communities rather than suburbs. Baby boomers downsizing from suburban homes should find a walkable/bike-able community downtown more attractive in their retirement years. People concerned about the environment, and particularly global warming, should be enticed into walkable communities by the much smaller carbon footprint of living downtown.

There is still hope. We just need to educate the masses. It's been done before. Look at the progress in the environmental movement over a period of four short years between 1969 and 1972 that I *outlined in Chapter Three.*

Of course, economics and congestion will eventually become the natural guardrails of our wasteful living preferences. When gasoline finally runs out or becomes too expensive to service this suburban way of life, people may be able to turn to electric vehicles. But even electric vehicles may become too expensive to service these suburbs for centuries to come.

Autonomous vehicles, discussed in *Chapter Twenty-Two,* may provide a less expensive way to service suburbs long term, but it is very likely that the value of properties in suburbs requiring automobiles will decline as their cost increases and more people turn toward more walkable/bikeable communities. Hopefully the worst-case scenario of dilapidated suburbs, slums and abandoned properties never becomes a reality.

CHAPTER TWENTY
Burlington Segways

During my last year at Georgetown Law School I took a trip to Kitty Hawk, North Carolina, and took a hang gliding lesson. I had always been fascinated with flight. I was hooked. I bought my first hang glider the first opportunity I got shortly after settling in Burlington. The problem was that there was nowhere to practice flying a hang glider in northern Vermont.

In 1984 I solved that problem by buying Cobble Hill in southern Milton, ten miles north of Burlington. Cobble Hill is one of three knobs, or monadnocks, in the Champlain Valley, the other two being Mt. Philo in Charlotte and Arrowhead Mountain in northern Milton. All three of these monadnocks have a summit of approximately 900 feet above sea level. All three were islands in Lake Vermont 10,000 years ago, a lake in the Champlain Valley at about 600 feet above sea level, formed by an ice dam to the north that finally melted at the end of the last Ice Age.

The advantage of a monadnock is that it allows launches into the wind in all directions. All aircraft need to launch and land into the wind. Prevailing winds in the Champlain Valley are westerlies. Arrowhead has a cliff on its western flank with a road and houses at the bottom. That wouldn't do for hang gliding. Mt. Philo is a state park and I knew they would never allow me to clear the side of the hill for hang gliding. That left Cobble Hill, and fortunately it was for sale.

I set about the task of clearing the northwest side of Cobble Hill with friends I hired to convert the second growth forest into firewood, which I sold to pay for the property. It took us five years to clear all the way to the top of the hill. My first and only flight from the top of the hill in a hang glider occurred in 1989. Due to a sloping landing zone, the hang glider didn't want to land. I finally stuffed the control bar out to full extension at 40 feet over my neighbor's back yard to stall the glider rather than face power lines on the other side of the house. The resulting crash destroyed the glider's downtubes and the control bar. I hit my head, but didn't get hurt. That proved hang gliders wouldn't work at Cobble Hill.

Fortunately for me, paragliders were invented in 1985, a year after I bought Cobble Hill. Paragliders work great at Cobble Hill because they are 15 feet overhead. They land more like a helicopter than an airplane. My wife, Ruth, and I took lessons in Utah and became paragliding instructors in 1992.

Rick Sharp flies a paraglider at Cobble Hill in Milton in 1995. *R. Masters.*

In 1996, while leading a paragliding tour in Mexico, I crashed into a cliff and broke my back and my right leg. I was fortunate to have survived the crash and made it back to San Diego for medical treatment. I was initially paralyzed below the chest. I spent four months in a wheelchair and I lost a nerve in my right leg that forces me to walk with a limp and use a cane for stability. I can walk, but I can no longer ride a bicycle — certainly an irony for "Mr. Bikepath" — but that has not kept me from using the path in other ways or from remaining passionate about issues of public transportation and infrastructure, as evidenced in part by this book.

I was vaguely aware of the efforts of others to extend the Bike Path northward across the Winooski River in the 1990s, but I was content to let them take the lead on that. I had two young children and a long recovery from my accident. It was great to see others getting involved as biking in our area seemed to gain popularity. Howard Dean had become Governor and his Administration was pressing for a bridge across the river. Local Motion began the bike ferry across the river, and before we knew it, we had a bike path bridge into Colchester and a pathway all the way out to the Causeway.

Although I attended many of the dedication ceremonies on the bikepath during this time, including the dedication of the bridge in 2004, it was difficult for me to get to these ceremonies because I had to park a long way away and walk in with a limp and a cane. It's very difficult for me to walk more than a hundred yards now. Since I couldn't ride a bicycle and I hate wheelchairs, I had never been out onto the Causeway after it was converted to a bike path in the early 1990s. That changed when I acquired a Segway PT in 2009.

My wife, Ruth, and I tried out Segway PTs at Clark's Trading Post in Lincoln, New Hampshire, and I immediately knew that this machine would give me back the mobility of my youth and allow me to get out onto the Causeway and a lot of other places on the Bike Path that I hadn't visited in a long time. I've always felt that a wheelchair puts me in a compromised position, and I hate that. When I greet people in a wheelchair, my eyes are at their crotch level. When I greet people on a Segway PT, I am usually a little taller than they are. Our eyes meet at the same level. The dignity that the Segway PT provides is important to me.

I enjoyed taking my Segway PT out onto the Causeway from our home, just off the Bike Path a half mile north of the bike bridge in Colchester. We decided to purchase a few more and offer an off-road Segway PT Experience at our property in Milton which we called Sharp Park.

In 2009 Jeff Snyder went before the Burlington Parks Commission seeking a permit to offer Segway PT tours downtown on the Bike Path. We learned of his proposal in the press and attended the hearing to support him. He ran into a stone wall. Several members of the Parks Commission were adamantly opposed to Segway PTs on the Bike Path. Most of that opposition seemed to come from an aversion to motorized vehicles on the path. The Parks Director at the time, Mari Steinbach, was an avid bicyclist and seemed determined to keep Segway PTs off the Bike Path. She tried to ignore her way out of granting a permit. She didn't return Snyder's phone calls or emails.

Snyder finally got so frustrated that he gave up. He sold his four Segway PTs to me. I started the application process for a permit from the city. Steinbach stonewalled me too. In the meantime, Doug Robbie had opened a small shop to rent electric bikes at the April Cornell building at the corner of Main and Battery Streets, and he was getting a lot of flak about motorized bicycles on the Bike Path. He gave up as well.

Mari Steinbach was an appointee of Progressive Mayor Bob Kiss, whose days were numbered due to a scandal involving an illegal loan of $17 million to Burlington Telecom. We weren't sure whether Steinbach's opposition to Segway PTs was due to her preference for bicycles or a socialist aversion to private business. Either way, it was apparent that we were in for a battle to change the minds of people at Parks and Recreation.

Miro Weinberger was running as a Democrat in the March 2012 race for mayor. He held breakfast meetings with the public at the bagel shop on North Avenue every Wednesday. I started attending and often got to engage in one-on-one conversations with him. I found Weinberger to be surprisingly approachable, very intelligent and, with a background in urban planning, just what the city needs. He certainly didn't disappoint me after his election as mayor. After stabilizing the city's finances and bringing its credit rating back from near junk status, Weinberger has completely rebuilt the Bike Path north of downtown and tripled the size of Waterfront Park, among many other accomplishments. Recently the Weinberger administration came up with an innovative plan to reuse at least the I-beam framework of the old Moran electric generating plant on the waterfront after over 30 years of failed plans to redevelop that structure.

We finally got a hearing on an application for a permit to conduct Segway PT tours on the Bike Path. Two or three Parks Commissioners were adamantly opposed. They didn't want Segway PTs on the Bike Path, period.

I told the Commission I would be riding a Segway PT on the Bike Path whether they liked it or not. I told them they could not prevent me. Since I am disabled, I am entitled to use a device to assist my mobility under the Americans with Disabilities Act (ADA). I cited some great language out of a case from Disneyland where the judge ruled that the advancement of technology did not end with the electric wheelchair. As technology advances the ADA requires consideration of more advanced devices to match the experience of the disabled as closely as possible to that of the able bodied.

The Commission still refused to issue a permit. They decided to study it more. I appealed to the Parks and Recreation Committee of the City Council. Councilor Karen Paul, chair of the Committee, gave us a hearing that happened to get scheduled for the first day of work for the new Parks Director, Jesse Bridges, appointed by Mayor Miro Weinberger. We presented our case. Councilor Paul directed Bridges to check out our Segway PTs and see if they were safe for use on the bikepath.

Jesse Bridges met with us and tried out a Segway PT on the Bike Path. He had no difficulty controlling the machine. Parks Commissioners John Bossange and Nancy Kaplan completed their review of the safety studies I supplied them, together with other information they gathered on their own. Bridges, Bossange and Kaplan all recommended permit approval. In the end the Parks Commission decided it would be better to have the cooperation of a responsible Segway PT tour operator on the waterfront, paying a 5% fee for use of the Bike Path, rather than fighting it out in court. We began Segway PT tour operations in downtown Burlington in April 2013.

Although Segway PT tours are offered at several ski areas in the northeast, tours of cities in New England are limited to Boston and Burlington, Vermont at this time. Our goal was to introduce the public to these machines with the hope of popularizing them as an alternate means of getting about the Queen City. Eventually we hope to replace some cars downtown with Segway PTs. We also brought electric bikes to Burlington after

THE BURLINGTON BIKE PATH & WATERFRONT PARK

a two-year effort to get a permit to use them in a rental fleet on the Bike Path. Ebike safety studies and a California law enacted in 2015, recognizing ebikes as the equivalent of ordinary bikes on all recreation paths in the state, seemed to finally win over the Parks Commission.

I quit my law practice after 30 years to concentrate on Segway PT tours downtown. I wrote a narrative of the history of the waterfront with an emphasis on the Bike Path and Waterfront Park. We have our interns learn the narrative and deliver it on tour by radio as they roll along. It turned out to be a lot more fun riding Segway PTs about the waterfront, downtown Burlington and UVM all summer with a bunch of college interns than practicing law in a stuffy courtroom into my late 60s.

Being on the waterfront on Segway PTs on a daily basis, the remaining deficiencies in the Bike Path downtown became apparent fairly quickly. The most important of these is that the Bike Path crosses the railroad tracks twice in two blocks. Remember, the city only had $750,000 to build the Bike Path originally. Corners had to be cut. It was a lot cheaper to paint a bike path over existing pavement on the east side of the tracks between King and College Streets then it would be to route it down the west side of the tracks like the rest of the path.

My understanding is that the Lake Champlain Transportation Company has refused to grant the city the easement it would need over its property to relocate the Bike Path to the west side of the tracks through that area. We see the results on a daily basis, with congestion at the Local Motion Trailside Center bike rental shop and Ice Cream Bob's, and bike crashes at the College and King Street crossings. Skate boards can't be ridden over the tracks, and the tracks are also a big challenge to inline skates. Some people get a running start and jump

the tracks at King Street and/or College Street on inline skates and even skateboards.

We became members of the Tourism Committee of the Lake Champlain Regional Chamber of Commerce and the Burlington Business Association. I began lobbying both of those groups, plus Local Motion, the Mayor, Public Works, anyone who would listen, about getting the Bike Path relocated to the west side of the tracks between College and King Street. Easements for this purpose would have to be obtained from both ECHO and the Lake Champlain Transportation Company. Phelan Fretz from ECHO agreed to an easement across the ECHO property. The hang-up was Lake Champlain Transportation.

Trey Pecor, the owner of Lake Champlain Transportation, would not grant the city an easement across its property on the west side of the tracks. Rumors were that Pecor wanted to build a hotel on the property. After two years of getting nowhere with this relocation effort, I decided that it was worth trying to move this along by getting it onto the city ballot in November 2016, a presidential election year.

We wanted to specifically address the issue of taking the easement from Lake Champlain Transportation through application of the Public Trust Doctrine or by eminent domain if necessary. A recent Superior Court decision had applied the laws of eminent domain to a bike path in Colchester. We felt it was time to do so in Burlington in order to eliminate the two railroad crossings in two blocks.

Each summer we hire six to eight interns to conduct Segway PT tours downtown at Burlington Segways. In between tours the interns are often bored and looking for things to do. We send them out to be seen around town. An important part of our branding is interns with red shirts and Bern helmets riding Segway PTs downtown. And 15% of our business comes from people seeing our interns out and about during the summer. It occurred to me that we could use the interns to collect petition signatures to get the issue on the city ballot. We knew that the Mayor and the City Council would never support a ballot item with wording that included eminent domain. So we didn't even ask. We just began collecting petition signatures.

The March city election provided us with the ideal location to collect petition signatures because every person passing by is a registered voter in Burlington. I stationed interns at each of the polling places, and Ruth and I collected petition signatures all day. By that evening we had over 700 signatures out of the 1,800 we would need. We knew there would be a primary in August where we would be able to collect a lot more signatures in one day as well. We collected the rest at the Farmers Market on Saturdays and at local morning coffee shops like Speeder and Earl's and Handy's Lunch. Earl Handy was especially cooperative, allowing me to approach customers at the counter. We also collected signatures at the Friday night Truck Stop food event behind Arts Riot and at the Art Hop.

I took out a full page ad in the *Burlington Free Press* and *Seven Days* and we mailed a flyer to those who had signed the petition. A copy of the flyer appears here and on the next page.

The measure passed by a slim majority. It suffered from a lack of exposure, appearing on a ballot with a lot of candidates and other issues. One of those issues was the redevelopment of the failing

RELOCATE THE BIKE PATH VOTE YES ON QUESTION #6
(And tell your friends!)

The Burlington Bicycle Path is still a work in progress 36 years after Howard Dean, Tom Hudspeth and I began advocating for a continuous recreation path separate from automobile traffic along the shore of Lake Champlain. We did that just like we are doing so again today, with an advisory ballot item.

That ballot item in 1980 got 75% support of city voters, eventually creating the Bike Path we all enjoy today.

The current ballot item is: "**Should the Mayor of Burlington and the City Council be advised to relocate the Burlington Bicycle Path to the west side of the railroad tracks between College and King Streets even if that means utilizing the public trust doctrine or eminent domain to accomplish this task?**"

THE BACKGROUND

The City has done a great job of upgrading the Bike Path as it snakes through the heart of the downtown district. It is currently in the process of relocating the path to the water's edge through the "north forty reserve." The only remaining realignment necessary to finally accomplish the City goal of a "world class bike path" is the two block stretch that is the subject of this ballot item.

For the past 28 years the bike path has been diverted eastward across the railroad tracks at College Street and then back west across the tracks at King Street. This route was a compromise necessary because the City only had $750,000 to install the entire pathway. It was a lot cheaper to paint a bike path on existing pavement east of the tracks through this area than it was to do it right and route it down the west side of the railroad tracks. This compromise route resulted in two hazardous railroad crossings that have caused hundreds of crashes and injuries to people on bikes, skateboards and inline skates. It has also resulted in congestion on the bike path at the Local Motion Trailside Center and Ice Cream Bob's. Realignment of the path to the west side of the tracks would eliminate both track crossings and alleviate congestion at these bottlenecks.

Burlington Town Center two-story enclosed shopping mall into a 14-story residential and office complex with shops on the main floor facing the street instead. Opponents of that development also seemed to oppose our initiative, probably because of the eminent domain language.

I haven't pressed the Mayor or the City Council on this issue since the November 2016 election. The Mayor was embroiled in a re-election campaign with substantial opposition from opponents of the downtown development project and the installation of bike lanes on North Avenue through the New North End. Apparently, there is a plan to bring Amtrak service back to Burlington by 2020. That will require a realignment of the tracks between College and King Street, possibly with the addition of an additional set of tracks. If nothing else, our efforts raised awareness of the need to move the Bike Path to the west side of the tracks between College and King Streets and should ensure that this realignment occurs when the tracks are installed in the near future.

At the same time, it would be great to get Lake Champlain Transportation to renovate its property. The condition of this property over the last 30 years, while the rest of the waterfront was undergoing its transformation into the park and bike path we all enjoy today, is still deplorable. On our Segway PT tours we sometimes direct tourists to look at the Lake Champlain Transportation property as an example of what the waterfront looked like prior to its recent rebirth.

I had a conversation with Mayor Weinberger about the Lake Champlain Transportation property recently, and his comments and questions prompted

---

THE LAKE CHAMPLAIN TRANSPORTATION PROBLEM

So far Lake Champlain Transportation (LCT) has been unwilling to convey an easement to the city for relocating the Bike Path to the west side of the tracks in this area. This ballot item is intended to apply public pressure on LCT, the Mayor and the City Council to relocate the Bike Path to the west side of the railroad tracks as soon as possible.

I was 28 years old when we started the public campaign to create the Bike Path. I'm now 64. I'd like to see it complete while I'm still here to enjoy it.

The cost of this relocation will be a small fraction of the cost to reconstruct the bike path from Perkins Pier to North Beach now in progress. This cost can be covered with Tax Incremental Financing (TIF) funds at no additional expense to taxpayers.

The Bike Path is the #1 Attraction for Burlington on Trip Advisor. Waterfront Park is #2 and the Church Street Marketplace is #3. Completing the Bike Path and upgrading it to "world class" status will attract even more tourists to Burlington.

The investment the City made in these three facilities over the past 30 years has resulted in a better quality of life in Burlington and economic prosperity downtown. For 30 years the only hotel downtown was the Radisson (now the Hilton). The Marriott opened in 2007. Hotel Vermont opened three years ago and our fourth hotel downtown, the Hilton Garden Inn, opened last year. Hotel rooms downtown fetch $400 a night and there are no vacancies during the summertime. Compare that to $250 a night at the Sheraton out by 189. That is a hotel building boom that Burlington won't experience again for 200 or 300 years, if ever.

THE PUBLIC TRUST DOCTRINE

The Public Trust Doctrine is a legal concept that says the bed of Lake Champlain belongs to all the people of the State of Vermont. Approximately 60 acres of land has been created over the years by filling in the lake, including the LCT ferry dock. In 1989 the Vermont Supreme Court ruled that the land filled into Burlington harbor is subject to the Public Trust Doctrine and must be used for public purposes.

So the filled land that the ferry docks are located on belongs to the people of Vermont and must be used for public purposes. A ferry is a public purpose, but does that mean LCT has a license to maintain this property in its current derelict condition indefinitely and deny the relocation of the leading tourist attraction in Burlington to a safer location without bottlenecks west of the railroad tracks? Isn't it time to take back a small sliver of this property to eliminate a major safety hazard in the existing bike path?

EMINENT DOMAIN

No one likes to employ eminent domain to create a public right of way such as a highway, a railroad, a pipeline, a power line or a bicycle path. Eminent domain is the taking of private property for the public good, with due compensation to the owner of course. It should only be employed in rare cases where the private property owner will not voluntarily yield to the greater public good.

Eminent domain was recently employed by the Town of Colchester to acquire four small pieces of private property necessary to construct the bike path along Holy Cross Road. The Vermont Superior Court upheld the application of eminent domain to the bike path in Colchester.

If the small sliver of property the city needs to relocate the Bike Path cannot be obtained from LCT voluntarily then eminent domain should be used to move the Bike Path west of the tracks between College and King Streets.

VOTE YES ON QUESTION #6

This advisory ballot item will shine a light on this relocation. A large yes vote on this item will likely move this relocation along faster.

This ballot item is being sponsored by Burlington Segways. Come visit us.

I can be reached at **(802) 489-5113** for more information. Please call if you have questions.

Rick Sharp

---

me to send him a memo about the future of this property.

I wanted to write you a memo to set out my thoughts about development of the Lake Champlain Transportation (LCT) property at the foot of King Street.

You know how passionate I am about the bike path, and I am eternally thankful for your contribution which I refer to as Bikepath 2.0. Once that work is complete, the most important remaining improvement to the bike path is to move it to the west side of the railroad tracks between King and College Streets. That means the City needs a strip of land from LCT. And as you know, a majority of voters in November supported this rerouting of the bike path, even if that means eminent domain.

I know you have discussions with Trey Pecor. I'm hoping you can get a deal done with LCT to acquire the strip of land needed to relocate the bike path sometime during your third term as Mayor. And you can be sure I will be pressing you for that. But redevelopment of the rest of the LCT property is also very important to the future of Burlington.

Burlington has come a long way since the 1980s when the waterfront was a derelict wasteland. The bike path and waterfront park are now the two leading attractions in Burlington, according to Trip Advisor. Certainly, the future of Burlington's waterfront is tourism, not grimy industrial uses. The LCT property is an eyesore that needs to be redeveloped in a way that generates revenue for LCT, but also serves the community by providing much needed services on the waterfront.

We have all heard rumors that Mr. Pecor wishes to build a hotel on the LCT property.

As you know, I spent a lot of time in the 1980s arguing that hotels and condominiums could not be located on land filled into Burlington harbor under the Public Trust Doctrine because the bed of the lake belongs to all the people of Vermont and must be put to a public use. Private homes and hotel rooms are the most private uses imaginable.

This has already been publicly settled during the Alden debate in 1985. Mayor Bernie Sanders made the same argument then that if Burlington voters said a hotel and condominium project was in the public interest, suddenly black becomes white and private becomes public. The end result was the 1989 Vermont Supreme Court ruling applying the Public Trust Doctrine to the filled land in Burlington harbor. Filled land must be used exclusively for public purposes.

So you can go back and relitigate that issue, arguing that the hotel lobby is open to the public. Not really. If a hotel guest lingers in the lobby, no problem. If a nonguest did so, she would likely be thrown out. And the hotel rooms upstairs are clearly private. In my opinion there is no way to make it otherwise. You are on the wrong side of history making that argument.

There is no doubt that the LCT ferry dock property is filled land. I've studied the historical maps. The entire property is too low and must be raised out of the floodplain of Lake Champlain. The Legislature is powerless to give away public trust (filled land) to private uses. That's the whole concept of the trust. The former bed of the lake is held in trust for public uses. Ferry docks, railroads, water plants, museums, restaurants, bars, even shops and art galleries work fine for me. I draw the line

THE BURLINGTON BIKE PATH & WATERFRONT PARK

at hotels and condominiums. I think the public does too.

I support dense development and taller buildings downtown. That's where they belong. And that's where hotels belong also — in between Battery and Church Street. That supports the Church Street Marketplace, putting it within walking distance of hotel rooms, along with the bike path, Waterfront Park and the best restaurants in the State.

More and more of the people we see at Burlington Segways have flown into Burlington Airport and gotten a shuttle to their downtown hotel. They don't bother to rent a car because they can walk everywhere downtown from their hotel room. If the hotel is located on the LCT property, it would be a long walk uphill to Church Street and downtown restaurants from there. And where would they park the cars they now need to get about?

It just doesn't make sense to build a hotel on the LCT property from a city planning perspective. The hotel building boom that's going on downtown now between Battery and Church Streets is great for the City. Keep it there. A lot of the people that supported the development downtown would be opposed to a hotel on the LCT property. The constituency in favor of an LCT hotel is one — Trey Pecor.

Although I know I have no right to tell Trey what to do with the LCT property, I must point out that it is currently an eyesore reminiscent of the grimy industrial past Burlington recently overcame. In its current condition it is an unsightly drag on the beauty of the waterfront and therefore on the tourism we all wish to promote. The LCT property needs to be raised out of the flood plain. Now is the time to redevelop the property into something that is more attractive to tourists and serves the community.

The bike path and Waterfront Park are great attractions enjoyed by thousands. What is sorely needed on the waterfront now are more small shops, restaurants and bars to service visitors after their walk on the bike path and through the park. The LCT property is very well suited for that purpose. By redeveloping the property with small shops, art galleries, restaurants, bars, etc. in low, 2 to 3 story structures right on the bike path you get the best of both worlds:

1. The bike path gets relocated and becomes integrated into the new development.

2. The property starts earning income for LCT.

3. The property is transformed from an eyesore to an asset to the community and tourism.

4. And if the developer brings in the local arts community, they could have art galleries there with guided tours of the south end Arts District only two blocks away.

That would be a project that would be supported by a large portion of the community. It would be a very important addition to Burlington that you could be proud of as the mayor who brought that kind of development to the waterfront. The alternative proposal of a multistory hotel on the LCT site would fly in the face of the best decisions the city has made to date to site hotels between Battery and Church Street rather than on the water's edge downtown. And you would be on the wrong side of history supporting that project. It would face significant opposition and, in my opinion, ultimately fail.

Ruth and I have traveled the world looking at what works and what doesn't on waterfronts and downtowns. The best example of what I think would work well on the LCT property is a small fishing village that was converted to shops, restaurants and bars called Port Lucaya at Freeport in the Bahamas. Check out this website (http://www.portlucaya.com/). The old fishing village is located behind a 10 story Sheraton on a beautiful white sand beach. Despite all the great shops and restaurants at the Sheraton, we spent our time in the old fishing village dining, shopping and conversing with locals because it had so much more character.

I truly hope you can have an influence on Mr. Pecor and steer him in the right direction for LCT and for the City as well.

Port Lucaya, Freeport, Bahamas, before it was lost to Hurricane Dorian in September, 2019.

I spoke to the Mayor about the LCT property at the bagel shop on North Avenue in late December 2018, and he assured me that discussions are ongoing with LCT and that relocation of the Bike Path will occur when the railroad is realigned, probably in 2020.

The "Greenride" bikeshare program landed in Burlington with a thud in 2018. This bikeshare program is run by a vendor called Gotcha selected by the Regional Planning Commission. It uses a smart phone activation and payment system. It was designed to assist local residents with short term, point to point transit between 17 hubs located at UVM, Champlain College, Church Street, the foot of College Street in front of the Boathouse and various other locations throughout the city.

Local Motion and the local bike shops were brought into the process very late. We all raised concerns about this bikeshare program competing with local shops and cannibalizing the summer tourist market all the local bike shops depend upon for their survival. Representatives of Gotcha and the Regional Planning Commission assured us all that the Greenride program would not compete for tourists during the summer.

Nonetheless, the pie charts produced by Gotcha depicting bike use in the summer of 2018 clearly indicates that almost half of all bike trips systemwide came from and returned to the waterfront rack. The Church Street hub was the second busiest hub. Although Gotcha's pricing was supposed to encourage only short trips by making longer rentals very expensive, GPS tracking indicated that 107 Greenride bikes were taken all the way out to the Causeway 10 miles north of downtown, a trip that requires at least two and a half hours, during the summer of 2018.

Although Gotcha and Bryan Davis from the Regional Planning Commission both insist that the Greenride program was a success in 2018, it is clear that it failed miserably in its goal to provide bikes for short trips from hub to hub downtown. This program can't be allowed to survive by cannibalizing existing bike rentals by Local Motion and local bike shops.

The program cost $400,000 for a three-year planned duration. This money was raised from sponsors like Ben and Jerry's and Seventh Generation, who got to put their logos on the bikes and advertise their support for environmentalism. The program did not come from grass roots supporters. It is being imposed on the city by Gotcha, which of course is a for-profit company more interested in their bottom line than what's best for Burlington. Personally, I think the $400,000 could have been better spent by buying a bunch of cheap bicycles and giving them to the targeted riders for free.

Gotcha is planning to add electric bikes to the program in 2020. There is no doubt that those ebikes would be used primarily to travel out to the Causeway. The summer tourist market for ebikes in Burlington is in its infancy at this point. It would be too bad to kill the business of local shops through cut throat competition in this market.

I believe this Greenride system is ill-conceived and will not work in Burlington. Most of these bike-share programs are located in larger cities where they extend a public transportation system an additional mile or two. And many of them seem to work well. They can work at colleges as well, but a point-to-point system for short trips must stand on its own and not cannibalize the tourist market local bike shops rely on for their life's blood in Burlington.

Our summer interns at Burlington Segways listened patiently to a presentation about the system. All of them had their own bikes and couldn't understand why a student would rent bikes for short trips instead. I don't believe the system will survive in Burlington.

Finally, I'd like to mention electric scooters. We saw the first batch of these machines to hit the streets a few months after they were first introduced in Venice, California in March 2018. Everyone seemed to be having a ball on the beach front bike path. No helmets of course. These machines don't need a docking station. They are activated with a smart phone. The rental company rounds up the

escooters each evening for recharging. And, of course, they are causing problems, including severe injuries due to collisions with cars, pedestrians and other objects. They require good balance and are challenging to control. Escooter companies often flood tourist areas with fleets of hundreds of escooters that get left about helter skelter.

This has become a major problem in San Diego where a private company now collects escooters that have been left on private property or on sidewalks and holds them hostage until fees are paid.

In Burlington escooters would undoubtedly be popular on the Bike Path. The problem is they may overwhelm the pathway if the escooter companies insist on bringing in fleets of hundreds of machines that get left about. It is possible to introduce escooters through local bike shops in smaller numbers so they don't overwhelm the Bike Path. Bike shops could also provide helmets and a lesson in Bike Path etiquette. I would oppose unleashing a fleet of hundreds of escooters in Burlington that clog the Bike Path and are left all over with riders without helmets.

But in my opinion, the introduction of fleets of escooters, if that's where Burlington is going, will hasten the relocation of the Bike Path to the west side of the railroad tracks between College and King Streets to reduce accidents going over the tracks twice in two blocks. The wheels on escooters are small and can get caught on the steel rails.

Escooters would also probably hasten the installation of a separated multiuse path up Main Street to UVM in order to get escooters off the street. Remember these riders will not be wearing helmets. Even more than bicycle or Segway PT riders, who generally use helmets, escooter riders need protection from automobiles. It would be unfortunate if it takes a serious accident to get this infrastructure installed.

CHAPTER TWENTY-ONE
Jane emily Clymer

As the battle over the Alden plan was headed into the final showdown in the fall of 1985, Jane emily Clymer was an 18-year-old junior at the University of Vermont. She had skipped a year in high school and entered UVM at 16.

Jane emily was the only child of Adam and Ann Clymer. Adam was an editor of the *New York Times*. According to the article about her in the September 19, 1985 *Vermont Cynic*, the UVM student newspaper, Jane emily spent her first two years at UVM in the Living/Learning student housing complex where she participated in "Center Council." She enjoyed photography, horseback riding, traveling, riding her bicycle and poetry.

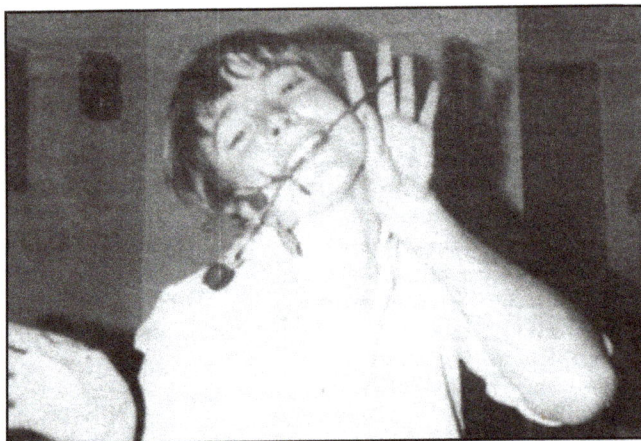

Jane emily had spent a summer in the Soviet Union. Her classes at UVM included Russian language, culture and history. She was treasurer of the Russian Club. She had spent the summer of 1985 in an apartment she shared with a friend in Burlington. In August she had acquired a ten-speed bicycle which

she rode everywhere, according to her friends. Her best friends at UVM described her as mature for her age but perhaps too young at 16 to enter college.

"She never grew up," said Tamara Nestler, a close friend. "She was like a little sister to me. She came to me for advice more probably because I wasn't a direct peer."

"She grasped naivete and lived it. She wanted to hold on to a naïve, youthlike character. She tried to preserve it, and she did."

"She wasn't studious," said Kris Kaye, another close friend. "In fact she hated studying," said another.

"She would tell me that I studied too much and then get better grades than me," said her roommate, Sarah Banges.

According to Banges, Jane emily left their apartment at about 3:30 p.m. on Saturday, September 17, 1985, on her ten speed. At approximately 4:15 that afternoon she was struck by a car driven by Theron Webster on the side of Route 116 in Hinesburg.

The accident occurred three-quarters of the way up a steep hill. Apparently Jane emily had gotten off her bike part-way up the hill. The road had a shoulder of perhaps five inches beyond the white line marking the edge of the driving surface of the highway. There was significant brush along the side of the road. Apparently Jane emily was walking up the hill on the pavement with the bike in the sand and gravel and low brush on the side of the roadway.

Webster and his passenger later testified that they were traveling southbound on Route 116 behind three other cars. According to the two of them, none of the other cars moved left in front of them before they hit Jane emily. Neither of them saw her before the collision. After he struck Jane emily, Webster crested the hill and came back to find her on the side of the road with the bicycle nearby.

Jane emily suffered severe injuries to her left leg at the height of Webster's bumper. She had damage to her left hip and severe head injuries. Apparently her body had been hurled over the car. Her head hit the rear window. She wasn't wearing a helmet.

She was admitted to the Medical Center Hospital at 4:30 p.m. and was officially declared dead shortly after her parents arrived from New York at 7:30 a.m. the following morning. Her organs were donated to science. Jane emily had been born in Washington D.C. on October 25, 1966. She was only 18 years old.

Webster was charged with driving while intoxicated and subsequently did some time in jail for DWI, death resulting. The Clymers won a wrongful death action against him and the bar that had served him before he hit the road that afternoon, and they successfully lobbied the Vermont legislature for tougher laws on drinking and driving.

I had an intern named Ann Saurman working with me from Jean Flack's Environmental Law class at UVM that semester. We were looking into getting funding for a 1974 Vermont law that was supposed to fund bicycle paths statewide when we learned of Jane emily's death. I asked Ann to focus on the circumstances of her accident to determine if a separate bike path in that area would have made a difference. Ann contacted the two officers involved in the investigation and arranged for a meeting at the site of the accident so we could understand exactly what had happened. Ann contacted Jane emily's roommate, Sarah Banges, and other friends and invited them to join us, but none of them did.

The officer parked the squad car at a small turnout at the foot of a steep hill on Route 116 just before the blinking light at the road to Champlain Valley Union High School. We walked up the steep hill to the location of the accident. The officer explained that Jane emily's body had been found in the roadway perhaps ten yards north of the bicycle. There was no damage to the bicycle. It was found perpendicular to the highway in the brush on the side of the road. That led to the conclusion that Jane emily had been walking on the pavement with the bicycle on her right just off the pavement when she was hit.

Route 116 is a rural highway similar to so many in Vermont. Although there is plenty of room on the side of the road there for a wider shoulder or breakdown lane, or even better, a separated bike path, that investment was never made. You can blame Webster for drinking that afternoon, and perhaps Jane emily would have been hit anyway, even if the shoulder was wider, but there is no doubt she would have survived that bike ride if there had been a separated path in that area. Perhaps she would be alive today if the Burlington Bike Path had existed at that time and Jane emily had decided to take a ride along the lake that day instead of heading south on Hinesburg Road. How many lives have been saved by the Burlington Bike Path? What is each of those lives worth?

It's just a matter of funding. We will continue to suffer this senseless and heartbreaking carnage on our roads until we make the investment in infrastructure necessary to make them safe by separating 2,000-pound cars from pedestrians, bicyclists and light-weight electric devices.

Ann Saurman contacted the State Highway Department to inquire about why the 1974 law had not been funded. She was told by Val Leach that this law had never been funded because there was "no need as yet" to develop bicycle paths. Ann got the statistics from the Vermont Department of Transportation. Twelve bicyclists or pedestrians were killed on Vermont roads in 1984. Ten were killed in 1983. We both disagreed with Leach that separated bike paths were not needed yet. Ann began to contact people surrounding Jane emily's death to testify in Montpelier in an attempt to get funding for the 1974 law enacted, but never funded, by the legislature.

The September 19, 1985 *Vermont Cynic* article ended with one of Jane emily's poems:

"... Perhaps in the morning
You'll stand in the sun.
Perhaps in the morning,
You'll see what has gone
Perhaps you'll be stronger
And look braver at the day
Perhaps you'll be stronger
And see all that you may."

I sent a letter to the *Cynic* the following week:

Student's death points to a need for safe bicycle paths

I was deeply moved by your article about the death of Jane emily Clymer. Her poem, which you printed at the end of the article, said something to me personally.

For over five years now I have worked hard to create a bicycle path in Burlington, separated from car traffic, that would be safe for bicyclists. I have often traveled the back roads of Vermont and noted their narrow shoulders and the dangers of mixing slow moving bicyclists with fast, heavy cars.

I read about a young lady being struck by a car a short time ago and learned only yesterday that she died. "A truly senseless and tragic loss," I thought, knowing all the while that the Vermont Legislature directed the devotion of highway funds to bicycle paths along state routes several years ago.

Obviously, very little, if anything, ever came of this legislation.

This fact I've known for quite some time, and yet somehow, I've always been too busy to do anything about our failure to construct separate bike paths along these narrow rural roads. "Perhaps in the morning...Perhaps you'll be stronger." Perhaps you'd still be alive, Jane, if I had acted earlier...

Certainly it is high time to act now. Concerned students should demand that the Vermont Agency of Transportation install these low cost lanes along rural routes close to Burlington. Don't let Jane's death be in vain. Get involved. If you're interested in testifying before a Transportation Committee to bring an end to this senseless slaughter, please contact me...Together we can make a difference.

All of this was going on right in the middle of the final months of the Alden campaign. My focus shifted to the fight over Alden, and I spent almost all my time on that for the remainder of the fall of 1985. Although Ann Saurman contacted a lot of people, we never did get a group together to testify in Montpelier. Jane emily faded from memory over time and the bike path along Route 116 never got built. Perhaps some group of concerned students at UVM or CVU will take up the cause after reading this book and finally get the Jane emily Clymer Memorial Bike Path along Hinesburg Road built. Perhaps. I would certainly be willing to help establish and fund a bicycle advocacy group called the Friends of Jane emily Clymer to get a path built along Route 116. That's long overdue.

Similar groups could be established in towns throughout the county and the entire state to create a network of separated multi-use paths along rural roads, making them safer and thereby greatly increasing the use of alternatives to the automobile for local transportation.

Our current road system is simply unsafe for bicycles, pedestrians and light-weight electric vehicles. When our children were young, we lived at the corner of Route 7 and Severance Road in Colchester for years. We tried to take our children on a bike ride along Route 7 only once. It ended in disaster when Dori, at about 6 years old at the time, fell off her bike on the side of the highway with 18-wheel trucks whizzing by a few feet away. Yikes! That just isn't safe. Whenever we wanted to go bicycling with the kids, we loaded the bikes in the car and drove to the Burlington Bike Path. I know a lot of parents who do the same thing. That is probably the most important reason for the success of the Bike Path — safety.

Thirty-four years after Jane emily's death, in the early years of an entirely different century, the bike paths along rural roads in Vermont I had talked about in 1985 still haven't been built. I pass by bicyclists in my 2,500-pound truck on narrow roads without a shoulder in Colchester and Milton and Essex all the time. On average every year another 40 bicyclists or pedestrians are slaughtered or seriously injured on Vermont roads. Many of these deaths could be prevented if we had a system of safe separated pathways along most of these roads.

That may seem like an impossible task, but Burlington isn't the only community in Vermont that has come together to create a multi-use path separated from car traffic. The Stowe Bike Path is perhaps the best known outside Burlington. The effort to create that path actually began three years before our efforts in Burlington, in 1977. The initial effort failed, but in 1981 Stowe hired then clothing designer, Anne Lusk, to promote the path. Lusk did not have a background in planning or preservation. Nonetheless, she was hired as a "preservationist" for $5,000.

Lusk admits that she had no idea how to create the Stowe trail at first, but she decided to take a different approach from the town engineer who had just taken a "black magic marker to a map over private land." The reaction of property owners, many of them who ran hotels and inns along the Mountain Road to the ski resort, was not favorable. Lusk went door to door, meeting with homeowners and businesses along the proposed path face to face and sold the project as a way to increase property values by stabilizing riverbanks. She wrote about her progress on the path every week in the *Stowe Reporter*.

"By the time I was done," she says, "there wasn't a single person [in town] who didn't know all about it." Before she finished, Lusk had notarized 27 deeds of easement for the trail.

"When the town moderator asked if anyone objected to the path at the town meeting to vote on it," Lusk recalls, "there was silence, and then laughter." No one objected. The whole town was behind the project. That's the very best you can do in gathering community support. The Stowe Bikepath is a smashing success which has improved the quality of life along the Mountain Road. That process can be repeated all over Vermont; $5,000 is a small investment to get the ball rolling.

According to the *Burlington Free Press* in an article dated September 7, 2016, Lusk "credits her experience coordinating the path as part of her transition from designer/preservationist to where she is now, a fellow at Harvard University's School of Public Health, studying the effects of bicycling on Alzheimer's patients."

In 2017, the Lamoille Valley Rail Trail (LVRT) launched a $3 million capital campaign to generate the private funding necessary to finish and maintain the trail. The LVRT is a project of the Vermont Association of Snow Travelers (VAST) in partnership with the Vermont Agency of Transportation. Eventually the trail will span all 93 miles of the old Lamoille Valley Railroad, and it will then be the longest rail trail in New England. As of this writing in 2019, thirty three miles of the trail are complete with a compacted crush stone aggregate surface suitable for bicycle use in the summer and cross country skiing, snow shoeing and snow mobiles in the winter. It is very popular in all seasons. Small businesses catering to rail trail visitors, renting bikes and ebikes, providing fuel for snow mobiles, food, guidance and other services, have sprung up along this trail, breathing fresh life into the tourism industry in the Lamoille valley.

On May 13, 2018, UVM research professor, Richard Watts, a member of the Transportation Committee of the Chittenden County Regional Planning Commission, posted an article online entitled *From Forty To Zero*. "Next year, 40 Vermonters are expected to die or be seriously injured while stepping out for an evening walk, riding their bike to work or crossing the street," it begins.

Mr. Watts dissented from a VTrans Safety target of 39.5 deaths or serious injuries for pedestrians and bicyclists on Vermont roads next year. "Does it make sense to endorse a plan that calls for a goal of 40 people dying or being seriously injured simply because they choose to walk or ride a bike? Or for 280 people to die or be maimed because they are going somewhere in a car? Why have we settled on the idea that traffic deaths are accidents — inevitable and beyond our control?"

Watts goes on to advocate for a strategy called Vision Zero. Vision Zero refocuses the approach to road safety, placing the emphasis on the transportation system itself rather than the individual. Sweden pioneered the idea. Its pedestrian deaths have been cut in half, producing one of the lowest pedestrian death rates in the world today. The twenty U.S. cities that have adopted Vision Zero have also sharply reduced deaths and injuries. In New York City, traffic deaths and injuries fell by more than 30 percent after instituting Vision Zero. Separated multiuse paths along rural roads is an important part of the Vision Zero effort in Vermont.

And I am extremely encouraged by progress in the development of Autonomous Vehicles, AVs, with technology that could one day soon completely eliminate collisions of cars with pedestrians, bicycles and other objects. Although complete AV technology is not here yet, partial systems, including collision avoidance sensors and emergency braking systems capable of detecting pedestrians and bicycles, are available on some cars today and will be installed on all cars manufactured in the United States by 2022. *(See Chapter 22)*.

But beyond safety, separated multiuse paths provide a better quality of life for everyone. Motorists get less traffic and congestion on roads because bicyclists will actually use this transportation system since it is now safe. That means fewer internal combustion engines, less pollution, less use of fossil fuels, less greenhouse gases, and less obesity as people get out of their cars and get more exercise. Separated multi-use paths will also increase the value of properties in communities with this infrastructure investment just as it did in Stowe and in Burlington.

The problem of course is funding. There is a lot more funding for separate multi-use paths today, and transportation funds are now available for a wide range of projects. Federal highway spending on bike and pedestrian-related improvements was $915.8 million in 2018. But that simply isn't enough. Municipalities can't afford the cost of building this infrastructure by themselves, although some have taken on this task. South Burlington recently passed a referendum to add a penny to the property tax to fund bicycle path construction. More state funding would certainly help. But what is really needed is a nationwide effort similar to that championed by President Eisenhower in the 1950s that resulted in the national Interstate Highway System.

By adding only a few pennies to the federal gasoline tax, it would be possible to build this infrastructure over a period of time. In a lot of ways, it comes back to the same mechanism I had studied as an undergraduate at USC — opening the Highway Trust Fund to use for mass transit. But this time the fund would be used to install a nationwide system of separated multiuse paths.

The money could be collected at the gas pump nationwide by the federal government. Funds could then be granted to municipalities that could decide how best to use the money to create separated pathways in their communities. This is the mechanism we used to get the first leg of the Burlington Bike Path paved. A federal community block grant in 1982 was used to pave the northernmost portion of the rail bed in Burlington. This exercise actually brought several communities in Burlington together behind the Bike Path because several Neighborhood Planning Assemblies from separate neighborhoods, some of which did not include the Bike Path, agreed to devote their limited block grant funds to paving the path in another area of the city.

A foot bridge connecting a neighborhood in Plattsburgh, New York (across Lake Champlain) to a nearby school fell into disrepair in 2017. The Web Island Bridge has been closed for over a year now. The cost to repair it is almost half a million dollars. Plattsburgh is struggling to repair or replace it because this foot bridge saves students over a mile on their walk to school. That is walk, not ride. The town would like to replace the bridge, but it doesn't have the funds. The state of New York has offered to cover $450,000 of the cost to repair it, but the town is worried about maintaining it afterward. If grant funds were available from the federal government, the problem would be solved. These kinds of decisions on how to provide paths separate from car traffic to communities across the country should be made on a local basis. They just need the funding provided by the federal government.

Looking back on this much later, my letter to the *Cynic* was ridiculously optimistic of course, but it was heartfelt. I felt blame for not doing more to prevent a senseless death of a beautiful UVM student with her whole life in front of her. We all should. I may still have a decade or two left to devote to the cause. But now it's time for others, like Richard Watts and a whole new generation of UVM students, to take up the torch. I'm more optimistic than ever before about where this is all going next. Read on.

CHAPTER TWENTY-TWO
The Autonomous Vehicle

The autonomous vehicle (AV), or driverless car, is about to revolutionize transportation systems around the world. In a lot of ways, it's almost impossible to imagine the changes right around the corner due to the arrival of the AV.

Deaths and injuries due to human fallibilities, like drunk driving, distracted driving, carelessness, slow reactions, medical emergencies or falling asleep at the wheel, will be almost entirely eliminated when AVs are fully implemented, potentially saving over 35,000 lives and over $220 billion dollars a year due to automobile accidents in the U.S. alone. The World Health Organization estimates that the number of people killed in automobile accidents world-wide every year now exceeds 1.3 million. The AV will completely change the way we live and eliminate the vast majority of those deaths. That's a really big deal. It is nothing less than the final revolutionary phase of the automobile on this planet.

I have already described the worldwide evolution/movement away from auto-centric development late in the 20th century called New Urbanism (*See Chapter Nineteen*). The pendulum of public opinion, so long in favor of the automobile, finally began to swing back to alternatives to the car such as bicycles and pedestrians and more "livable cities" with "sustainable transportation alternatives." So by the early decades of the 21st century leading city planners had already turned away from the automobile, even before the invention of the AV. Now let's examine how the AV will accelerate the New Urbanism movement that began late in the 20th century.

Very few people today understand how far the AV has come in the last decade. And even fewer people have a clue as to the amazing changes the AV is about to bring to human mobility worldwide. Perhaps the best insider account of the progress of the AV revolution is a book co-authored by former GM executive, Lawrence Burns: *Autonomy — The Quest To Build The Driverless Car — And How It Will Reshape Our World* (2018). The conclusion to his ground breaking book is stunning.

Looking back, I can't stop marveling at that moment in Victorville, California, after the DARPA (U.S. Defense Advanced Research Projects Administration) Urban Challenge in 2007 — when everything changed. That race set up the battle between incumbents and disruptors that will define the future of the auto industry — and personal mobility in general. At Detroit's darkest hour, you had these bold plays from Google, Tesla, Uber and Lyft. The timing's remarkable.

If we pull it off, and we will, we're going to take 1.3 million fatalities a year and cut them by 90 percent. We're going to eliminate oil dependence in transportation. We're going to erase the challenges of parking in cities. All that land will allow us to reshape downtowns. People who haven't been able to afford a car will be able to afford the sort of mobility only afforded to those with cars. And we're going to slow climate change.

In other words, we are about to witness the greatest change to human mobility since the invention of the automobile over a century ago.

Very few people are aware that fully autonomous vehicles are currently cruising the streets of Phoenix, Arizona, Pittsburgh, Pennsylvania, San Francisco and even New York City.

There are dozens of major companies hard at work perfecting the AV now. Google's Waymo AV is perhaps the furthest along, operating a fleet of 100 minivans in Phoenix on a test basis. Waymo began the first commercial AV-for-hire venture in the world in Phoenix in 2018 with a select group of "early riders." They plan to add 20,000 Jaguar I-PACE electric SUVs to their fleet by the end of 2020 and they recently concluded an agreement with Fiat Chrysler to purchase up to 62,000 Pacifica minivans.

In addition to Waymo, GM, Uber, Toyota, Tesla, Ford, Lyft and Volvo all have advanced programs to develop AVs that will be on the road by the early 2020s, if not sooner. So the age of the AV is not just on the horizon, it's already here.

The AV revolution will be concentrated in the largest cities at first, as driverless Uber-like vehicles provide taxi services on demand, ordered by smart phone. But because these AVs have no driver, Waymo, Uber, Lyft and others like them will be able to offer these services at a substantially lower cost than present-day ride hailing services with live drivers. It is very likely that the annual cost of this AV service to get anywhere you want to go beyond reasonable walking or bicycling distances (7 miles) within the city you live may be as little as $2,000 to $3,000 a year, less than a quarter of the cost of owning a car for most people.

A leading transportation analytics firm out of the Seattle area says that the average cost of operating a car in the U.S. in 2017 was $10,288. Parking is the largest portion of this expense, almost doubling the cost of owning a car in New York City.

Check out the chart of the cost to own a car in various U.S. cities in 2017 below.

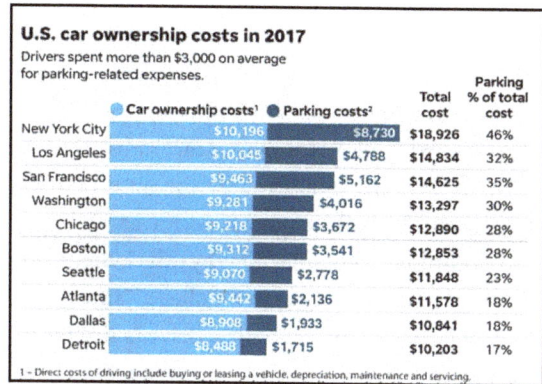

U.S. car ownership costs in 2017
Drivers spent more than $3,000 on average for parking-related expenses.

	Car ownership costs[1]	Parking costs[2]	Total cost	Parking % of total cost
New York City	$10,196	$8,730	$18,926	46%
Los Angeles	$10,045	$4,788	$14,834	32%
San Francisco	$9,463	$5,162	$14,625	35%
Washington	$9,281	$4,016	$13,297	30%
Chicago	$9,218	$3,672	$12,890	28%
Boston	$9,312	$3,541	$12,853	28%
Seattle	$9,070	$2,778	$11,848	23%
Atlanta	$9,442	$2,136	$11,578	18%
Dallas	$8,908	$1,933	$10,841	18%
Detroit	$8,488	$1,715	$10,203	17%

1 – Direct costs of driving include buying or leasing a vehicle, depreciation, maintenance and servicing.

Note that the cost of parking can be up to 46% of the total annual cost to operate a car.

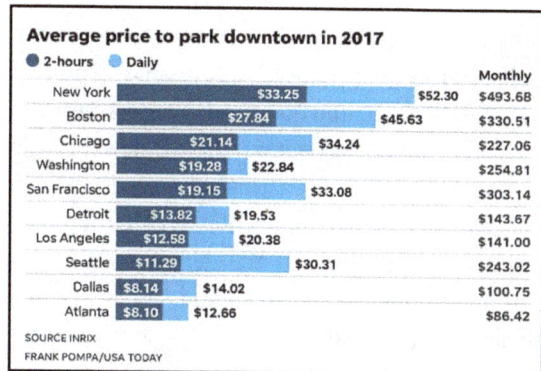

Average price to park downtown in 2017

	2-hours	Daily	Monthly
New York	$33.25	$52.30	$493.68
Boston	$27.84	$45.63	$330.51
Chicago	$21.14	$34.24	$227.06
Washington	$19.28	$22.84	$254.81
San Francisco	$19.15	$33.08	$303.14
Detroit	$13.82	$19.53	$143.67
Los Angeles	$12.58	$20.38	$141.00
Seattle	$11.29	$30.31	$243.02
Dallas	$8.14	$14.02	$100.75
Atlanta	$8.10	$12.66	$86.42

SOURCE INRIX
FRANK POMPA/USA TODAY

So, for less than a quarter of the annual cost of owning a car in a big city, or less, you can have a carefree ride wherever you want to go in minutes with a few quick taps on a smart phone. And remember the AV doesn't need parking. It simply drives to the next customer, probably only a block or two away. So right off the bat it saves 17% to 47% of the cost of owning a car in these ten American cities.

Timothy B. Lee has written several articles recently on the evolution of AVs for *VOX*. Like Lawrence Burns, he insists that car ownership is about to pass into history like a dinosaur of the 20th century: "Driverless cars will virtually eliminate the concept of private car ownership altogether. Instead almost everyone will get around in driverless taxis." Because cars are so ubiquitous today, they are no longer status symbols for most Americans. The love affair so carefully cultivated by the auto industry throughout the 20th century is now over.

According to research done by Julia Fiore, a Theodore Kheel Fellow at Hunter College, "since 1983, the percentage of people with a driver's license [in the U.S.] has steadily decreased among sixteen- to forty-four-year-olds. In 2005 vehicle-miles-traveled in the United States per capita began to decline. In 2017, it was 5.4 percent below the 2005 level, mainly because of the shift in millennials' travel and living habits." In 1983 almost 90 percent of nineteen-year-olds had a driver's license. By 2014 only 69 percent did. One survey found that 10 percent of Americans who trade in cars do not purchase a new one and opt instead to use ride-sharing services.

The U.S. Public Interest Research Group contends that "millennials are demonstrating significantly different lifestyle and transportation preferences than older generations." Many millennials and members of Generation Z living in American cities today don't own a car and have no desire to. Many of them don't even bother to get a driver's license. My 29-year-old daughter, Catia, is one of them. She lives in Boston after finishing her graduate studies at Harvard. She gets around town, to her job, shopping, dining in great restaurants all over town and living a very fulfilling life, by walking, bicycling, using the T and Uber. When she comes home to Vermont, she grabs a ride with a friend or takes a bus. If we had train service from Boston to Burlington she would use the rails. She is my model of the young professional living in a large American

city today. She has a driver's license, but with AVs due in Boston in only a few short years, it is very likely she will never own a car. Most children born in 2018 will never get a driver's license.

Although the most compelling reason for implementing AV technology worldwide is the safety that comes with removing the human factor from the driving equation, and all the mistakes humans make, it is the economics of AVs that will lead to their swift adoption. Earlier in this book I introduced you to Jane emily Clymer and Bill MacLeay, two people killed by drunk drivers on Vermont roads near Burlington. Both of them would be alive today if AVs had been invented in 1980 instead of 2020. Five students from Mount Mansfield Union High School were tragically killed in a head-on crash on Interstate 89 in 2017 by a driver speeding northward in the southbound lane of the highway, presumably on a suicide mission. That "accident" would be impossible once AVs are fully adopted.

So it doesn't take a rocket scientist to figure out where the evolution of the AV will take us shortly. What is one of those lives I just mentioned worth? The answer is that they are all priceless. Ultimately that is the real reason for adopting AV technology. But let's take a look at a few other aspects of this revolution that perhaps you haven't even thought about yet.

Burlington is about to exponentially increase the number of housing units downtown with the completion of City Place (319 residential units) in the heart of the city and Cambrian Rise (730 residential units and possibly a hotel) on the former Burlington College campus on North Avenue just north of downtown. Hundreds of other residential units are either in construction now or in the planning process. The addition of these residential units downtown should go a long way to stabilizing rents, finally tackling a problem that has plagued the city for decades. For over 40 years the city has suffered from a chronic shortage of new housing downtown as student demand for housing exceeded the supply during the late 20th and early 21st centuries. Mayor Weinberger understands that rent control proposals put forth by the Progressives in the 1980s and Infinite Culcleasure, a left wing candidate in the 2018 mayoral election, will not solve the rental problem in Burlington. Only the addition of new housing units downtown will do that.

Fortunately for Burlington, Weinberger has a background in urban planning. He is committed to increasing housing downtown as the real solution to the rent problem. His policies will lead to the construction of even more housing downtown over the next 3 years (and hopefully beyond). Once a critical mass of housing is built downtown, the demand for local services will lead to grocery and hardware stores, cinemas, dry cleaners, specialty shops and a host of other services now only available at shopping centers at the edge of the city or in nearby communities. Someone living downtown with all these services within walking distance of the ground floor elevator door will have very little need for a car. If that person wants to visit the Shelburne Museum or go skiing in Stowe, inexpensive AVs will be available to take them anywhere they wish to go with a couple of taps on a smart phone.

But let's examine the life of a young professional who lives on the 12th floor of one of the towers at City Place with a fantastic view of Lake Champlain and the Adirondacks in upstate New York. She needs to commute to her job at the State House in Montpelier, Vermont's capital, a 45-minute drive from Burlington, every day. She doesn't own a car, of course. She spends the money she saves on local restaurants, shops, performances, entertainment and travel. Her job sometimes requires her to stay late at the office, not getting back to Burlington until 9 p.m. or later.

The AV bus to Montpelier is available for her at the new downtown bus station less than a block away. But she also has the option of a smaller AV minivan for almost the same price, shared with 4 or 5 others, on a much more flexible schedule, almost on demand.

Let's say she has stayed late at her job and it's after 10 p.m. She has missed the last bus or six passenger minivan back to Burlington. She's tired and hungry and in no mood for small talk on the 45-minute commute back to Burlington with others. So for a few dollars more, she orders a one or two-person AV with her smart phone and tells it to pick up a pizza and a soft drink for the ride home. When the AV picks her up at 10:30 p.m. in front of the State House, the hot pizza and a cold soft drink are on a table waiting for her. By the time she arrives home in Burlington, her stomach is full and she is fast asleep. The AV gently wakes her and wishes her a good night.

The reason those trips by AV are so much cheaper than owning your own car is obvious. According to Lawrence Burns and a lot of others, when you own a car, it sits idle in your driveway or in a parking lot or garage near where you work or shop 95% of the day. In contrast to this idle transportation vehicle, the AV can be utilized perhaps 20 hours a day if necessary. (It will have to be recharged.) And unlike a taxi, there is no driver to pay. That's what will make Uber-like ride-hailing services so much less expensive than they are today, and most importantly, much cheaper and more convenient than owning your own car.

And when you get to your destination and the AV drops you off, there is no car to park. Eliminating the cost of parking in a major city is a big deal. As indicated in the Pompa graphs on the previous pages, the cost to park a car in a dense urban environment is one of the biggest costs of owning a car. So the cost of a parking space ($40,000 to $50,000 in some urban centers), and up to 50% of the cost of operating a car, can be completely eliminated. According to MIT professor of urban planning, Eran Ben-Joseph, in *Rethinking a Lot: The Design and Culture of Parking* (2012), "in some US cities, parking lots cover more than a third of the land area, becoming the single most salient landscape feature of our built environment." Just imagine a city with almost no parking garages downtown.

All that very expensive parking space can now be devoted to other uses, such as more living, office or retail space. The streets can be shared with separated bike paths and pedestrian plazas. All those parking lots can now be replaced with shops to service people living downtown. That's the walkable city Speck, Langdon and the New Urbanists are promoting. We are talking billions and billions of dollars in real estate in every American city that bought into the auto mania of the 20th century. That's 100% of American cities.

Traffic consultant, Samuel Schwartz, advises those who are building parking garages downtown to build them with 10 to 12 foot high floors, instead of the 8 foot ceilings in most parking structures being built today, in order to facilitate their conversions to office or residential space when they are no longer needed for parking after the arrival of AVs in a few years.

And just imagine the reduction in congestion in cities worldwide. Lawrence Burns calculates that all the transportation done by the fleet of privately owned cars clogging American cities today could be handled by a fleet of Uber-like AVs only 15% that size. What would a Los Angeles freeway at rush hour look like with 15% of the cars? That's probably overly optimistic, but stop and go, bumper to bum-

per traffic will probably be a thing of the past. What is now an excruciating and frustrating two hour commute each way every day, requiring all of the drivers' attention, could instead turn into a 20 or 30 minute commute, working, reading, connected to the internet or simply relaxing, listening to music or watching a movie or TV program.

For camping trips or other remote activities, AV rentals would last a bit longer, and people will need larger vehicles or trucks to accommodate do-it-yourself projects. Other folks might opt to own their own AV vehicles, but far fewer than own automobiles currently.

But that's not the only benefit of the AV world I am describing here on the rush hour commute. Because AVs can be controlled much more precisely by a computer than a car driven by a human being, cars can be packed together much more tightly than they are today, with absolutely no accidents. That's because human drivers need 40 or 50 yards separation from the car in front to safely react to drastic changes in speed at 60 to 80 mph. The computers of the AV can do that job safely with only 20 feet of separation. That will allow freeway traffic to move along at the speed limit with up to ten times the number of AVs packed into the same space. And that occasional traffic jam costing you an extra half hour on the commute home for no other reason than someone hit the brakes too hard in extreme congestion is completely eliminated. Computers don't freak out at the sight of brake lights or an accident in the traffic going in the other direction.

In his recent book, *No One At The Wheel: Driverless Cars and the Road to the Future*, (2018), Samuel Schwartz notes that the lanes on most highways in the U.S. today, and all of the Interstate system, are 12 feet wide (the width of a tank to be transported on that military Interstate Highway System). Ten feet is usually plenty for six-foot-wide cars and up to 8-foot-wide trucks. According to Schwartz, AVs could be operated in lanes 7 or 8 feet wide, allowing up to 6 lanes of AV traffic in the place of 4 twelve-foot-wide lanes.

Schwartz paints a darker vision of the future, worrying that most people will own AVs rather than hailing them on demand. He believes that their low cost and convenience will lead to more cars on the road, not fewer, as people opt for AVs rather than public transportation. And he believes AVs may actually encourage sprawl and cause a host of other problems.

I disagree with his speculation of doom and gloom. Schwartz was chief engineer at the New York City Department of Transportation. He has a healthy skepticism of the professed benefits of AVs, "hyped" by others. But sometimes that skepticism leaves him doubting the technology, which in turn leads to a more pessimistic view of the future. I tend to side with Lawrence Burns, who acquired his understanding of AVs while immersed in their development. That seems to have resulted in a more profound trust that AV technology will eventually work out all the kinks.

It will take a big change of attitude away from car ownership and toward ride hailed AVs instead, but that change is already in progress, only a few short years since the invention of the smart phone. The economics of the AV and its impeccable safety record, over time, will change hearts and minds around the globe, even in auto-crazy America.

However, that isn't the end of the discussion. Think of all the people who can't drive a car, such as children, the disabled, visually or mentally impaired, the elderly or people with severe medical conditions. According to the U.S. Census Bureau, about 28 million people in the United States say that they have a severe disability that prevents them from driving today. All of these people are suddenly

as completely mobile as an able-bodied driver. Instead of driving your daughter to ballet or soccer practice, you just order an AV with your smart phone to take her there and return her home safely afterward, at a fraction of the cost.

The AV also takes the car keys out of the hands of the person who shouldn't be driving but does so anyway, because they insist on doing so even when their condition demands that they give up driving altogether. My sister falls into that category. When her eyesight deteriorated in her early 60s, she became a hazard to herself and everyone else on the road. She continued to drive for several years beyond the time her doctors advised her to completely give up driving. She was lucky and didn't experience an accident before she finally sold her car at 64. She now relies on family, friends and Uber instead. The AV was the perfect solution for her years ago. We are all thankful for the convenience of Uber, even if it is a bit expensive for her at this time, because it still requires a driver as of this writing.

Tragically, two small children were killed in a crosswalk in New York City in 2018 by a woman with a medical condition that caused her to lose control of her car at a critical moment. By all accounts, she should not have been driving that day. It's only human nature for people with questionable driving abilities to want the same mobility that capable drivers enjoy. The AV will provide that mobility to those people at a cost they can afford, completely eliminating their mobility problem and allowing all the rest of us to breathe more freely.

Of course, the path to a fully autonomous system will have some bumps along the way. The first death in a partially autonomous vehicle occurred on May 7, 2016, a mere seven months after Tesla began offering their "Autopilot" system, when a Tesla slammed into a tractor trailer making a left turn at 78 mph. The driver had been warned several times by the Tesla to keep his hands on the wheel. He failed to take control and avoid the accident. Lawrence Burns has a detailed account of this accident in his book, along with a thorough discussion of the dangers of partial AV systems that turn control of the vehicle back to the occupant when the system becomes overwhelmed.

The second death occurred at about 10:00 p.m. on March 18, 2018, when an Uber AV hit a bicyclist walking her bicycle across the northbound four lanes of a highway in Tempe, Arizona. The NTSB report on this incident indicates that about 6 seconds before impact the system detected an unusual bag-laden bicycle, first as an unknown object, then a vehicle and finally a bicycle. Approximately 1.3 seconds before impact, the AV decided the situation warranted application of emergency braking. Unfortunately, Uber had previously disabled the emergency braking system on this AV due to its erratic driving behavior caused by false positives, or ghost objects.

The backup safety driver reported that the first she knew of the woman with the bike was when the vehicle struck her, causing a loud thump. She applied the brake after the collision. Dashboard video reveals that the bicyclist appeared very suddenly. However, the video camera pointed at the driver caught her looking down, distracted by an electronic device, in the moments before the accident. But the most disturbing aspect of this incident is that Uber had disabled a safety system on the AV that might have detected the woman with the bike and saved her life. Obviously, there are a few kinks to work out in these systems. Short circuiting the system when it doesn't work properly is not the answer.

Those deaths are tragic and they will likely slow down the adoption of AV technology. Although the reaction to those two incidents has been measured to date, the public will not feel safe in AVs until they are close to 100% safe, both for those inside the vehicle as well as those outside. It is probably impossible to achieve no accidents at all, but that's not really the question. The real question is how many lives can be saved by this technology, even if perfection continues to elude the engineers.

Fortunately portions of this autonomous technology are already available for installation in cars today. Collision avoidance systems and automatic breaking when sensors determine that a collision is imminent have been available for several years now. These sensors put the brakes on automatically, completely avoiding a collision or making the impact much less severe.

Volvo has been installing sensors on their cars that can detect pedestrians since 2012. In 2014 Volvo introduced sensors that can detect bicyclists as well. These collision avoidance systems have already saved lives on highways in the U.S. and around the world. They aren't perfect. Some of these systems only stop the car before hitting a pedestrian or a bicyclist less than fifty percent of the time. And these sensors are even less effective immediately after turning a corner. But over time, they will improve and save thousands of lives a year. All U.S. car manufacturers are currently committed to the installation of automatic collision avoidance systems in all new cars by 2022. The results of this safety advancement should show up as a huge reduction in highway death and injury statistics by the mid 2020s.

Waymo has racked up over 10 million miles on public streets to date with only one minor fender-bender. It has taken a very cautious approach to testing these vehicles. Uber and the others may have some catching up to do. Those companies should follow Waymo's example for a safe introduction of AV technology in the early part of the 21st century. Once the data is in, and it is demonstrated that far fewer people are killed or injured per mile driven in AVs compared to cars with human drivers, the rush to adopt this technology will accelerate very quickly.

One unintended consequence of AVs will be the loss of jobs currently employing people as taxi, bus and truck drivers. Those operating airplanes, ships and trains will follow. The U.S. Navy already has a 132 foot long ship called the Sea Hunter which is capable of traveling long distances at sea with no human operators on board. Insurance agents, car repair shops, even litigation attorneys will lose employment. Job losses will be significant and there will be widespread dislocation of hundreds of thousands of workers. The problems caused by this dislocation cannot be minimalized. The solution, of course, is to anticipate this dislocation and provide retraining for individuals displaced by the AV revolution. Eventually demand for new automobiles will be greatly reduced as people stop buying cars and start using AVs on demand. That will lead to a big disruption in automobile manufacturing with widespread job losses. A lot of auto workers will need to be retrained as well.

How long will this process take? The extremely short duration of the evolution of AV technology is well documented by Lawrence Burns in his book, *Autonomy*. It started with a challenge from the U.S. Military (DARPA) to design a self-driving vehicle for use in war zones. The one million dollar prize attracted some very talented teams of engineers to take on the problem in 2004. In the decade and a half that followed, tremendous advances in AV technology have made AVs more reliable than human drivers.

But it wasn't just the development of this incredible hardware and computer software that made the coming revolution in human mobility possible. Smart phones are also an essential element in this new AV-on-demand realignment of mobility. Smart phones

weren't invented until 2007 and didn't become widespread until 2011 or 2012. That made Uber and Lyft and other ride-hailing systems possible. The final piece of the puzzle was in place. Now all that's left is the roll out of this revolutionary technology.

As of this writing, over 15 million miles have already been driven by AVs in several cities in the U.S. The adoption of AVs will occur first in cities, particularly those embracing the New Urbanism previously discussed at length. Some futurists believe that AVs will be ubiquitous in American cities within ten years. I believe there will be some unforeseen events that will slow widespread AV adoption to more like 15 to 20 years out. I would be very surprised if an AV ride hailing Uber-like service doesn't arrive in Burlington by 2030.

Some people will resist this revolution, wishing to retain their cars. Car aficionados will always cherish classical internal combustion automobiles. Antique car shows will only grow in popularity. Those living in rural areas will probably be the last to adopt this technology and some never will. That's fine. To each his own.

People living in suburbs are also likely to resist adoption of AVs, clinging to their auto-centric lifestyle instead, until the safety or economic advantages of AVs convince them otherwise. Over time the mix of human driven cars versus AVs will shift toward AVs until very few cars will depend on a human driver. When will that be? Perhaps 2050, maybe before that.

One ironic result of AVs may be that they allow low density suburbs to survive peak oil and the changes that will result from vastly increased prices for petroleum products. The efficiency of the AV may overcome some of the inefficiency of suburbs and allow them to avoid being abandoned as some have predicted. Let's hope the AV doesn't lead to more sprawl.

CHAPTER TWENTY-THREE
Final Observations

PERSISTENCE

"Nothing in this world can take the place of persistence. Talent will not: nothing is more common than unsuccessful men with talent. Genius will not; unrewarded genius is almost a proverb. Education will not: the world is full of educated derelicts. Persistence and determination alone are omnipotent."

— President Calvin Coolidge

Perhaps the most important lesson to be learned from all this is the value of persistence. Even in the face of incredible opposition it is so important to persist. Once you get committed to a project it is essential to continually pursue it and see it through to completion.

It often takes only a very small number of dedicated people to get a project started. The C&O Canal in Washington D.C. was saved by Justice William O. Douglas almost single handedly. Howard Dean and I lead the way on the Burlington Bicycle Path together with a very small dedicated group of volunteers. The Stowe Bicycle Path came to be mainly because of a lot of hard work and dedication by Anne Lusk. The High Line is the consequence of the chance encounter of Joshua David and Robert Hammond at a meeting about the future of a derelict elevated rail line in New York City. Local Motion and the Island Line Trail are the result of the efforts of Brian Costello and Chapin Spencer. Ryan Gravel's plan to transform the railroad beltline around downtown Atlanta into a set of communities connected by pathways and street-cars is yet another example. The effort to repurpose the Reading Viaduct in Philadelphia is being led by Sarah McEneaney and John Struble. There are plenty of other examples worldwide. Someone needs to take the bull by the horns and wrestle the beast into existence.

Most of these projects start out as wild ideas that most people declare impossible. Nonetheless, someone takes on the impossible dream and slowly but surely, step by step, the project picks up momentum and support. Every project is different. With the Burlington Bike Path we took a fairly low key approach, raising just enough money to fund printing inexpensive materials for distribution. Fortunately for us, the city and the state fell in behind this project and supplied all the legal representation and funding to build the Bike Path, and over time, a 60 acre waterfront park. Joshua David and Robert Hammond took a very different approach to fundraising for the High Line. They went with fancy and expensive materials with professional photography and expensive promotional events focused on the New York elite they needed to fund the High Line. Eventually they took paid positions with the organization they created to operate and maintain the High Line.

There is still so much more to do. Most of our transportation infrastructure nationwide was designed in the twentieth century at the height of the Auto Dominant Era. The infrastructure for bicycles and lightweight electric vehicles like electric bikes, Segway PTs, and more recently, electric scooters, was never built. Of course electric bikes and Segway PTs didn't exist until about a decade ago. Escooters first started showing up in cities across the country in 2017. Bicycles were just expected to share the road infrastructure with automobiles. The result has been thousands of needless deaths as two-ton automobiles collide with pedestrians and bicyclists on transportation infrastructure almost exclusively designed for automobiles.

As noted numerous times in this book, our entire system of roadways needs to be redesigned to add separated paths for pedestrians, bikes, ebikes, escooters and Segway PT-like devices. That means ten-foot-wide pathways to replace five-foot-wide sidewalks wherever possible. And it means the installation of thousands of miles of separated pathways along rural roads throughout Vermont and the rest of the country.

Cambridge, Massachusetts was the first community in the nation to make separated pathways for these devices mandatory on all streets as they are reconstructed over time. All Vermont communities should follow that example and make separated pathways mandatory in their communities.

EDUCATION

"A mind that is stretched by a new experience can never go back to its old dimensions."

— Oliver Wendell Holmes, Jr.

This is where I disagree with the quote from Calvin Coolidge above. Education is extremely important, and not only for the increased income that comes with it. A good education will stretch the mind. Both my undergraduate and graduate educations changed my thinking by exposing me to concepts I never would have been exposed to if I had remained in Bellows Falls after high school graduation working in the family furniture factory. It changed my

perspective and the course of my life. It also led to a much more meaningful and fulfilling life for me.

There is no doubt that I could not have contributed what I did to the Bike Path without a legal education. That education was even more important when it came to preserving the filled land in Burlington harbor for public uses under the Public Trust Doctrine. The ability to do legal research and find the cases that were critical to the Alden debate allowed me to put forth a credible argument that there was a way to reclaim the land filled into Burlington harbor for the public uses we were insisting upon. We took an obscure legal principle that no one had ever heard of and made it a household word in a few short years, resulting in a ballot item in 1986 that received 76 percent support from city voters. The decision of the Vermont Supreme Court in 1989 proved we were right and that it's possible to popularize an obscure legal concept and use it for the betterment of our community.

My faith in the legal cases we uncovered fueled and fortified my determination to prevail in locating the Bike Path in a waterfront park along the lakeshore despite a very strong and determined campaign to cover the waterfront with buildings. Howard Dean lacked that determination because he was educated as a physician not as a lawyer. And that's why he eventually supported the Alden plan.

So the lesson here is to get the very best education you can. That education will serve you well in your pursuit of the environmental, or any other cause you believe in. And it will also enrich you spiritually and financially as well.

THE PIVOT POINT WAS ALDEN

Looking back on it all now, it's easy to see that Alden was the pivot point for the Burlington waterfront. If Alden had received the necessary two thirds vote on December 10, 1985, there would be a hotel within

25 feet of the lake's edge just north of College Street, and what is now Waterfront Park would be covered with the dense development previously described.

The proponents, led by Mayor Sanders, started with a sizeable majority of city voters. They had twelve out of thirteen city councilors, all three political parties and the entire business community behind the project. They were well funded and had the best PR people money could buy. Without organized opposition that could counter their public relations and put out an opposing point of view at public hearings and in printed materials, there is little doubt that Alden would have achieved the two-thirds majority it needed. That was the mood of the city after almost one hundred years of a junkyard on the waterfront.

Even after our campaign, along with the opposition of the School Board and allies like Bea Bookchin, Paul Lafayette, Maurice Mahoney, Sandy Baird and others, Alden received 53.4% of the vote. Without that opposition, it seems highly likely that much of what Alden was proposing would cover Waterfront Park today. The Bike Path would be a wide sidewalk wedged between Lake Street and the railroad in a "transportation corridor" advocated by Peter Clavelle at CEDO at that time. One of Clavelle's often repeated arguments during the debate over Alden was that if buildings were set back from the water's edge with park space up front, those buildings would form an unsightly "Chinese wall" on the Burlington waterfront.

Although the Public Trust Doctrine certainly turned out to be a savior for public access to the filled land in Burlington harbor as things eventually turned out, it is entirely possible that the outcome would have been much different if the Alden bond had passed. Remember that at that time there was a collusive lawsuit going on in the Superior Court. The city, the state, the railroad and Alden all agreed that the Alden project would satisfy public trust concerns. The Citizens Waterfront Group had been frozen out of this litigation except as *amicus curiae. See Appendix 10* for my Bench Memorandum to the Chittenden Superior Court.

If Alden had been successful at the polls, the Chittenden Superior Court would have rubber stamped the Alden plan and that would have been the end of it. Remember that the Superior Court judge in the trial court after it turned adversarial ended up finding fee simple title in the railroad. That's quite a different result than what the Vermont Supreme Court found on appeal. Unfortunately, this case would never have gotten to the Vermont Supreme Court because the case would have been settled at the Chittenden Superior Court. The Vermont Supreme Court would never have heard a word about the Public Trust Doctrine.

And even if the Public Trust Doctrine had somehow been resurrected years later by some unknown plaintiff who somehow obtained standing, and the Vermont Supreme Court heard such a case, at that point there would be a hotel, condominiums, parking garages and a lot of other development on the filled lands. What is the likelihood that the Vermont Supreme Court would find all that filled land belongs to the people of Vermont under a strict *res publicum* decision and order the removal of those buildings? Although the *Illinois* public trust case works great for the Burlington waterfront when it is a junk yard, it doesn't if it has millions of dollars of new buildings sprawled all over the filled land.

The legal outcome of building on filled land throughout the country is not as simple as the *Illinois* case would make it seem. The *Appleby*[24] case out of New York City comes to a different conclu-

---

24. *Appleby v. City of New York, 271 U.S. 364 (1926).*

sion, allowing buildings on filled land. Similarly, the state of Massachusetts has had to deal with buildings on land filled into Boston's back bay centuries ago. The Massachusetts legislature dealt with buildings on filled land by allowing title to pass between private owners.[25]

The state of Maine allowed old piers in Portland harbor to be converted to high priced condominiums. There are cases out of California where shopping malls and other commercial uses were allowed on filled land under the Public Trust Doctrine.[26]

Even if the Public Trust Doctrine as applied to the filled land in Burlington harbor had somehow reached the Vermont Supreme Court, once the Alden buildings were in place, it is highly unlikely that the Vermont Supreme Court would have issued the strong public trust (res publicum) pronouncement it did. The Court had the luxury of an undeveloped waterfront when the case got there. It's much easier to come to a strong public trust conclusion under those circumstances.

Had Alden's plans come to fruition the Vermont Supreme Court could have found plenty of precedent to allow the buildings to remain. So the crucial factor that saved the filled land in Burlington harbor for public uses was political, not legal — the failure of Alden to achieve a two thirds majority from city voters on December 10, 1985. The minority had prevented the majority from making a big mistake. That says something about carefully considering a strong opposition opinion to any public policy. Democracy demands rule by the majority, but not tyranny. It is both foolish and inefficient to completely ignore a sizeable minority.

---

25. *Boston Waterfront Development Corp. v. Commonwealth*, 378 Mass. 629 (1979).

26. *City of Berkeley v. Superior Court of Alameda County*, 26 Cal. 3rd 515 (1980).

IN THE NICK OF TIME

So many of the projects I have talked about in this book were saved in what I would call "the nick of time." There is no doubt in my mind that the Burlington Bike Path would not exist today but for our very early start. We began our campaign to repurpose the old railroad right-of-way through the New North End at an extremely early time — 1980 — three years before the railbanking provisions of the Rails-to-Trails Act.

It was only a matter of time before adjacent property owner, Paul Preseault, would be swooping in to gobble up the railbed in the backyard of his luxury lakefront condominiums. He filed his lawsuit in 1981, shortly after the city-wide referendum on the Bike Path. The proceedings he triggered before the ICC resulted in the first set of federal regulations for the conversion of railbeds to recreation trails nationwide. And the landmark U.S. Supreme Court case of *Preseault v. ICC* in 1990 was the first to apply the Rails-to-Trails Act to a railbed in America. As we have seen, the Alden plan was a project that was killed in the nick of time.

The trail out to the Causeway in Colchester was saved in the nick of time from becoming hopelessly overgrown in the early 1990s to almost being washed away by the floods in 2011 and 2018. If the Causeway bike path had not been reclaimed when it was in the 1990s and made a part of the infrastructure of the Town of Colchester, it would not have received FEMA funding or the private donations necessary to turn it into the world class bike path it is today after the floods of 2011 and 2018.

Funding for the bridge across the Winooski River was jammed through by the Dean Administration in the closing hours of his term as governor of Vermont. The following governor would have eliminated that funding if construction had not started in the nick of time. Similarly, the demolition permit for the High Line in New York City had already been signed when the Bloomberg Administration saved it from the wrecking ball.

Back in the 1950s, Justice William O. Douglas saved the C&O Canal from becoming a freeway at the last second. The Mineral King Valley in California was saved by the enactment of NEPA in 1970. And there are so many other examples of places we cherish today that were saved at the last minute.

The universal lesson in all of these examples is that the sooner you get going on your project the more likely it will be saved, and with a lot less hassle and complications with a lot less money.

If we had saved rail beds back in the 1960s when many of them fell into disuse, the "nick of time" problem would have been solved. But the Rails-to-Trails Act wasn't enacted until 1983 — way too late. That allowed thousands of miles of rail beds nationwide to revert to private ownership, including the Biscayne Heights subdivision in Colchester and the 37 mile line through the Islands in the 1960s.

It's too late to do anything about Biscayne Heights other than to run a bike path along town streets in the area. The rail bed through the Islands is still intact in most places, but the task of reconstructing Humpty Dumpty by putting all those privately owned parcels back together is daunting, but also doable. It's just much more difficult and expensive. One day, as bicycle travel and recreation become even more popular than they are today, there may be a string of B&Bs and small shops along the old rail bed catering to the biking crowd and breathing economic life into the Islands just as Fred Sargent had envisioned with his String of Pearls proposal in 1964.

If an unused rail bed runs though your community, by all means, reclaim it for public use.

AN ENVIRONMENTAL RUDDER

The environmental rudder I developed early in my life steered me through the battle over the railroad right-of-way and Alden and fortified my determination to see those battles through to a successful conclusion. The reason Bernie Sanders got sucked into the Alden plan was that he lacked that environmental rudder. His rudder, which is also the foundation of his political career, is the class warfare he continually champions. It's so ironic that he is now one of the one percent at the top that he has railed against his entire political career. For a long time he was reluctant to release his tax returns, probably because he didn't want to reveal that he is now a millionaire, after loudly deriding millionaires and billionaires for over 40 years. Now it's only the billionaires that are offensive. As I noted earlier in this book, that passage from the comic strip Pogo applies here as well: "We have met the enemy and he is us!"

Although Sanders has taken up the global warming mantra recently, his support for the Alden plan over the bike path and waterfront park we were proposing in the early 1980s demonstrates his lack of an environmental rudder. And by the way, one would think a self-avowed socialist championing class warfare would never support a development like Alden on the Burlington waterfront, especially after espousing the flaming rhetoric he put forth in his campaign for mayor in 1981: "No enclaves for the rich on the Burlington waterfront."

So what happened? Obviously, even when it comes to his socialist beliefs Sanders lacked the rudder necessary to steer clear of the Alden plan. The lesson here is to set your environmental rudder early and keep a firm grip on the tiller until you prevail.

BUILD IT AND THEY WILL COME

Vermont has a big demographic problem in the early years of the 21st century. Our current population is the oldest in the nation with the lowest birth rate as well. More people are dying every year in Vermont than are born. Our population is shrinking.

Our high school and college graduates are leaving the state in droves for greener pastures elsewhere. This problem has become so acute now that state government twenty is employing gimmicks to attract young people and get them to settle here. The state now offers people willing to move here with an out-of-state job that allows them to work remotely up to $10,000 to assist them in their move here.

Perhaps the better solution is to build the kind of communities that will attract millennials and members of Generation Z. As noted earlier, young people today often decide where they want to live, move there and then look for employment. In my opinion the best way to solve this demographic problem is to make our communities as attractive to young people as possible.

Burlington has already gone a long way toward doing just that. The Bike Path, Waterfront Park and the Church Street Marketplace make Burlington much more attractive to young people than it was when I arrived here in 1978. Installing a system of separated pathways for pedestrians, bicycles and light electric vehicles will make the city even more attractive to young people by increasing bike usage and enhancing the lifestyle of those moving and living here.

The New Urbanism I have championed here, where people can live downtown with all the services they need within walking distance, will allow those young people to live a fulfilling life without being tethered to an automobile. The lower carbon footprint of this lifestyle will be very attractive to younger generations concerned about climate change and global warming.

Burlington is one of the first cities in the U.S. to generate all its electricity from renewable sources. That will also be very attractive to this younger generation. The installation of separated pathways citywide will enhance Burlington's reputation as a city on the cutting edge of the environmental movement today.

The University of Vermont and Champlain College are thriving in the early years of the 21st century. They add so much vitality to Burlington, providing enlightened cutting edge thinking that makes a city vibrant.

The marathon, the Jazz Festival, the Grand Point North concert, Mardi Gras, the Art Hop, the Festival of Fools, the Dragon Boat races, the Brew and Food Festivals, the state's largest farmer's market, the Flynn Theater, the Mozart Festival and Lane Series, First Night and all the other events that happen in Burlington on an annual basis make this city a very attractive place to live for the younger generation. Burlington is on the right track. Investing in our communities to make them more attractive places for these new generations to live is the ultimate solution to our demographic problem. Welcoming refugees and immigrants is another solution that has the additional benefit of providing more cultural diversity to what is still one of the whitest states in the nation.

These investments are so much more important than promoting gimmicks like subsidies to move here. As the movie *Field of Dreams* so elegantly points out: "Build it and they will come!"

EXTREMISM

Unfortunately, in order to prevail on many environmental issues, it is often necessary to take a more extreme position than one would prefer. It's not enough to meet the opposition half way. The opposition will run right over you if you do that.

Throughout the Alden debate I was continually forced to take a more extreme position than I would have preferred in order to drive the point home. It wasn't enough to offer to settle for an 80-foot setback. That got us nowhere. Paul Flinn and his attorney, Charles Shea, just snickered at my offer to compromise. So it was all or nothing.

That forced me to insist that all the land filled into the lake was subject to the Public Trust Doctrine and that hotels and condominiums were absolutely prohibited on that filled in land. The Vermont Supreme Court eventually agreed with that "extreme" position, but it took four years to obtain that result and there was a substantial risk we would not prevail. In fact, if the Alden vote had gone the other way, I'm pretty sure there would be a hotel on the lake's edge just north of College Street today.

But just to be clear, although extremism may include "direct action" such as a group of bicyclists clogging the roads in protest to make a point, it must never cross the line into disrespect or violence. The lessons of Mahatma Gandhi and Martin Luther King, Jr. always apply. A lot can be accomplished through non-violent protest without resorting to violence.

I have devoted a lot of print in this book to praising Local Motion and that praise is well deserved. They are the most effective bicycle advocacy group I know of. But because Local Motion receives public funding through various grant programs, they are prohibited from political activities and thus prevented from taking controversial positions like relocating the Bike Path to the west side of the railroad tracks between College and King Streets through application of eminent domain powers.

That's why Local Motion would not support us in the petition drive to get that relocation onto the ballot in November 2016. That also prevents Local Motion from taking part in "direct actions" to support bicycling in the Burlington area such as gathering groups of bicyclists together in order to gain attention for specific projects for improving biking in our community.

That's why we need a "more radical" group like Bikeable Burlington Now to press for these changes. Bikeable Burlington Now is the brain child of Liam Griffin, a devoted bicycle advocate who continually shows up at planning meetings for a more walkable/bikeable city with great ideas and a wealth of relevant information to fuel these discussions. Griffin maintains a Facebook group for Bikeable Burlington Now which includes the following mission statement:

> We are a group of individuals joined together for the common purpose of helping make Burlington a better city for people on bikes. We were founded on the concept that ideas executed on the street level can create change, by being positive, visible, constructive, action-based, and respectful. New members are as important as old ones, and everybody in the group has a right to their own perspective and ideas. The best way to get involved is to BE involved. Speak up, come to an event, post your ideas on what you'd like to do, or things you would like help doing. This is a place to talk about ways we can change things we don't like, instead of just complaining about how things are. Together we can help move things forward.

"A dream you dream alone is only a dream. A dream you dream together is reality. "

— John Lennon

No one could have said that better than John Lennon. What a great conclusion to this book!

ACKNOWLEDGMENTS

First, I want to thank Ira Allen as the ultimate father of this book and a lot of really good things that have come about in Burlington due to his foresight in contributing the land that became the University of Vermont in 1791. For it is UVM that has contributed so much to what Burlington is today, and in my opinion, made this city the "place of consequence" that Ira foresaw over two centuries ago. Although his remains lie in an unmarked grave somewhere in a pauper's field in Philadelphia, his ghost still wanders the streets of the Queen City, in all those associated with the University Ira created.

The idea for the Burlington Bicycle Path was first pitched to me by Tom Hudspeth, a UVM professor. UVM students assisted me with legal research and so many other ways in our quest to create the Bike Path and Waterfront Park.

And of course, my wife, Ruth Masters, was a UVM intern for me from Jean Flack's Environmental Law class at UVM. Without her, there would be no book. She did all the typing through countless drafts, did much of the research, gave me good advice, and navigated the world for me. I am eternally grateful. The University has certainly had an exaggerated impact on this book and on Burlington itself.

I also want to acknowledge the contribution of Mark Pendergrast in writing, rewriting and editing portions of this book and for great advice and encouragement, and Amber Vaillancourt for her research into the extension of the Bike Path across the Winooski River out to the Causeway.

Also, a big thank you to all those who contributed to the Bike Path. First and foremost among those is Governor Howard Dean. He is the real hero of not only the Burlington Bicycle Path, but also the bridge across the Winooski River and the Causeway out to the

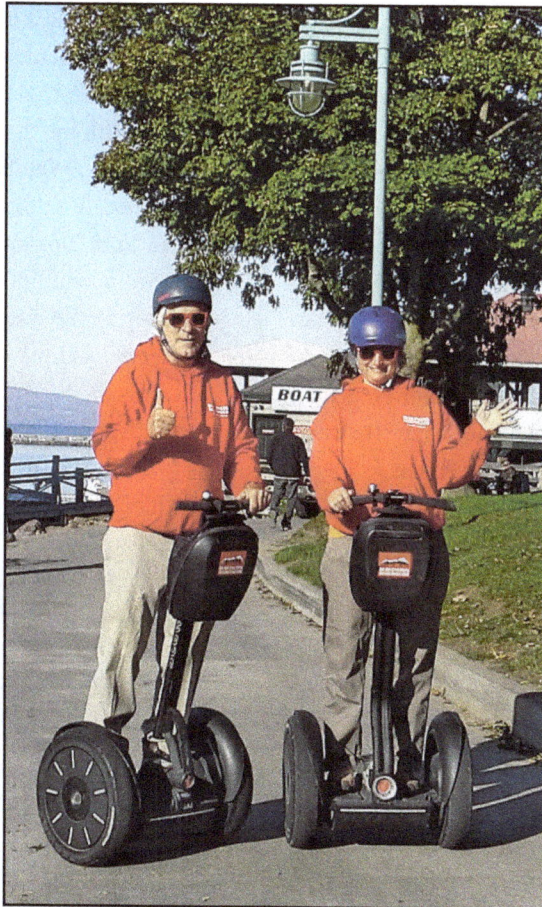

Rick Sharp and Ruth Masters in front of the park at the foot of College Street in 2019. *M. Corr.*

Champlain Islands. He has been a tireless advocate for alternatives to automobiles his entire adult life.

Attorney John Leddy represented the city in the litigation with Paul Preseault. Attorney John Dunleavy represented the state of Vermont throughout all that litigation all the way up to the federal Circuit Court of Appeals and the U.S. Supreme Court. He wrote portions of the chapters explaining the tortured path of that litigation for me. And I suppose we should thank Paul Preseault for all that time, money and energy he spent in establishing a whole new body of law critical to reclaiming abandoned railbeds across the country for recreation trails.

I am forever grateful to Dorothy Hunt, Del and Karen Martin, Alderman Allen Gear, Morton Lamden, Robert Bensen, the publisher and editor of *That Paper*, Bob Devost, and so many others for their early contributions to the creation of the Bike Path. UVM interns Shep Johnson and Ann Saurman stand out as leaders of a much larger group of students from the University who assisted me in my research into the Public Trust Doctrine and the death of Jane emily Clymer. Bea Bookchin, members of the Green Party, Maurice Mahoney, attorney Sandy Baird and Alderman Paul Lafayette were essential to our success in defeating Alden.

Although he made mistakes supporting Alden and putting forth a "Chinese Wall" argument against 80 feet of park space along the water's edge, Mayor Peter Clavelle succeeded in snaking the Bike Path through the south end and negotiated the "Sale of the Century" with the railroad, finally reclaiming the filled land for public use forever.

Long serving City Councilor and State Representative, Kurt Wright, deserves to be mentioned for his unwavering support of the Bike Path more recently. And I'd like to acknowledge the contribution of an intern at Burlington Segways in 2013 by the name of Harry Neuert who went through dozens of old files to organize the material that became the backbone of this book. I also want to thank Burlington Segways interns for their efforts collecting petition signatures for relocating the Bike Path in 2016.

Bill MacLeay, Betsy Terry, Buzz Hoerr, Charlie Auer, John Ewing, Brian Searles, Joe and Kathy Frank must be acknowledged for their contributions to extending the path across the Winooski River and out onto the Causeway to the Islands. And a special thanks to Brian Costello and Chapin Spencer for their tireless contributions to the bike ferry across the Winooski River and the Cut in the Causeway. The smashing success of Local Motion is directly attributable to their efforts. I also want to thank Local Motion for generously sharing maps and photos with me that appear in the book.

Mayor Miro Weinberger and Parks and Recreation Director, Jesse Bridges, as well as Parks Commissioner John Bossange, deserve a lot of credit for their work rebuilding the Bike Path and moving it closer to the waters edge through the north forty reserve to triple the size of Waterfront Park in 2016. Together with John Bossange, Parks Commissioner, Nancy Kaplan, carefully evaluated proposals to bring Segway PTs and electric bikes to the Bike Path and eventually approved both.

I want to thank all those Bike Path users that I see on a daily basis with big smiles on their faces. Those smiles are my greatest reward for the work I did.

Finally, I want to thank my daughters, Catia and Dori, for their contributions and support, and particularly Dori for what will probably be the epitaph on my tombstone: "My dad doesn't take no for an answer."

BIBLIOGRAPHY

Ben-Joseph, Eran. *Rethinking a Lot: The Design and Culture of Parking.* Boston: MIT, 2012.

Burns, Lawrence D. and Christopher Shulgan. *Autonomy: The Quest to Build the Driverless Car.* NY: Harper Collins, 2018.

Carson, Rachel. *Silent Spring.* NY: Houghton Mifflin, 1962, 2002.

David, Joshua and Robert Hammond. *High Line: The Inside Story of New York City's Park in the Sky.* NY: Farrar, Straus & Giroux, 2011.

Dunham-Jones, Ellen and June Williamson. *Retrofitting Suburbia: Urban Design Solutions for Redesigning Suburbs.* Hoboken, NJ: John Wiley & Sons, 2011.

Fallows, James and Deborah. *Our Towns: A 100,000 Mile Journey into the Heart of America.* NY: Pantheon, 2018.

Feeney, Vincent E. *Burlington: A History of Vermont's Queen City.* Bennington, VT: Images from the Past, 2015.

Fitzgerald, F. Scott. *The Great Gatsby.* NY: Scribner, 1925.

Gravel, Ryan. *Where We Want to Live: Reclaiming Infrastructure for a New Generation of Cities.* NY: St. Martin's, 2016.

Jacobs, Jane. *The Death and Life of Great American Cities.* NY: Vintage, 1961.

Langdon, Philip. *Within Walking Distance: Creating Livable Communities for All.* Island Press, 2017.

Owen, David. *Green Metropolis: Why Living Smaller, Living Closer, and Driving Less Are the Keys to Sustainability.* Riverhead Books, 2010.

Pendergrast, Mark. *City on the Verge: Atlanta and the Fight for America's Urban Future.* Basic Books, 2017.

Sadik-Kahn, Janette and Seth Solomonow. *Streetfight: Handbook for an Urban Revolution.* NY: Penguin, 2017.

Schwartz, Samuel I., *No One at the Wheel: Driverless Cars and the Road of the Future,* Hachette Book Group, 2018.

Speck, Jeff. *Walkable City: How Downtown Can Save America, One Step at a Time.* North Point Press, 2012.

Speck, Jeff. *Walkable City Rules: 101 Steps to Making Better Places.* Island Press, 2018.

APPENDIX INDEX

McNEIL, MURRAY & SORRELL, INC.

ATTORNEYS AT LAW

111 ST. PAUL STREET

BURLINGTON, VERMONT 05401

JOSEPH C. McNEIL (1919-1978)
JOSEPH E. McNEIL
FRANCIS X. MURRAY
WILLIAM H. SORRELL

MARSHA J. SMITH
ROBERT E. FLETCHER, JR.
RICHARD C. WHITTLESEY
JOHN T. LEDDY
NANCY GOSS SHEAHAN

TELEPHONES 863-4531
862-8989
AREA CODE 802

MEMO

TO: Alderman Allen F. Gear

FROM: John T. Leddy, Esq.

RE: Bike Path Lawsuit

DATE: August 19, 1982

You have asked me to evaluate the City of Burlington's position and the likelihood of prevailing at the trial on the merits of the Bike Path litigation. The case presently before the Chittenden Superior Court is, I believe, a matter of first impression in the State of Vermont. Hence, a quick and facile answer is not readily obtainable.

Nevertheless, based upon the extent of the research that I have done to date, it is my opinion that the Defendant City of Burlington may have a better than even chance of prevailing in the lawsuit. That is not to say that the Plaintiffs' claim to the former railroad right-of-way is frivolous. To the contrary, Plaintiffs' action may be substantiated at common law, however, I believe that the Vermont Legislature may have changed the common law by certain statutory enactments specifically pertaining to the former Rutland Railroad right-of-way passed in the last two decades. Absent these special legislative acts, the City's position appears much weaker at a trial on the merits.

I. State of the Title--Easement or Fee Simple.

A controlling question in the litigation is whether the railroad, in originally taking the land by right of eminent domain pursuant to public laws, 1898, No. 160, "An Act to Incorporate the Rutland-Canadian Railroad Company," held merely an easement or took title to the fee. The railroad appears to have taken an easement only.

In the case of Dessureau v. Maurice Memorials, Inc., 132 Vt. 350 (1974), the court, in dicta, stated that a taking, pursuant to statutory authority, gave the railroad only an easement, and not a fee. Id. at 351. The statutory authority referred to, §§3356-3362 of the Revised Laws of Vermont (1880) [now 30 V.S.A. §§1303-1310] is presumably the same condemnation authority utilized in the taking of the Rutland Railroad right-of-way.

Several Vermont cases lend precedent to the proposition that when a railroad condemns land it takes only an easement. An early decision dealing with this issue was Quimby v. Vermont Central Railroad Co., 23 Vt. 387 (1851). In Quimby, the court noted at the outset that railroad charters granted in New York provided that the railroad take fee title to the land. However, the defendant railroad's charter, although copied in large part from New York charters, adopted different language as to the defendant's title reciting that the railroad "shall be 'seized and possessed of the land;' that is, seized of such an estate as is necessary for [its] uses--a right-of-way." Id. at 393.

In the case of Rutland Railroad Co. v. Chaffee, 71 Vt. 84 (1899), it was provided in the charter of the railroad company that when it took land by right of eminent domain, the railroad shall be deemed to be seized and possessed of such lands appraised by the commissioners. The court held: "The right of the plaintiff to the land in question is an easement; the only purpose for which it had a right to take it, was for a right-of-way." Id. at 85. See also, Connecticut and Passumpsic Rivers Railroad Co. v. Holton, 32 Vt. 43, 47 (1859) (the right acquired to land taken under charter is merely an easement); Troy & Boston Railroad Co. v. Potter, 42 Vt. 265, 274 (1869) (easement, not a fee); Jackson v. Rutland and Burlington Railroad Co., 25 Vt. 150, 158-159 (1853) (nothing more than a right-of-way).

A review of the language of the charter incorporating the Rutland-Canadian Railroad Company, Public Laws, 1898, No. 160, fairly indicates that only so much of the land as is necessary, could be taken.

> Sec. 1 . . . Said corporation shall have and enjoy the right of eminent domain . . . ; may receive, take, hold, purchase, use and convey such real and personal estate as is necessary or proper in the judgment of such corporation, for the construction, maintenance and accommodation of such railroad as aforesaid, and its structures and appurtenances, and as the purposes of the corporation may require . . . .

Public Laws, 1898, No. 160, Sec. 1. Compare, Quimby v. Vt. Central Railroad Co., supra and Rutland Railroad Co. v. Chaffee, supra.

In 1900, the Legislature passed No. 153, entitled "An Act to Consolidate the Rutland Railroad System". Included therein was the Rutland-Canadian Railroad Company. Public Laws, 1900, No. 153, Sec. 1. Section 4 of the Act provides in relevant part:

> Upon consummation of such act of consolidation, . . . all of the property, both real, personal and mixed of such consolidating corporations shall be taken and deemed to be transferred to and vested in said Rutland Railroad Company without further act or deed; and all claims, demands, property, rights-of-way, and every other interest shall be as effectually the property of the Rutland Railroad Company as they were of the other corporations, parties to such agreement and act, and the title to all real estate taken by deed or otherwise under the laws of this state . . . vested in either of such corporations, parties to said agreement and act, shall not be deemed to revert or be in any way impaired by reason of this act or anything done by virtue hereof; but shall be vested in said Rutland Railroad Company by virtue of such act of consolidation.

> *   *   *   *

Public Laws, 1900, Act No. 153, Sec. 4. Hence, the Legislature addressed the question of reversion in Act No. 153. At least arguably, Act No. 153 may have effectively abrogated any subsequent right of reversion in the adjoining landowners. See discussion below, III.

II. <u>Abandonment.</u>

Another overriding issue in the litigation is the question of abandonment. In Vermont, upon abandonment of a railroad right-of-way which is only an easement, such abandonment causes the property to revert to its former owner. Dessureau v. Maurice Memorials, Inc., 132 Vt. at 351.

To constitute an abandonment, the intention to abandon must exist on the part of the railroad, coupled with an external act by which the intention is carried into effect. 65 Am. Jur. 2d, Railroads, §83. The lapse of time and non-user are competent evidence of intent to abandon, and, as such, may be entitled to great weight considered with other circumstances. Id. Evidence of the requisite intent to abandon has often been found in the deliberate removal of tracks or other facilities from the land whereby the running of the trains is rendered impossible. Id.

The question of abandonment is one of fact for the determination of the jury, depending upon all the facts and circumstances disclosed by the evidence of each particular case. Id., §83. In the case of Stevens v. MacRae, 97 Vt. 76 (1923), the court found that the mere lapse of time and non-user for railway tracks of a portion of a railroad right-of-way for a period of about ten years did not in themselves operate as an abandonment as a matter of law, the question being one of fact to be determined on the evidence. 97 Vt. at 80.

Based upon the facts of the instant suit, the trier of fact could be presented with persuasive evidence of an intention to abandon. The State of Vermont has asserted in its filings that an abandonment at law may occur only upon the issuance of a Certificate of Public Convenience and Necessity by the Interstate Commerce Commission, pursuant to 49 U.S.C. §10903. Indeed, the United States Supreme Court recently reaffirmed that the ICC has plenary and exclusive authority to regulate, in the interest of interstate commerce, the abandonment of rail lines. Chicago and Northwestern Transp. Co. v. Kalo Brick & Tile, 101 S.Ct. 1124, 67 L.Ed.2d 258 (U.S., 1981).

III. Reversionary Rights in Adjoining Property Owners.

The question as to the extent of the interest acquired by the railroad has an important bearing on the effect of the cessation of the use for which the property was taken. Generally speaking, if an easement only was acquired by eminent domain, the right to the possession reverts to the owner of the fee, regardless of whether the taking was by the state or by an individual or a corporation. 26 Am. Jur. 2d, Eminent Domain, Sec. 147.

However, a qualification of this rule as to reverter is found in those cases which hold that land in which an easement has been condemned for one public use may, with the consent of the Legislature, be applied to another use of the same kind without working a reversion to the owner of the fee. State v. Maine, 27 Conn. 641 (   ); 26 Am. Jur. 2d, Eminent Domain, Sec. 147, n. 1.

On at least four different occasions, the Vermont Legislature has enacted statutes dealing with the Rutland Railroad right-of-way. (1) Public Acts, 1963, No. 162, pertains to the acquisition, by purchase or condemnation, of portions of the line necessary and required for the continued operation of a railroad. The maximum amount appropriated for this purpose, $2,700,000.00 may militate against the notion of a mere easement. (2) Public Acts, 1965, No. 197, pertains to the sale of "State-owned former Rutland Railway Corporation property" north of Burlington. Section 1 of the act provided in part: "In the sale of such land, wherever practicable the board [of forests and parks] shall give priority to municipalities and then to persons owning property rights therein or adjacent thereto." (3) Public Acts, 1971, No. 113, is entitled, "An Act to Authorize the Sale or Lease of Certain State-Owned Property". Act No. 113 makes reference to the sale of a fee interest in the former right-of-way. (4) Public Laws, 1900, No. 153, discussed above.

Arguably, the above four legislative enactments, are in derogation of the adjoining property owners' common law right to reversion upon abandonment. Accordingly, the above stated exception to the rule of reversion - that is, with prior legislative consent, an easement condemned for one public use may be applied to another use of the same kind without effecting a reversion. See, 26 Am. Jur. 2d, Eminent Domain, Sec. 147, n. 1.

Arguably, any one of these legislative provisions, or a fortiori, all four laws taken cumulatively, may demonstrate that the land in question is held in fee simple absolute by the State of Vermont.

Given the public policy behind these enactments that ownership of the right-of-way should be retained in the public domain, the defendants may have a slight advantage in the pending litigation. Nonetheless, it is important to note that in order for the city and the other defendants to prevail in this action, new law will likely have to be made. If the common law is found to be unchanged, a reversion may have occurred, thereby extinguishing all rights of the defendants in the former right-of-way.

IV. Conclusion.

In sum, there is no well-settled rule of law which controls in this litigation. Although I will continue to research the issue, the City may have a slightly better than even chance of prevailing at the trial on the merits in this suit.

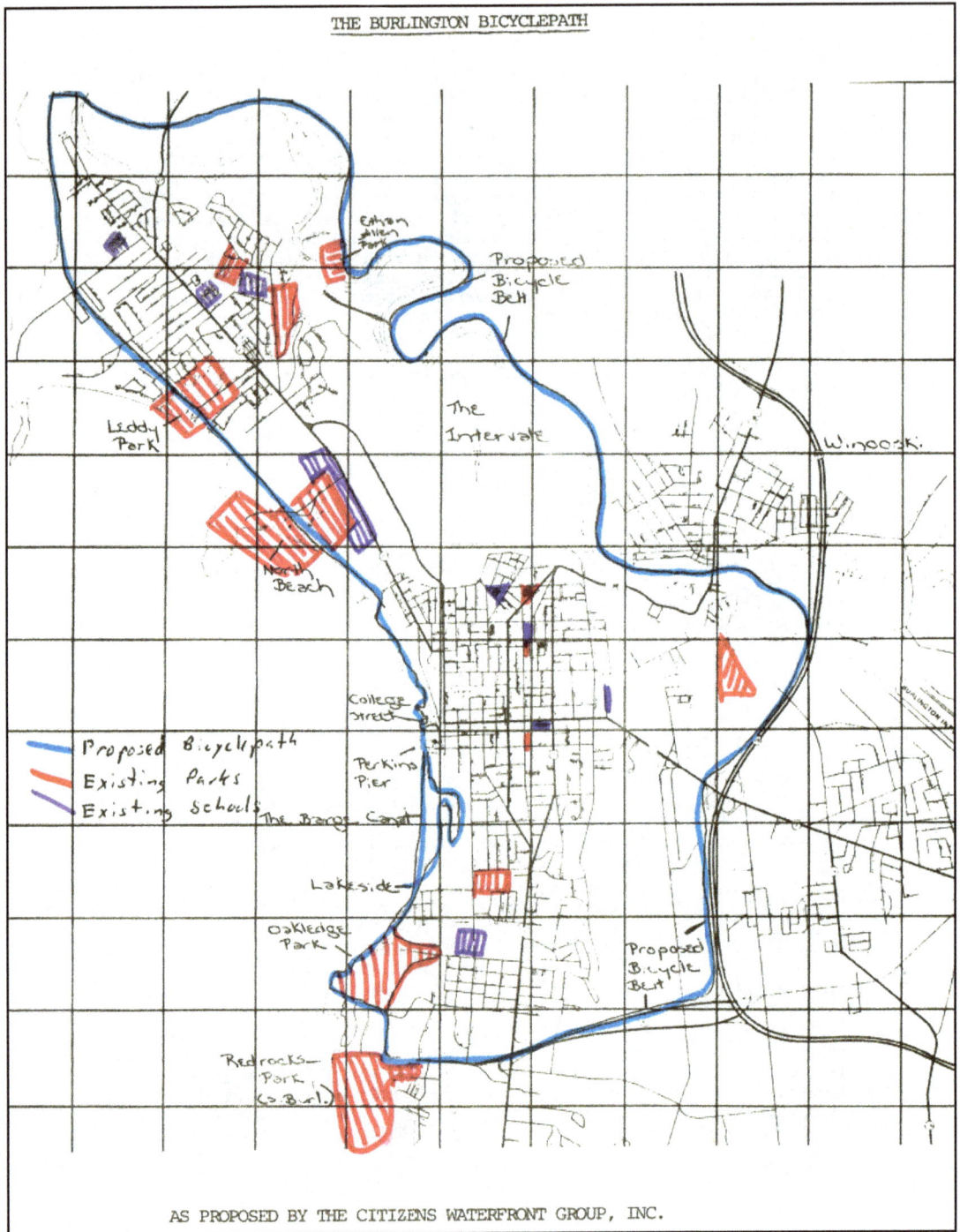

THE BURLINGTON BICYCLEPATH

AS PROPOSED BY THE CITIZENS WATERFRONT GROUP, INC.

Introduction

We are at a critical point in the development of the City of Burlington. Like many other American cities, Burlington has long neglected its waterfront, allowing it to deteriorate into a wasteland of deserted railroad yards, oil storage tanks and dilapidated buildings. And like so many other cities, Burlington will soon turn to its waterfront in an effort to reverse decades of urban decay and to rejuvenate the heart of the downtown district.

Pressure for development of the lakefront grows each day. Waterfront acreage is the most expensive in the State, currently estimated to be between $200,000.00 and $400,000.00 an acre. Over the past five years, two plans for major private developments at the foot of College Street have been submitted to City planners. Still more plans are sure to follow. Once the first project is constructed on the waterfront, land values are likely to skyrocket and still other developments are sure to follow.

Certainly the City will benefit from the development of its waterfront. The potential for increased tax revenues is staggering. In fact, it may be possible to avoid any increase in real property taxes throughout the City for the rest of this century through proper development of the waterfront alone. But, the real value of the waterfront is far greater than the sum of its tax receipts. We would be extremely shortsighted to view this precious resource in terms of potential tax revenues alone.

The waterfront represents an unparalleled opportunity to revitalize the downtown and achieve economic prosperity. With proper planning and development, large portions of the waterfront could be left open to public access, as an attraction to area residents and tourists. With no planning or poor planning, private waterfront development may exclude the public from a large portion of the Burlington lakeshore. The real question is not whether there will be development, but instead, the form that development will take. Land use patterns established on the waterfront in the near future will greatly affect the use of this area for 50 to 100 years, or even longer.

Our City is at a crossroads. One road leads to widespread public access to the lake within the City's borders. The other leads to a lakefront of private enclaves, expensive and exclusive, and accessible to only a few.

The Problem

One of the key problems to overcome in providing for public access to the lake is that land ownership along the Burlington lakefront is highly fragmented with no cohesive force to co-ordinate development of the various privately owned parcels. The Burlington lakefront is 9.1 miles in length. Only 1.2 miles of the lakeshore is currently open to the public. The remaining 7.9 miles, representing some 86% of the Burlington shoreline, is divided between numerous private interests and, therefore, inaccessible to the public.

Public access points within the City are divided and often difficult to locate. Visitors to our City often have an extremely difficult time locating points of public access to the lake. Marina space is very limited with waiting lists of seven years or even longer for dockspace. The only boat launching facility in the City is simply inadequate to handle even existing traffic.

Although public interest in the waterfront is high and land values continue to appreciate, this area remains a wasteland today. Part of the failure to develop this resouce can be placed upon the fragmented pattern of land ownership, but a substantial portion of the problem is attributable to the City's failure to take the initiative in waterfront planning and development.

The approach of the City to date has been mainly a passive one. Although the City has taken some important initial steps in zoning and land use planning, and although the planning office has assisted private parties in their attempts to obtain federal funding for portions of proposed projects, the City has, for the most part, felt confined to reviewing plans submitted by private developers. It has not come forward with its own plan for public access. It has, instead, choosen to deal with this issue on a project by project basis with no overall plan.

The City's failure to formulate an overall plan for providing public access to the lake has resulted in confusion as to what is acceptable waterfront development. This confusion has in turn caused private developers to withdraw plans for waterfront development until the City sets a firm policy on this critical issue.

Although the withdrawal of plans which are not right for the Burlington waterfront is preferable to proceeding, we can no longer afford to lose millions of dollars in taxes each year while the waterfront remains as an undeveloped eyesore.

The Solution

We in the Citizens Waterfront Group, Inc., believe that the solution to the public access problem is to take the initiative by proposing a plan to insure public access to the lake before private development begins.

We further believe that maximum public access to the lake would be achieved through the creation of a continuous strip along the lakeshore open to the public. City voters overwhelmingly supported such a public pathway in an advisory ballot item in 1981.

Additional marina space open to the public and additional boat launching facilities could be acquired and developed with the bicyclepath. Installation of the pathway and associated public facilities might even spur private development of the waterfront and increase tax revenues.

We in the Citizens Waterfront Group, Inc., support the concept of "strip zoning" in the downtown waterfront. Strip zoning would insure the creation of such a public strip, satisfying public access and at the same time laying solid ground rules for private developers.

The Burlington Bicyclepath

Depicted on the cover is the bicyclepath and pedestrian corridor proposed by the Citizens Waterfront Group, Inc. The proposed pathway is to run along the shore of Lake Champlain, from Oakledge Park, at Burlington's southern border, to the mouth of the Winooski River, the City's northern boundary.

The envisioned pathway would be paved and open to the public for bicycling, jogging, cross-country skiing or strolling. It would be a "green strip" woven through existing and future lakefront development - a nine-mile park along the Burlington waterfront.

The pathway would link existing City Parks at Oakledge, Perkins Pier, North Beach and Leddy Park. Other parcels currently owned by the City, or acquired from private holdings along the lakeshore, could be added to the pathway over time. The end result would be a whole system of public parks woven between private development in a well-planned and aesthetically pleasing urban community.

How Could Such A Pathway Be Created?

We are fortunate here in Burlington to have history on our side. In 1899, a 80-foot wide strip of property was condemned for a railroad line along the lake through Burlington's new north end. This railbed is no longer used by the railroad. It is now owned by the State of Vermont and the City of Burlington. A portion of the old railbed has already been converted into a bicyclepath by the City, and on many City maps the entire roadbed is depicted as a bicyclepath. This old railbed could be used by the City to create more than one-third of the pathway.

The remaining two-thirds could be acquired from several different sources. There is an existing railroad line that runs along most of the remaining Burlington shoreline. Although this line is currently being utilized for railroad purposes, it may be possible to acquire an "easement" for the pathway along this railroad right-of-way, beside the existing tracks.

The City could require private developers to set aside a right-of-way for such a pathway through and between all new construction. Toward this end, the City could "rezone" such a strip as recreation/conservation (strip zoning), thereby insuring its inclusion in all future development plans. Most private developers will accomodate reasonable requests for public access if properly approached. The Citizens Waterfront Group was successful in obtaining a commitment for such a right-of-way from the Pomerleau Agency when it submitted plans for waterfront development in 1981.

A more ambitious scheme would be for the City to acquire rights to install such a pathway, together with proper shoreline protection, all along the lakeshore in the City's southern end. A large waterfront park, adjacent to the old barge canal, could be created by filling a shallow portion of the lake there. There is currently an excess of clean fill material from construction projects in the City. More than 200 truck loads of such fill material was acquired by the Citizens Waterfront Group, Inc., at no cost last year for the proposed City park at the foot of College Street. This fill material could be stock piled by the barge canal and used to create a large park in this area of the City. Although this approach would be considerably more expensive, it would result in the creation of a large City park on the waterfront at a minimal cost and in the installation of proper shoreline protection in the southern end of the City, where lake errosion has long been a costly problem.

Acquisition and Funding

The two obstacles to be overcome in implementing such a plan are acquisition of necessary rights and funding of development.

A. ACQUISITION: The necessary right-of-way could be acquried from private developers as each project came up for review before the Planning Commission. The problem with this approach is that it might take 20 years and it is peicemeal. The refusal of a single developer to cooperate could leave the City without an essential link in the pathway.

The better approach appears to be to zone the necessary strip onto City planning maps as recreation/conservation, thereby insuring the availability of the necessary right-of-way in advance of any construction. This approach has the added benefit of providing advance notice, to developers as to the City's plans for waterfront development.

Toward this end, the Citizens Waterfront Group fully supports the proposal currently before the Planning Commission to rezone the railroad right-of-way from North Beach to the mouth of the Winooski River recreation/conservation. We support the extension of this zone into the downtown area.

We believe that the City should rezone the entire downtown waterfront into "strip zones." Under this plan the first 60 to 100 feet along the entire waterfront downtown would be rezoned as recreation/conservation. Only existing structures would be allowed in this zone. The bicyclepath would then be woven between these existing structures in a new recreation/conservation zone.

We also feel that the next 100 feet, or more, of waterfront property should be rezoned mainly as commercial space. High density residential zoning should be restricted to the bank below Battery Street. We feel that it is important to separate residential areas from the bicyclepath as much as possible in order to avoid conflicting interests that would generate pressure to restrict public access to this strip.

Resolution of the legal action now pending over the railroad right-of-way in Burlington's north end is necessary prior to the development of this portion of the pathway. The Citizens Waterfront Group believes that the State and the City will eventually prevail in the proceedings now pending in the Courts. In the event that the State does not prevail, the Group favors condemnation of this property for use as a bicyclepath. Adjoining landowners would then have to be compensated but this is a key link in the proposed pathway, and well worth whatever price we must pay for it.

From Perkins Pier south a decision must be made as to whether to pursue a shoreline approach or to settle for a route along the existing railroad right-of-way or next to the southern connector, if it is constructed. If the shoreline route is to be selected, a study must be completed to estimate the cost of constructing the pathway and adequate shoreline protection. If the cost of this approach is deemed to be worthwhile, then the City will have to negotiate with private parties along the lakeshore to acquire rights to install the pathway and shoreline protection. If one of the other paths are selected, the City may wish to rezone this property and it may be necessary to acquire additional rights-of-way.

B. FUNDING: Preferably, funding for this project could be acquired from federal sources. The Citizens Waterfront Group fully supports earmarking a portion of the federal block grant money allocated to the City for acquisition and development of this pathway. The Group is submitting an application for block grant funds to pave the portion of the railroad right-of-way north of Starr Farm Road next summer. Additional federal and state funds may be available from several different sources for the construction of the pathway. We would request that the Planning Commission take an active role in pursuing federal and state funding of this project.

Private funds may also be available and the Citizens Waterfront Group is willing to raise funds in the community from individuals and local businesses.

Public funding in the form of a bond issue is also a possibility. City voters have often supported public bonds for worthwhile projects in the City, including the Fletcher Free Library expansion, the new water filtration plant and the woodchip plant. Public interest in the waterfront is high and it is likely that Burlington voters would support a bond for the creation of such a pathway.

Certainly, we should not fail to ask the public if they support a bond simply out of fear of rejection. Nor can we wait too much longer before providing such a funding mechanism for the pathway. If no other funding mechanism is available by March of 1984, the Citizens Waterfront Group will propose for placement on the ballot a bond in the amount of two million dollars to establish a public trust fund for acquisiton and development of the pathway.

Two million dollars is a small amount to pay to insure public access to the water-front for the next 100 years. This figure represents only two years of tax revenues from a single ten-acre site on the waterfront. The City spent more than a quarter of a million dollars on a parking lot at North Beach last fall. For the price of eight parking lots, the public could have unlimited access to the waterfront in Burlington.

Won't you help us make the Burlington Bicyclepath a reality?

RICK SHARP
ATTORNEY AT LAW
108 SOUTH WINOOSKI AVENUE
P.O. BOX 191
BURLINGTON. VERMONT 05402

RICK SHARP
JAMES A HUGHES*
ATTORNEYS AT LAW
———
DAVID R COWLES
SUSAN GILFILLAN
LAW CLERKS
*ADMITTED IN NY ALSO

April 1, 1985

TELEPHONE
AREA CODE 802
864 7490
863 1040

Charles Shea, Esq.
Gravel, Shea and Wright
P.O. Box 1049
Burlington, VT 05402-1049

RE: Alden Waterfront Development

Dear Charlie:

As you well know, the waterfront development proposed by the Alden Corporation, for the foot of College Street in Burlington will undoubtedly become the centerpiece of Burlington's new image for a generation to come or longer. It will certainly set both the tone and the pace for future growth in the Queen City throughout the rest of this century. The Citizen's Waterfront Group (CWG), which I represent, therefore views this particular segment of the Burlington waterfront as the standard by which all others will be measured. It is, therefore, critical that the development at the foot of College Street set a good example for all subsequent developments that will follow.

To date, the CWG has been most successful in obtaining adequate access and park space along the water's edge as developments come up for review. We did very well with Rod Whittier and his project at North Shore, with uniform setbacks of over 200 feet from the water's edge throughout the project. I might add that the final result at North Shore is much better for the public in terms of usable open space along the water's edge due to the participation of CWG in this process.

It is not unusual for a development office of a City and a potential developer to share ultimate goals that lead them to agree on a level of public access that environmental groups might find lacking. Especially when it is learned that we, the public, actually own large segments of the area to be developed. It is not unreasonable under these circumstances for a legitimate disagreement to develop that finds its way into a legal struggle.

I do not intend to use the process of this appeal to delay what I consider to be a very viable project that will benefit this City immeasurably in the long run, through economic as well as social and cultural opportunities, all blooming out of what is now an untaxed eyesore.

I do not wish to unnecessarily delay such a benefit to this City. But it is so critical that we do it right the first time, for there will be no second chance, possibly for several generations to come. That is why the CWG views the public trust property, on which much of this development will be located, as a key to assuring that the citizens of the City and the State of Vermont will have access to the shoreline in the form of parkland and green areas forever.

Through the neighborhood planning and public comment processes, the people of Burlington as well as its surrounding communities have displayed a great deal of interest in making certain that a "greenstrip" of public access parkland exists along the water's edge.

Although Alden has taken many of these comments into consideration in moving the so-called "Inn" out of the water, the fact that the Inn will still be within 20 feet of the water's edge under the current proposal concerns many of our members and we feel that the proposed development is not in keeping with the overwhelming majority of public comment recieved to date. Alden representatives have admitted that the "filled lands" in dispute are as wide as 400 feet in some areas. CWG merely asks that the shoreward 30-foot strip of this land, held "in trust for the public", be preserved for truely public activities.

CWG's strongest objection to the final draft Stipulation and Agreement are the placement of other then primarily public use structures within 80 feet of the water's edge. CWG is not asking that the Alden plan be altered in any way other than the granting of this green strip, with no encumbrances, as a public area. If more space is needed for the construction of buildings because of the 30-foot set back, CWG would support a move to have the City deed any interest it holds in the bank below Battery Street to Alden in exchange for the 30 feet along the water's edge.

Of this 80-foot greenstrip, we envision the shoreward 20-foot strip to be an area where people can sit and relax and watch the sunset without being disturbed by nearby movements. The next 40 feet would be trees and grass, and would help create a "feeling" of serenity, the essance of Vermont itself. The eastward most portion of twenty (20) feet would include a walkway in front of shops, restaurants and other primarily commercial property. Woven between the trees and grass in the 40-foot strip would be a low speed bicycle path and possibly a bridal trail. This pathway would not be the primary thoroughfare that is planned for the major transportation corridor. This would be a meandering path for walking and bicycle travel would only be allowed under highly restricted speeds.

CWG members have suggested that this greenspace or greenstrip be planted with many sugar maples by City residents at no cost to the City all along its 9.1 mile length. In the spring the City could establish a maple sugar harvest festival with the collection of sap by local residents, possibly with horse drawn carts or sleighs, along this same meandering path which we intend to use as a bicycle path in the summertime.

In effect this waterfront park would become a "maple gateway" to Vermont's Queen City from Lake Champlain. This gateway park would be in keeping with Vermont's unique maple tradition. What could be more Vermont? And just imagine the colors in the fall. Truely this would be a waterfront for all seasons!

That's what we in the CWG call long range planning for the quality of life of our own children and our children's children.

The Stipulation and Agreement, though good generally, lacks specificity as to the "public ammenities" which will be provided. The Agreement does not mention construction of a public boat house which I was of the understanding was to be an essential part of the plans already. Such primarily public uses as this would not be prohibited in the 80-foot setback CWG is requesting. Other ancilary uses, such as a hotdog stand/snack bar, open to the public at a truely nominal cost, would not be objectionable either. CWG sees a major distinction between uses which are primarily public, such as the above-mentioned, and primarily private uses such as condominiums, hotels, or other commercial space.

The only other problem CWG has with the proposed Stipulation and Agreement is with some of the provisions in the Easement and Warranty Deeds, Exhibits C and D respectively. Both documents declare a 10-day notice period before rules and regulations drafted by Alden become effective. CWG believes that 10 days is a woefully inadequate amount of time, unless some emergency exists, and requests the timing be modified to allow for a 60 day public comment period. Furthermore, the City Council should be the reviewing body, not just the Mayor and City Attorney, as it more widely represents the public and is the proper forum for such review. The paragraph in the Easement Deed giving a reversionary interest to Alden should be eliminated in its entirety. This land should forever be devoted to the maple gateway park.

CWG is anxious to see the commencement of construction on the waterfront. CWG is not, however, willing to sacrifice what it sees as the public's right to at least the shoreward 80 feet for the maple park in order for development to begin. If Alden and CVR agree to CWG's requests as stated herein, CWG will withdraw its Motion to Intervene, making the appeal moot, and assist in a speedy approval process.

Burlington has only one waterfront. CWG wants to assure that the development of this waterfront area is done in a manner that reflects the public's long range interest in the preservation of open space along the water's edge as a major consideration in its design. This area should "feel" like park space. CWG is not hiding behind a facade to endlessly delay construction. CWG has been consistent in its approach and is sincerely interested in helping the project win approval at all levels.

As a final note, I would suggest that the minimum setback issue be put to a public vote at the next City election, to once and for all settle this delicate issue. CWG will propose this route to the Board of Alderman if this issue can not be resolved in the near future. I will also release a copy of this letter to the press and to the Board of Alderman.

I'm looking forward to your response.

Sincerely,

RICK SHARP

RS:kt

cc: City of Burlington-Board of Alderman
    John Franco, Esquire
    Wallace Malley, Esquire

STATE OF VERMONT

HOUSE OF REPRESENTATIVES
STATE HOUSE
MONTPELIER, VERMONT 05602

TELEPHONE (802) 828-2231

July 17, 1985

Paul Flinn, President
Alden Waterfront Corporation
120 Lake Street
Burlington, VT 05401

Dear Paul:

I've been following the prevails of the Alden Waterfront Corporation in the
paper, and I must agree with your conclusion that it's time to get the project
moving.

I also agree with your statement that tax incremental financing is the appropriate way to go. When that bill came to the Legislature, I worked very hard,
along with Bob Walsh of South Burlington, to get it passed, because while it
is not suitable for frequent use because of the forward pledging of tax revenues, it is ideal for special situations such as the Alden Development.

As you know, I've spent a tremendous amount of time on the various issues
surrounding the development of the Burlington waterfront. While I have not
always agreed with the Alden Corporation, I believe the Alden Corporation has
presented by far the best plan, and in fact a plan which is so good that it is
unlikely to be duplicated. It is my view that if the Alden Corporation does
not develop the waterfront, it will lie undeveloped for some years, and then
will give way to a far less people oriented waterfront.

I would be happy to do whatever I could to encourage the city to use the tax
incremental financing plan for this project. While I agree with Mayor
Sanders' comments that it is not the best of all possible worlds to pledge tax
receipts for the development to pay for the infrastructure, I do think that
the benefit gained by beginning this project as soon as possible far outweighs
the demerits of the incremental financing plan.

I am looking forward to hearing from you at your convenience.

Sincerely yours,

Rep. Howard Dean, M.D.
Assistant Minority Leader

HD:cat
124k
cc: Stephen Crampton
    Rick Sharp
    Peter Clavelle

APPENDIX 5

Resolution Relating to

FILLED LANDS IN BURLINGTON HARBOR

CITY OF BURLINGTON

In the year One Thousand Nine Hundred and ___Eighty-five___

Resolved by the City Council of the City of Burlington, as follows:

That ___WHEREAS, there has been extensive discussion of what
constitutes a proper setback from the lakefront on filled lands
in Burlington Harbor; and

WHEREAS, 75% of those responding to a survey distributed
during the presentation of the Alden Corporation's plans for
waterfront development were in favor of the plan; and

WHEREAS, the Alden Corporation Master Plan was revised
to locate buildings further back from the lakeshore but still
closer than 80 feet; and

WHEREAS, the Burlington Board of Aldermen approved the
revised plan and authorized the signing of a pre-development
agreement which affirms the concept of a 30-80 foot setback;
and

WHEREAS, the issue of appropriate setback was discussed
by the Waterfront Board prior to their recommendation to the
Planning Commission of a setback which is consistent with the
proposed Planned Unit Development Ordinance (PUD) which states
that there shall be an average 50 foot setback with no building
closer than 25 feet; and

WHEREAS, the Planning Commission has held public hearings
on the proposed PUD and no negative comments on the setback
provisions were received; and

WHEREAS, establishing substantially more severe restrictions
at this time will seriously undermine the City's efforts to
date, as well as make it more difficult to thoughtfully evaluate
proposals on specific sites with unique site characteristics.

Resolution Relating to

CITY OF BURLINGTON

In the year One Thousand Nine Hundred and ....
Resolved by the City Council of the City of Burlington, as follows:

That ....

NOW, THEREFORE, BE IT RESOLVED that the Burlington Board
of Aldermen believes that this issue has been thoroughly discussed
and that a rational and coherent policy has been developed.

AND BE IT FURTHER RESOLVED that the Board of Aldermen
are opposed to requiring a minimum 80 foot setback on so-called
filled lands in Burlington Harbor.

AND BE IT FURTHER RESOLVED that the Board of Aldermen
hereby voice their opposition to Article III of the June 11,
1985 Special Meeting which states "Should the City of Burlington
require a minimum set-back of 80 feet from the water's edge
for any future private development on the filled lands in the
Burlington harbor?".

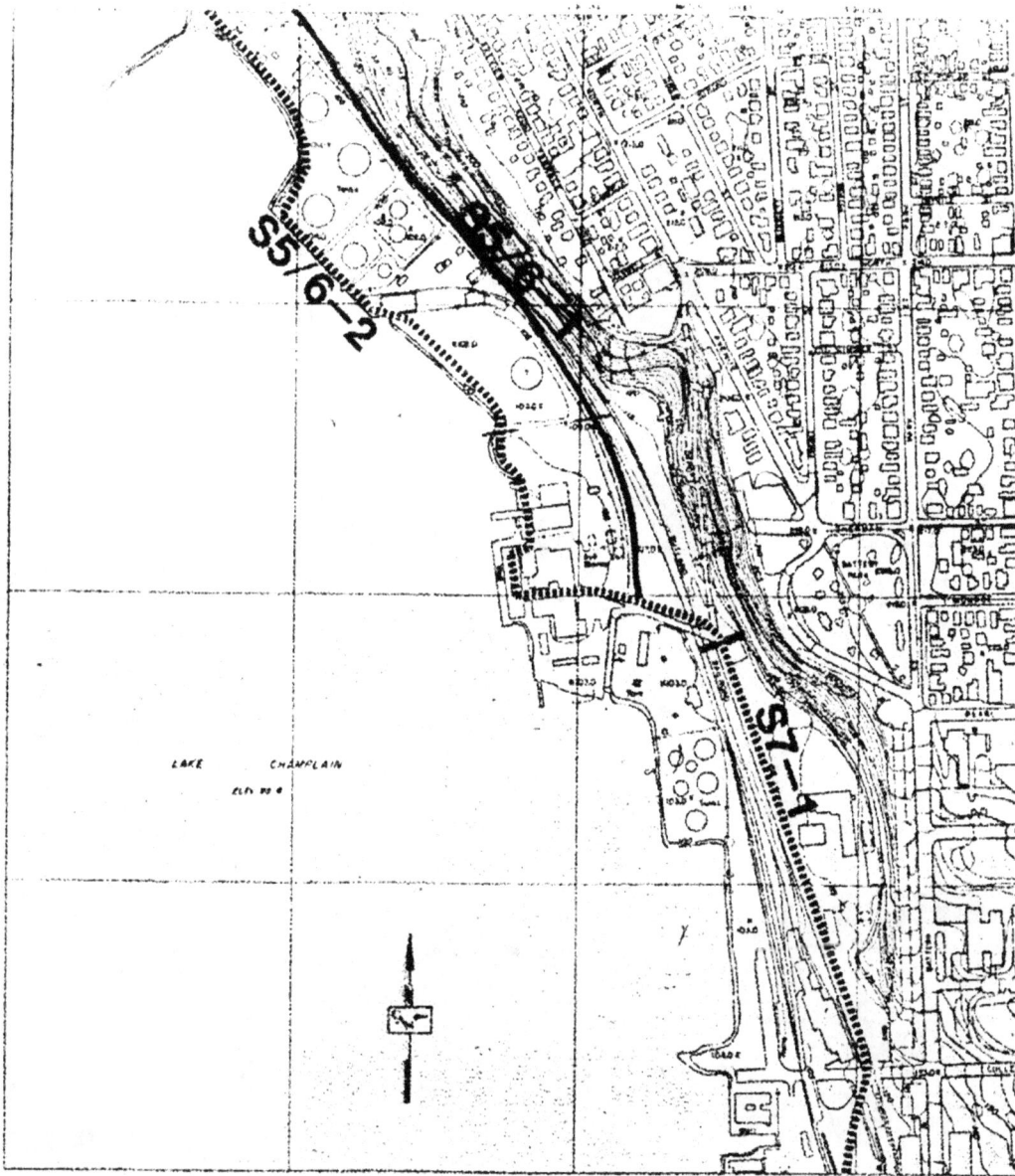

Page 20 of the Boyle/Boehm Association Report of 1984 (the Boehm Report) depicts possible routes for the Bike Path from Texaco Beach in the north to the ferry dock. The entire report is available from the CEDO office. The report presented various routes for the pathway for the length of the waterfront downtown. But for the area Alden had under contract north of College Street only one route is presented (S7-1) along the east side of the railroad tracks and the Pease Grain Building, no doubt at the direction of the Sanders Administration.

UNANSWERED QUESTIONS!

● Our full faith and credit is behind this general obligation bond. The Development Agreement with Alden contains no guarantee for repayment of these bonds. How can we be sure in the face of development risks that Alden will in fact repay this debt?

● The cornerstone of the proposed public space is now occupied by the Naval Reserve station. The Navy has given no assurance as to when they will relocate.

● With the impact of Alden's plan already being felt in area real estate costs, how will Burlington citizens be able to continue to afford to live in neighborhoods around the waterfront development?

● The Community and Economic Development office says that one of the biggest problems facing the Burlington job market is low paying jobs. Why is public money being used to make this problem worse?

● Will the City's role be one of an entrepeneur partner with a developer rather than as protector of the public interest? Isn't this a blatent conflict of interest?

● Because there is no deeded right-of-way for the bicycle path, could it be eliminated by future development?

● The public trust doctrine is currently being considered by the Chittenden Superior Court. Shouldn't this issue of who owns this filled land be settled before we vote on this bond?

● Even the proponents of this plan agree this financing plan if flawed. Why don't we wait until this law is corrected to vote on this bond?

● These are just a few of the unanswered questions. If any doubts remain in your mind, we urge you to vote NO on December 10.

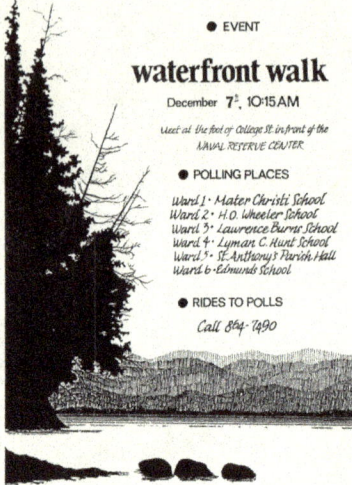

Citizens For A BETTER Waterfront

is a Coalition of...

Democrats • Citizens' Waterfront Group • Independents

Northern Vermont Greens • Republicans

Burlington Environmental Alliance

● EVENT

waterfront walk

December 7ᵗʰ, 10·15 AM

Meet at the foot of College St. in front of the
NAVAL RESERVE CENTER.

● POLLING PLACES

Ward 1 • Mater Christi School
Ward 2 • H.O. Wheeler School
Ward 3 • Lawrence Burns School
Ward 4 • Lyman C. Hunt School
Ward 5 • St. Anthony's Parish Hall
Ward 6 • Edmunds School

● RIDES TO POLLS

Call 864-7490

Box 191 Burlington, Vt. 05402 · Sandy Baird · Treasurer

Our Waterfront is still NOT FOR SALE!

PLEASE VOTE

NO

ON THE WATERFRONT BOND ISSUE

On December 10, 1985

sponsored by,

Citizens For A BETTER Waterfront

On December 10, City voters will be asked to subsidize the construction of an expensive hotel and luxury condominiums on our waterfront with a $6 million bond that will cost $13 million to repay out of future tax revenues.

WHAT ARE OUR TAX DOLLARS BEING SPENT ON?

● A 200 room so-called "inn", seven stories high with rooms costing $100 per night.

● Up to 300 luxury condominiums, so-called "neighborhood housing", with price tags up to $300,000 each. Packed into less than 10 acres, this will be one of the densest developments in Burlington's history.

● Expensive shoreline protection designed to protect and enhance the hotel and condominiums.

● A 50-foot wide paved walkway, 16 feet narrower than Church Street, that will be encroached upon by a 25-foot overhang on the third to seventh floors of the hotel.

● A total of five acres of park space. Two acres of this land already belongs to the City and is currently occupied by the Naval Reserve station. The other 3 acres are part of the 12 acres of filled land on the lakeshore which belongs to us under the public trust doctrine.

● An uncertain bicycle path that will run behind the seven-story hotel and luxury condominiums.

● Underground utility lines and the relocation of Lake Street, with a price tag of $1.8 million, costs usually borne by the developer.

● A half million dollar boathouse.

HOW WILL THIS BOND EFFECT OUR SCHOOLS?

● The Burlington School Board voted 8 to 3 against this tax incremental financing plan

because they realize our schools would be giving up future tax dollars for up to 20 years. The current plan places 24 acres of the most valuable land in this State in what amounts to a "tax dead" zone. Under the current law, which contains many flaws, all new tax revenues received from this zone must be devoted to repaying the bond. That could be the year 2005.

● Our schools are facing a $1.5 million deficit next year. We need these tax revenues now, not in 20 years. These future tax revenues should be devoted to teachers' salaries and text books instead of "infastructure" for the rich.

WHAT ABOUT GENTRIFICATION?

● An influx of money will inevitably drive up property values and taxes. This will displace local residents. Already, real estate brochures advertise area housing at inflated prices, urging potential buyers to "get near the Waterfront Development."

● No housing legislation is currently in place or being proposed to protect against inflated housing costs, increased rent, and displaced tenants.

● Development of the Alden Waterfront will threaten the cultural identity of many local neighborhoods, disrupting their family community atmosphere.

WHAT ARE THE HIDDEN COSTS OF THIS PROJECT?

Whenever someone says "this won't cost you a penny...", think twice...

● Police Chief Burke has estimated that additional police protection for this development would cost $66,000 per year.

● Add to that additional tax dollars for increased expenses in our schools, our fire, sewer and electric departments and other City services.

● And what about cost overruns, which could mean a reduction in public amenitites.

WHAT IS THE ENVIRONMENTAL IMPACT?

Despite what's been said, the land on the waterfront is not vacant. It is occupied by five-dozen species of trees, wild flowers and mammals. A hundred species of birds live on the waterfront. Half of these species would be dislocated under this plan. The waterfront is also currently used by a great number of ordinary Burlington citizens as a place to relax and view the lake.

We feel little effort is being made to protect and provide land for present and future ecosystems.

FORTUNATELY, THERE ARE ALTERNATIVES

In the last six years, this City has seen five major plans for waterfront development. Our waterfront will continue to attract developers who inevitably generate tax revenues. These tax revenues will be available immediately, not in 20 years. Our more difficult task is to restrain the developer and get what WE want on our waterfront for the next 200 years instead of what the developer wants.

Under Vermont public trust law, the "filled land" in the Burlington harbor belongs to all the people of this State and must be retained for public uses. This public trust doctrine could be used to move the high priced hotel and condominiums off our 12 acres of filled land so that this land could be preserved for truly public uses.

Revenues generated from a marina in which all 340 slips would be available to the public and from other rental fees could amount to more than half a million dollars per year by 1990 under this alternative plan.

● It had been said that 18% of the net profit will go to the city. Will the city's role become one of entrepreneur rather than a protector of public interest? Doesn't this set a dangerous precedent for future partnerships between the city and private developers?

● How much of Alden's land will be guaranteed for public use in the event of a transfer of ownership?

● One quarter of the proposed public access land is now occupied by the Naval Reserve station. When will the Naval station be relocated and thus relinquish this land over to public park space?

● With the impact of Alden's plan already being felt in area real estate costs, how will Burlington citizens be able to afford to live on and around the Waterfront development?

● Who will be employed? What are the guarantees that those employed will be Vermonters? Will the jobs provided be good paying and secure ones?

● The Community and Economic Development office says that one of the biggest problems facing the Burlington job market is low paying jobs. Why is public money being used to make this problem worse?

● Because the bike path is not on land termed "public access," what is its future should further development take place?

Please Join Us ....

December 2nd   7:30 pm.

■ *A PUBLIC INFORMATION MEETING—*

at the Fletcher Free Library Community Room

All are invited to an informational meeting and public discussion forum on the Waterfront issue.

December 7th   10:15 am

■ *THE LAST WALK ON THE WATERFRONT*

Featuring a nature walk and explanation of the layout of the proposed development plan.

Citizens For A BETTER Waterfront
say

Burlington is still ...
NOT FOR SALE

VOTE
NO

On December 10, 1985

Box 191 Burlington, Vt. 05402 · Sandy Baird - Treasurer

On December 10th, City voters will be asked to subsidize the construction of an "enclave for the rich" on our Waterfront with a 6 million dollars bond that will cost 13 million dollars in future tax dollars to repay over a twenty year period.

HOW MUCH WILL IT ACTUALLY COST BURLINGTON TAX PAYERS?

Lots! The actual cost of just the bond buy-back is 13,000,000 in future tax revenue. And this does not even include:

● Immediate loss of 300,000 dollars in revenue from the Moran Plant (150,000 from the city, 150,000 from the schools)

● 66,000 per year, minimum, in extra police and fire protection.

● 7,000 per year in park maintenance

●Unknown increase in Harbor Patrol

● Creation of a "Tax Dead" zone for twenty years!

Future tax revenues can not be applied for use by the Burlington Schools until the bond is entirely repaid. With Burlington schools facing an immediate deficit of 1.5 million dollars, and soaring costs...it's no wonder the School Board voted 8:3 in opposition to the Alden Plan.

WHAT ABOUT PUBLIC ACCESS?

Not much! Public access is limited to:

● a 300 yard, 25ft.wide promenade, part of which may be leased back to Alden for private use. Is this public park space?

● Our bike path has been relocated to behind the condos and a 5-7 story hotel, and this land has not even been deeded to the city.

● The future of the Haigh Mill, once promised to us as an arts center, is left uncertain.

● Also left uncertain is the possible development of low and moderate income housing.

● Future park space depends on the relocation of the Naval Reserve Station. By the city administration's own admission, the schedule of relocation is left uncertain.

● The community boathouse, which the city is paying for entirely, is only alloting 50% of its space for public use.

What exactly are the Alden Corporation's guarantees?

WHAT WILL HAPPEN TO THE AREA NEIGHBORHOODS?

● An influx of money, which will inevitably drive up property values, will displace local residents. Already, real estate brochures advertise area housing at increased value, urging potential buyers to "get near the Waterfront Development."

● No housing legislation is currently in place or being proposed to protect against inflated housing costs, increased rent, and displaced tenants.

● Development of the Alden Waterfront will threaten area neighborhood's cultural identity and family community atmosphere.

WHAT IS THE ENVIRONMENTAL IMPACT?

● Despite what's been said, the land on the Waterfront is not vacant. Not only is it occupied by a dozen species of trees, scores of wild flowers & plants, dozens of species of mammals, and over a hundred species of birds, but it is used by a great number of Burlington citizens as a place to relax and view the lake.

We feel little effort is being made to protect and provide land for present and future ecosystems

DO THE "YES" SUPPORTERS WANT A LOW VOTER TURNOUT?

● Apparently! They've scheduled the election at a very odd time, Dec. 10, right between two major holidays, and on the second day of Hanukkah.

FORTUNATELY, THERE ARE ALTERNATIVES

● The Waterfront will continue to be prime real estate land which can be developed in a way that will guarantee immediate tax revenues to the city and schools.

Alden's not the first plan and it certainly won't be the last. Precedent has already been set that the city can require 15% of private developer's land for public use. This would be land over and above what is already ours.

Construction currently slated for 12 acres of land, financed by the bond issue, legally belongs to the people of Vermont under the Land Trust Doctrine. This is an issue that needs some more investigation.

Transcript of Meeting of Citizens for a BETTER Waterfront, Fletcher Library, December 2, 1985 — "No on the Alden Plan 1985" — CCTV posted by Barrie Silver (https://www.facebook.com/cctv.vermont/videos/10204920595631957/)

John (Moderator): Ok I'd like to get something going here. Thank you all for coming. My name is John. I've been working with the Citizens for a Better Waterfront.

Rick Sharp: My name is Rick Sharp. I'm an attorney here in Burlington. Been practicing here for some six years and for five years I've been very active in waterfront development, attempting to preserve the lake's edge for public access and a waterfront park. We started in on that about five years ago. We've been very successful to this date in acquiring quite a bit of property along the lake to preserve for a bicycle path and the park. We got the $750,000 bond and that will allow us to put in the bicycle path in the railroad right-of-way. The railroad right-of-way itself was in danger of being taken over by some private property owners who wanted to use it for condominiums about four years ago. We got into a lawsuit over that railroad right-of-way and we went to the legislature and we got the law changed on railroad abandonments. The former law was that when a railroad is abandoned it reverts back to the adjoining landowners. We went to the legislature. The legislature changed the law. No longer will railroad rights-of-way revert back to adjoining landowners. They'll be retained by the state in perpetuity for use for public purposes. So it is possible to do something about your waterfront to preserve it for public access. The legislature can take acts to do exactly that. When we got into…that gave us the five miles that we needed along the lakeshore out in the north end of Burlington from the mouth of the Winooski River down into the downtown area – the filled land. We started to research the filled land in the Burlington harbor about two and a half years ago to see how we could acquire that strip of land that we needed down there to run this bicycle path and lakefront park along the lake there and we stumbled upon the public trust doctrine. I stumbled upon it at exactly the same time that John Franco, Assistant City Attorney stumbled on it as well and I don't have a copy of the article here tonight, but I'm sure that Bea does [laughter] because her daughter just happened to have been the reporter that interviewed John Franco about that. On August 23, 1983 there was an article that appeared in the Rutland Herald in which John Franco stated that the bed of lakes in the state of Vermont are owned by the state and they are held in trust for all the people. Now when an adjoining landowner fills in the lake, he does not acquire title to that filled land. He just filled in the state's land. Our Burlington waterfront was filled in over a period of the last 200 years. I have a paper that explains the public trust doctrine. It's at the back of the room if any of you want to pick it up. It says "The Public Trust Doctrine" right on it. But the basic concept is that… in the Burlington harbor we have about 400 feet of filled land because of the sawmills that were located there in the last century. They continued to dump saw dust, dump saw dust and they built up that area. So we're talking about basically all of the land which is flat and on the west side of Lake Street today has all been filled into the lake over that period of 200 years. It's about 400 feet wide. That consists of…the Alden project, the 24 acres that we're talking about in the Alden project - 12 acres, half of that, is the filled land in the Burlington harbor. So it is subject to the public trust doctrine. Now the public trust doctrine came about in a case that was decided in 1892 by the U.S. Supreme Court. What happened was that in 1872, the state of Illinois gave large sections of the Chicago waterfront to the railroads for use for railroad purposes and the railroad started to fill in the lake and then started to convey the property off. The state of Illinois decided that they wanted that property back because they didn't want the railroads benefitting from their lakeshore. They passed an act to take the property back. The railroads sued and it went all the way to the U.S. Supreme Court. The U.S. Supreme Court held that under the public trust doctrine the bed of Lake Michigan belongs to the state of Illinois and it cannot be given away to private people for private purposes. If the state of Illinois wishes to take it back, they can take it back at any time. They in fact took it back and today the city of Chicago has a wide-open waterfront with park space and bicycle paths throughout the entire waterfront area. Our legislature did the same thing that Illinois did two years later in 1874, we passed an act which gave that land to the railroads. What I'm saying is that our legislature could do the same thing. We could take that property back at any time by merely repealing Title 27 Section 1,003. And by reacquiring the land we could then devote it to public purposes such as an adequate buffer zone for park space and a portion of the land away from the lake, say 200 feet from the lake, could be used for public purposes such as restaurants, open air cafes, that kind of thing. I have strong objections to use of any portion of this land for purely private purposes such as hotels or condominiums because I think that they are clearly private purposes there. They have no public use at all. And that is what I have premised my drive for the public trust doctrine to reclaim this land and use it for public purposes in the future. That process would not cost the state or the city a dime. All the legislature has to do is act to take the property back. And it should do that now because the railroads are no longer using that for the public purpose of railroad transportation. It has been sitting idle for a long time. 100 years have passed and it is obvious that a different public use has to be made of that land. That's basically the public trust doctrine in a nutshell. If you'd like to read more about it and the cases that are cited it's on a sheet of paper entitled Public Trust and it's at the back of the room.

John: Questions for Rick on this particular item... In the back.

Member of the Audience: I think it would be great if the city did own that land. I think that would be fantastic. It's just...I'm wondering if that was indeed true that this doctrine is legal law,...on the other hand, how come it hasn't been acted upon yet?

Rick Sharp: That's a good question. John Franco found out about that in August of 1983. That was before the mayor went down and talked to the Alden Corporation about this. He made statements to the press at that point in which he said that the bed...the filled land is equal to the bed of the lake, it belongs to the state of Vermont and all the people. It's held in trust. He said that that could not be alienated. And Bea has a copy of the article here. I'll read you a portion of exactly what Mr. Franco had to say. He says "research suggests that the state is not competent to convey outright interest in the lake bottom. It's just something you can't sell. Franco said for legal purposes filled land is the same as the lake bottom itself." And what's happened since that time is that Mr. Sanders has made a deal with the Alden Corporation and he's told his assistant city attorney, John Franco, to sit down and don't tell the people about the public trust doctrine. He's got one problem and that is that I show up to all these meetings and I start waving around that article in which he was quoted. I believe the old John Franco was correct. The new John Franco who suddenly thinks this is a mysterious doctrine that nobody can understand is incorrect and is trying to withhold something from the public.

Member of the Audience: Are you insinuating there was a conspiracy at city hall?

Rick Sharp: That's correct. [Laughter, clapping.] There's a conspiracy to withhold information from the public.

John: Any other questions? This woman right here.

Member of the Audience: What's being done about it to get it back...to get the state to take it back?

Rick Sharp: What could be done is that we could go to our legislature and ask them to repeal 27 VSA 1003. That has not happened because I am one individual and I am the only one who's done the research on this other than John Franco, and John isn't talking. So that leaves it to me and it hasn't...I've been trying to tell a lot of people about that over the last two years, but it doesn't really come to the public forum and we don't get a public discussion of it until we get a bond issue like this on the ballot. That then gives me the opportunity to tell you about it. And I would hope that you all go back to your legislators and give them a call and tell them if this bond issue goes down on December 10th, PLEASE, let's settle the public trust doctrine and take this land back because they could do it in the next legislative session.

Member of the Audience: Rick, can't they do it now? I mean, can't you do it...I mean you're saying, excuse me if I'm not getting this right. If they pass it, if they pass it, if the bond gets passed, we go to our legislature and they bring it back or is it the other way around?

Rick Sharp: Well it's not...even if the bond issue passed the public trust doctrine is not dead. You're right that the issue is in the Court right now. It's over in the Superior Court. We have made a motion to get into that action and we are arguing on behalf of the public that that land cannot be used for private purposes of hotels and condominiums. The problem is that the Sanders administration has done a very tricky little thing here. The public trust doctrine does not prohibit anything located on that filled land. What it says is that that filled land has to be used for public purposes, ok Now public purposes can be interpreted in a lot of ways. Certainly railroads, public transportation is a public purpose. A ferry dock is a public purpose. A sewage treatment plant, a light department, a water plant. Those are all public purposes. I think even arguably you could even argue that a restaurant could be a public purpose because it's open to the public. A stadium can be a public purpose. A civic center can be a public purpose. But I draw the line when you get to hotels and condominiums. Those to me are private and they can never be converted into public uses. What the Sanders administration is trying to do is that if they get a two thirds vote on December 10th, they will go into court and they will argue that two thirds of the people in the city of Burlington support private hotels and condominiums on the waterfront. Therefore, what is a private use becomes a public use through public opinion, ok. And that's what they are going to argue and that's why I hope this bond issue goes down, so that we have an opportunity to go to the legislature and let them hear the issue there.

Member of the Audience: I also heard something else in what you said Rick...

John: I'd like to….Excuse me ma'am…

Member of the Audience: Excuse me, I just want to finish. The state holds it in trust for us, am I right? But it's for all of the people of Vermont.

Rick Sharp: That's right. It's not just the people of the city of Burlington. It's all the people of the state of Vermont. That's right.

Member of the Audience: Ok. Thank you.

John: Could we…I want to move this to the next topic. Could you save your question to the…?

Bea Bookchin: Go ahead.

Gene Bergman: Real specific. One is just a point. I don't see the difference between a hotel and a restaurant and I think that while most of your argumentations have been very, very persuasive to me, that is not persuasive at all because it's just as public as anything else, anybody can go there. But what I want to ask, …that was a point of information, …I think…selling point.

Rick Sharp: I'll talk to you after the meeting.

Gene Bergman: OK. I'd like to know what you as spokespeople think…I mean how can Burlington people convince the legislature to do anything, given the record of anti-Burlington sentiment and, you know, how can people who are from across the political spectrum impact on this, on this specific topic?

Rick Sharp: In a nutshell, my response to that would be that as this lady pointed out it's the state that owns the land, not the city of Burlington. This is something that should interest all the people in the state. I grew up in Bellows Falls, Vermont. I loved coming to Burlington. It was like going to the city of Oz on the hill. It was a big deal, ok. And there wasn't a waterfront that was open to the public. I think that I can go back to the legislators that come from Bellows Falls, Vermont, and tell them that in the interest of the high school kids that come up to this city, they should do something about preserving this land for their own kids from their own constituency because we all own that. We're all residents of the state of Vermont.

Maurice Mahoney: John, before we go on, Rick is probably not going to like me doing this, but I've known Rick for about five years or so and followed what he and the Citizens Waterfront Group have done in the city of Burlington and they have done more for bike paths and for public access to the lake than any city administration has ever done and I just think that he is owed a round of applause. [Applause]

Bea Bookchin: The thing that worries me about the plan as it stands right now is that I don't consider that it is a people-oriented waterfront. I really consider that a piece of that land that's down on the lake should be made… should be available to the ordinary people of Burlington, or the state, or elsewhere to be able to use, and the problem right now is, that the way it's being built, the only amount of land that people are going to be able to use along the edge of the water is this 50 foot promenade and I think it's really disgraceful that a 200 room hotel that's the size of the Radisson should be put 50 feet from the water. I think that's a terrible use of the land. I think that plain, ordinary people should have some amount of park space up close to the water where they can walk or bike or sit or talk and that whatever development takes place should be moved back further from the water so that people have some land of their own. That's my major criticism of the design. And I also feel that it's disproportionate with respect to the amount of housing that's there. There are 300 high priced condominiums that are going to be built there, so that from the point of view of the development of the design, what seems to have happened there is instead of taking this piece of land which is at the foot of College Street, at the foot of downtown Burlington, and saying what do the people of Burlington need from this piece of land, what is it that you could do for people with this piece of land, the question got turned around and the question was, how can you make the most money off the piece of land, how can you get the most profit off the piece of land and I think the balance between the land being available to people for use and making profit, I think that that balance has become much too skewed. So that's what I think the problem is. And I just wanted to answer the question, because it comes in here. There is talk. I mean, over and above taxes, if ever there is a net profit, if ever the Alden Corporation actually starts making a profit, the Agreement calls for the fact that the Alden Corporation is going to take 18% of this profit and give it to the city. In other words, what happens here is that the city is essentially being put into an entrepreneurial position. It's becoming the same as a developer. Now on the one hand it might seem very nice that the city is getting 18% of the profit, but on the other hand if the city starts making a profit like a developer, then the city can no longer play a mediating role between the needs of the ordinary people and the needs of making a profit and what the city should be doing is looking out for zoning. The city should be looking out for public trust doctrine. The city should be looking out for the interests of its plain, ordinary citizens. And if it's looking about the amount of money it can make, then problems start arising. And that's exactly why, I think this is one of the reasons that we are exactly left with a 50-foot paved promenade along the edge of the shore and buildings coming up to the edge of the shore. [Applause]

John: Some questions for Bea.

Member of the Audience: I heard at one of the workshops that they're thinking of renting that space…the promenade. That there's a possibility that they're going to rent that back.

Bea Bookchin: Well, that, of course…if they rent it back that would be even worse, but I mean to me, I mean then it's even less than 50 feet somehow. And by the way, it's these little things that bother me. It's not only that the promenade is going to be 50 feet which is bad enough, and the story, and the hotel is the size of the Radisson up there along the edge of the water… sort of that hotel standing where we should be sitting. But not only that but on top of that, the third story of the hotel is going to be an overhang which is going to jut out another 25 feet over into the 50 feet. So it's going to be 25 feet from the edge of the water also. I don't know if it's just the third story or the third to the seventh story. We haven't gotten that clear yet. But whatever it is it's bad enough. Yes.

Member of the Audience: Condominiums…also…along the lakeshore?

Bea Bookchin: Yes. Right, right. The condominiums also go along the edge of the lake. And there are many countries in which the people always have the right to walk along…to have a certain amount of space along the edge of the water. I mean there's just no reason for putting what I consider to be private buildings along the edge of the water when they can just as…I mean, even if one compromises…they can just as easily be moved back and let the people somehow have access…real access along the edge of the water and let the buildings be further back.

Member of the Audience: To the roadway?

Rick Sharp: Everything to the west of Lake Street is subject to the Public Trust Doctrine. It's all filled land.

Member of the Audience: And that could possibly be park land and whatever and public land and then behind that could be the hotels and condominiums?

Rick Sharp: They still have 12 acres…you know they're going to locate their hotels and condominiums on 12 acres of our land. We have said why don't they put their condominiums and hotels on their 12 acres that are back further.

Member of the Audience: …Burlington, we had problems with that…how can Burlington build stairways going down to the buildings?

Rick Sharp: You've made that point at a number of meetings…I've heard you make that point and I think it's an excellent idea that the hotels and condominiums could be tucked back up against the bank and leave a lot more space in the front. That's an excellent idea.

Maurice Mahoney: Plus, if I could…one thing that we haven't addressed yet…even that 50-foot promenade, where does it go? It's a dead end. It stops. And why isn't it at least connected to…land the city already owns, which is very, very close to it by the Burlington water department? I don't know, unless…we really don't want people to go down there.

John: I'm sorry, this gentleman in the middle had a question.

Member of the Audience: I saw in the paper that was handed out by Alden Corporation and the administration …. That none of the buildings was supposed to be above the level of Battery Street. But I've been down, right on the fill down there and they said they would have to fill some more to raise everything above the flood plain. And I don't think you can build a 7-story building that will not go above Battery Street. I don't think you can. I think you're…maybe 5 stories of fill. But I just have problems believing what they say.

Rick: So do we. [Laughter]

John: Yes, sir.

Member of the Audience: How does the public get access to this promenade? The main reason I bring this up…not too many years ago you used to be able to drive through Battery Park and see the view and they'd park for a little while and go on. This summer I drove down to Perkins Pier. There used to be a parking lot there where you could park. I was told that I could park there if I had boat space in the marina. Now, how are people going to get to this promenade? Are they going to walk over the bank from Battery Park or…? [Laughter]

Unknown: Hang gliders. [Laughter]

Bea Bookchin: There is access to the promenade. It will be from College Street. There will be access to it. The problem is…the problem is that the promenade will be exactly what will be the front street of the hotel and the front street of the condominiums. It won't be a kind of place that you can just comfortably sit in and enjoy the lake which is why Burlington is here in the first place. It won't be the kind of thing where you really have a chance to sit there and have space of your own. Your own public space.

Member of the Audience: However, you failed to mention

that beside the 50-foot promenade there's also going to be two adjacent parks. And that's why to get to the promenade is through the island park and another park which is on about a quarter acre of land. That's the million-dollar prize about where the public space will be placed, which is essentially on the shore front. I just want to address…about Maurice's plan about the tax incremental financing…

John: Wait. We can't do that now. If you could wait till the end, just because …

Member of the Audience: Oh, I see, Ok. I see, ok.

John: No, no, no, don't take us down there.

Bea Bookchin: Let him talk.

Member of the Audience: You know there's no way the state is going to take that without compensating the Central Vermont Railway for 12 acres of land and that could be as much as the ten million dollars …

Rick Sharp: That is not true. We paid no one any money when we changed the law on the railroad right of way out in the north end. All we did was we said the common law that said that it reverts back to adjoining landowners won't happen any more. And it's the same thing with the Public Trust Doctrine on the waterfront is that the railroads could continue to use that at the legislature's will as long as they used it for the public transportation purpose of a railroad. When they stopped using it for that purpose, the purpose that the legislature gave it to them for, it comes back to the state. They can take it back at any time. It was our land to begin with. They didn't pay anything for it. We don't have to pay them anything back for it. We just take it back. There's no compensation necessary.

Member of the Audience: Have you talked to any representatives about it?

Rick Sharp: Yes, I have talked to representatives about it. But they haven't heard a full debate yet. They will hear that very shortly. If all the people in this room go back and tell their legislators they want them to debate the Public Trust Doctrine.

John: Okay fine. I don't want to close this off to debate. That's not our purpose. But I did ask that we could address specific questions for specific topics and fine, if we can do this at the end but in fairness to two other people that have to give brief presentations. You know, is that fair to you?

Bea Bookchin: I'll just respond to the parks and then we'll let the two other people talk and then we'll…I certainly, I'm very conscious of…I don't want to stop debate. I mean other people do it to us and I certainly don't want to do

it here. So whatever we have to we'll finish the debate. So we'll just let the other two people make a brief presentation. But I just want to answer the parks. To me, walking along that shoreline…what's important is all the land along the shoreline. Now, what is going…what is being designated as park right now as part of this project is a piece of land that right now the naval reserve station stands on. Now it just so happens that this piece of land is owned by the city of Burlington right now and the city of Burlington could make this into a park if it wants to without any connection with the Alden Corporation. In other words, the piece of land that is the park of this development…that piece of land that the Naval Reserve station stands on is already outrightly owned by the city. And in order to turn it into a park, we first have to ask the Naval Reserve station to move. That is, it's got to take time for the Naval Reserve station to move itself. Now what Alden has given is an acre of land behind the Naval Reserve station land and that is going to turn into a park. I just…I don't think that's sufficient, both from the point of view of in a certain sense how much land Alden is giving and the back and forth compromise and second of all, for the fact that it's city land that is…that the brochure says there is going to be five acres of park in the project, but really it's city land to begin with that's the land that's being turned into a park and it's city land that has a Naval Reserve station standing on it right now. In other words, I think it's insufficient.

Member of the Panel: I'm here because nearly three years ago a group I was affiliated with gave a petition to the Burlington aldermen asking for a wetlands park in George Perkins Marsh memorial. George Perkins Marsh was born in Woodstock. He's the international conservation movement father. He was involved with the Central Vermont Railroad. He was appointed Ambassador to Italy by Lincoln in 1864. He stayed there for 20 years. The Italians loved him so much they didn't want to send his body home. His work is the book, Man and Nature. He, because he was interested, traveled as much as possible throughout the world…put all the information together…We asked this because Lake Champlain is the sixth largest lake in the United States and it has international significance. It is an international waterway. It's not simply Burlington or Vermont doing their thing. It's an international situation. Environmentalists, as you know, are much thinking. The situation for world climate is becoming critical. Man himself is an endangered species. I'll read you a quote from Edward O. Wilson who is a sociobiologist at Harvard University. He says, "Children can adapt to any kind of life. They can survive and reproduce the same way laboratory rats and caged tigers can. Human nature is something more. Our species evolved in open and uncrowded environments surrounded by living creatures. Our ancestors were hunters and gatherers who were intimately related to a diversity of other organisms as part of their living methods. At the same time no other species has moved so fast and so far from its origin. This is the human dilemma. We have traveled a great distance from the economic and social systems in which we evolved, yet many of our basic emotions are still rooted in the Pleistocene history, including our strong tendency to affiliate with nature." Albert Schweitzer's famous quote is, "It's no longer enough to love our own species". I'm taking a slightly different view than what is ordinarily proposed in presenting this idea to you. It's sad we have a landscape architect who is proposing buildings rather than landscapes. This is landscape [holds up a book]. This is landscape [Opens book to pictures and holds it up]. This is landscape [Holds up magazines]. The University of Wisconsin is the world center for environmental restoration. It's no pie in the sky idea. This is landscape [holds up another pamphlet]. Colorado has a formal urban program for promoting species diversity within their cities. These are all handouts…you may look at at your leisure. For your purposes, [holds up map of the waterfront] the green is all fill in Burlington. What we are discussing is 24 acres here, you see how much was filled and how busy our ancestors were. There are standards for park space. They are 78 acres per thousand. According to such, Burlington should have nearly 3,000 park acres. We have less than 400. It is no big thing to ask for park space at a time when tropical forests are being cut down worldwide and temperate forests are being asked to take over for them to keep world oxygen supply and climate moderation in balance. The best thing to do is to provide all the green space we are able to provide. What have other people done? I travel widely in Europe, in the United States, in the Caribbean, in the westerly Pacific Islands. All of these areas preserve their waterfronts. California has taken the entire ocean shoreline and said no buildings. It is for natural purposes. They are well aware of what the international significance is. I will remind you as well, there is something called the municipal planning and development act [holds up pamphlet]. This is where you write plans for cities and towns. I've got the purpose of the act and the definition for land development. (I will pass out to you) and if your plans do not adhere to the purpose what you are doing is not legal.

Member of the Audience: Is it unethical that environmental impact statements not be done simply because of that law?

Rick Sharp: No, but federal law states that you only have to do environmental impact statements…there's no state law for environmental impact statements. It only has to be done under federal law if there's a federal involvement in some manner.

John: Hendrick.

Hendrick: Yeah, I'd just like to point out a couple of things. One, there's going to be nature walks on Saturday morning, and a group of us did the nature walk about a year and a half ago and I also did a lot of research that I've done… English law…and there is a tremendous amount of wildlife that's down there right now that would be adversely affected. And filling in portions of the lake will cause, you know, detriment to fish spawning grounds, amphibians, birds, you know, like to feed along the lakeshore and things like that. And any development that's close to the waterfront or body of water, has a definite effect on what life it's going to have. Right now, there's over 100 species of birds that, throughout the course of the year, you know, have spent some time there, a great deal of them build a nest down there, others just come through to feed, or just come through during migration. There are owls, there are hawks, ducks, small songbirds, all different kinds of birds and wildlife are there and there would definitely be a negative impact if there is a lot of this development.

Member of the Panel: I should mention as well for those who do not know it…this filled land was once all a wetland and it was a major stop on the international fly way for geese and ducks. As you know, the Canadian and the United States government and Ducks Unlimited and other similar private organizations have been so successful in bringing back these species from near extinction… we don't know what to do with them all. We are building so there is no place for them to stop on the way. If you listen to the media, [laughter] you heard this year there were geese where there were never geese before. They're looking for a place. I say it's entirely appropriate to …

Member of the Audience: What does Bernie have to gain… or what does this…I mean, what are they trying…why are they doing this to the city of Burlington? …[laughter] I mean you guys…I mean…really?…I mean, just as a whim? …wants to…

Bea Bookchin: I could begin to answer that…I feel that what he has to gain is he…I can't speak for him, but…he probably thinks that he's putting down a good fiscal tax base, that he's…that the area that is going to…that it's an unused area…and it will start making a lot of money… that it will start generating tax dollars. I think it's a way of making money for the city. It's a way of making the city more fiscally balanced. It's a way, it's a method, I think it's what…

Member of the Audience: One thing…he's not working for the poor, as he says. He's working for the rich. And he's always saying he's helping the poor …

Gene Bergman: It's not just Bernie…Hey! Let's get it straight right now there are republicans…for all the die-hard republicans here, there are republicans, there are elected officials and leaders of the parties, there are democrats as far as I know…the democratic party…what I object to is the "Bad Bernie" thing. I have a lot of….

Member of the Audience: Oh please!

Gene Bergman: I do because it's not…

Bea Bookchin: Let him talk!

Gene Bergman: In principal I have a lot of problems with this plan and I fought the original waterfront plan in 1977, because redevelopment things. But I really take issue at this. If there's going to be an attack made on the proponents, it should be an attack on the proponents or an attack on all the political parties. Otherwise you discredit yourselves in my eyes and probably a lot more people.

John: Maurice?

Maurice Mahoney: Yeah. I don't think anyone here has attacked Bernie.

Gene Bergman: I heard it. I was sitting right here. Saying… the administration is not just the administration …

Unknown: May I just say something please? Let me just say something

Maurice Mahoney: OK, can I make a point, please?

Multiple people: [Unintelligible.]

Member of the Audience: He was the mayor…he is the mayor and he is very vocal and he gets what he deserves… he was the president of the board of aldermen…[Unintelligible]

Maurice Mahoney: Gene, Gene, let's just deal with this. I have not made that an issue and I don't intend to make that an issue. Bernie's going to be running for Governor. I don't know what he's got to gain out of this. I know we've got a lot to lose and that's the point I'm trying to get across.

Member of the Audience: Right, right, right.

Member of the Audience: …I can understand how you feel about that because I have the same issue with republicans that you have with us about this situation. The reason why the mayor's name got brought into this is because of questions he addressed. We…now, listen, I have been to republican meetings and I listen to the republicans trying to blame this all on the democrats [laughter] so I'm say-ing that if you just…there's plenty of room for people to throw things around if they want to throw it around. And we're not saying that this an issue, Bernie issue or progressive, republican or democrat…it's obviously across all the political factions if you just look at the formation of our group. We're not discussing politics here. What we're discussing is, is this really definitely the best deal for the taxpayers? We say no. Is it the best solution for the waterfront? We say no. And these are the reasons why we say no. And you know, personally speaking, we all have our own personal feelings about every different party in the city and one thing is for certain, this city is not boring and…you know, we're just saying this is what our positions are. This has nothing to do with a political battle on Maurice's part, on Rick's part, Gene's part or mine. It's simply we got together because we felt very strongly that this is not the best solution for our city regardless of what you call yourself, period. [Applause.]

Member of the Audience: Thank you. [Clapping]

Member of the Audience: On the west side of Battery Street between College and Battery Park there's a wide walkway. There's gravel put down, and there's concrete steps, I don't know, must be, I would say between 50, maybe even 75 feet wide. What is the Alden Plan for that? As I see from the map that I saw in the handout given from the Alden Company and the Administration, Alden takes possession of everything right up to Battery Street.

Rick Sharp: No. That's city owned land. That will remain as park space.

Member of the Audience: And it will remain?

Rick Sharp: Yup, yup.

Hendrick: I would just like to say…when you mention that Bernie thinks that this will be to the financial benefit of the city, there was a lot of applause back there. And I'd like to say that there, yeah, there are a lot of waterfront plans that will financially benefit the city and, in fact, the main problem is that they're saying [laughter] that this waterfront won't cost us a penny, and in reality, it will cost us a great deal. It will cost us ecological space and things that people need and it will cost us financially because of the bond…

Rick Sharp: Thank you all for coming tonight.

My note: Gene Bergman is a member of the Progressive Coalition. He later defeated me in two very heated campaigns for Alderman from Ward 2. Despite his loss on the Alden plan, Bernie Sanders went on to a long life in national politics as a U.S. Representative and Senator from Vermont and a serious candidate for president in 2016 and 2020.

The Burlington Free Press — Sunday, December 15, 1985

Rick Sharp Puts Image on Line For Environment

By MARK JOHNSON
Free Press Staff Writer

He has been dismissed as a dreamer, a political gadfly who pops up to spoil the plans of Mayor Bernard Sanders. His credibility has been challenged, his ideas labeled absurd and unrealistic, his motives questioned. When he walks the streets of Burlington, he knows some people look at him with genuine disdain.

Rick Sharp, lawyer and environmentalist, may not be a household word, but after leading the charge against a development project on Lake Champlain and, earlier this year, helping to defeat a landfill bond issue, he says he is a political force that cannot be ignored.

In an interview at his downtown office — where the cork-covered walls are dog-eared, file cabinets sit half-open and wall hangings and boxes rest on the floor — Sharp said his motives in fighting the landfill improvement bond and waterfront development have been skewed by his critics.

"I think there are a lot of people who don't understand where I'm coming from or why I'm doing what I'm doing," he said. "I do not like being opposed to bond issues. My public image in this community has been damaged. I guess I place the quality of the environment over my self-interests or looking good. ... I'll take that risk that people see me as just a spoiler and an obstructionist in order to get what I see as the greater long-range benefit, even if in the short range I have to pay the consequences of the backlash of being against something."

Sharp, 33, a Democrat cut from the Kennedy mold, sees nothing wrong with being a dreamer. Trounced in a 1982 bid for the state Senate, Sharp said his fights on the landfill and against the waterfront development were not driven by a desire to get ahead politically or because of personal animosity toward Sanders, whom Sharp admits he disagrees with on policy.

"We're in a time period where there is this 1980s mentality that power and success to the 1980s Yuppie means having a condominium right on the lake's edge with a huge plate glass window, with no one walking in front of you, with no trees to encumber the view. I think that's what I'm fighting against," he said.

He claims to have no firm political ambitions and even his supporters say he may be too idealistic and not pragmatic enough to be an effective politician.

In the past, he unsuccessfully fought the location of the McNeil Generating Station and earlier this year was thwarted on a move to block development within 80 feet of the water.

Sharp's harshest critics have been city officials, including Sanders and city Community and Economic Development Director Peter Clavelle, who say Sharp has the right to speak out but is unrealistic. in his nature, but that's part of the responsibility that comes with success."

Sanders said Sharp has been "loose with the truth" on occasion and stressed that on both the landfill and the waterfront, Sharp "thwarted" the majority. He suggested the bond opponents, including Sharp, might pay the political consequences later if the waterfront remains undeveloped or a worse plan comes along.

"Mr. Sharp or no Mr. Sharp, it is difficult to get two-thirds," Sanders said.

Said Sharp: "I know I will be the goat of Burlington if there isn't any development on the waterfront in the next three to five years."

When Sharp argued the city should reclaim the waterfront land through the "public trust doctrine," supporters of the Alden plan called Sharp's idea far-fetched. When Sharp called a press conference to suggest a maple tree park be built instead of condominiums and a hotel, Clavelle took apart the plan and wondered: "Who the hell is Rick Sharp to get all this attention?"

First and foremost, Sharp says, he is an environmentalist. The product of what he called a lower-middle-income family in Bellows Falls, Sharp got his first taste of environmental problems as a youth, disgusted by the dyes and chemicals being dumped in the Connecticut River by area paper companies.

He went on to the Univesity of Southern California, then Georgetown University Law School. One of his biggest thrills was meeting former Chief Justice William O. Douglas, a champion of environmental rights who convinced politicians to build a park instead of a freeway over an abandoned Washington canal.

"I see myself as one of those seedlings of Justice Douglas who has been transplanted to Burlington, Vermont, and who is going to create that same green strip if we can have the same sort of luck (as Douglas did)," Sharp said. "That's where a lot of it comes from. And I think it's good to dream a little bit."

When he graduated from law school, Sharp decided to skip the high salaries on Wall Street and returned to Vermont. He worked for three years for the Environmental Conservation Agency, where he learned the problems of placing a landfill near a wetlands area.

For the past three years, he has been known as "Mr. Bike Path," the leading advocate for the construction of a bicycle path along the lake from one end of the city to another. The idea for the path came from Howard Dean, a doctor and now a member of the Vermont House, who said the plan would have gone nowhere without Sharp.

"Three years ago, that (bike path) was a twinkle in our eyes. ... Now look," Dean said.

Together, they formed the Citizens Waterfront Group, an organization that city officials attacked — saying it had fewer members than Sharp claimed — during the debate over the Alden plan.

Dean considers Sharp a friend but said they sometimes disagree because of Sharp's admittedly more extreme views. On the Alden plan, Dean broke with Sharp for the first time publicly and supported the plan.

"Rick has been criticized as extreme and aggressive, but I think his integrity is beyond question. He's incredibly dedicated ... and a workaholic," Dean said.

Sharp calls himself a "non-materialistic Yuppie." He owns no car, preferring instead to invest his money in 100 acres in Milton where he dreams of building a hang-gliding recreation area. When he first moved to Burlington, Sharp shared a six-bedroom house for $43 a month.

"I think with Rick what you see is what you get," said Dean, saying he could recall only few occasions when he had seen Sharp dressed in a suit.

However, while Dean said he would encourage Sharp to run for political office, it may not suit his style.

"A few years ago, I talked him out of running for city Democratic chair. I knew he would be more interested in his interests than in the nuts and bolts of political work," Dean said. "With his idealism, he looks at things as right or wrong and it tends to be more difficult for him to compromise."

"If they'd given me the 80 feet at the beginning, I would have settled for that. Now I wouldn't. Now we're looking at 200 feet," Sharp said, referring to his stand on the waterfront.

Sharp admits oversimplifying his arguments in opposing the bond, but said the supporters were just as guilty.

During the waterfront debate, Sharp kept himself financially afloat with the one-third share of a $27,000 settlement he won for a former Burlington police officer, Wayne Hunt, who was struck by his landlord.

But during the campaign, he had to swallow a $400 printing bill for the first round of anti-Alden fliers that contained, he said, "gross inaccuracies." Eight thousand of the fliers still sit in his office.

Dean said Sharp, while not a gloating person, did enjoy the fight against the waterfront development.

"What he said to me was it was a case of the little guy taking it to the corporations. A lot of people who talk about those kind of things, you find out they're from the middle class and they have a trust fund. Rick's done everything himself," Dean said.

While Sanders questioned Sharp's strength, Dean and Sharp said environmentalists could no longer be ignored.

"He could make a lot with this or throw it all away," Dean said. "This is a new period of growth with him. It will be interesting to see if he can make the transition from idealist to being a bit more pragmatic It's not in his nature, but that's part of the responsibility that comes with success."

Free Press Photo by JYM WILSON

Burlington attorney Rick Sharp stands with the city's waterfront area in the background.

STATE OF VERMONT   CHITTENDEN SUPERIOR COURT
CHITTENDEN COUNTY, SS.   DOCKET NO. S966-84 CnC

STATE OF VERMONT and CITY OF   )
BURLINGTON,   )
          Plaintiffs,   )
)
              vs.   )
)
CENTRAL VERMONT RAILROAD, INC.,   )
ALDEN WATERFRONT CORPORATION and   )
McLEAN CORPORATION,   )
          Defendants,   )
)
              vs.   )
)
ALDEN WATERFRONT CORPORATION,   )
          Third Party Plaintiff,   )
)
              vs.   )
)
GREEN MOUNTAIN POWER CORPORATION,   )   BENCH MEMORANDUM
          Third Party Defendant,   )   OF
)   AMICUS CURIAE
              vs.   )   CITIZENS WATERFRONT GROUP
)
GREEN MOUNTAIN POWER CORPORATION,   )
          Fourth Party Plaintiff,   )
)
              vs.   )
)
STATE OF VERMONT, DEPARTMENT OF   )
TRANSPORTATION and CENTRAL VERMONT   )
RAILWAY, INC.,   )
          Fourth Party Defendants.   )

> "[T]he General Assembly cannot grant to
> private persons for private purposes, the
> right to control the height of the water of
> the lake, or the outflow therefrom, by
> artificial means, for such a grant would not
> be consistent with the exercise of that trust
> which requires the State to preserve such
> waters for the common and public use of
> all...The General Assembly being powerless to
> make such a grant, none can be intended as the
> basis of the decree."

Hazen vs. Perkins, 92 Vt. 414, 419-420 (1918) (citations
omitted).

INDEX

A. **The first issue that must be decided by this Court is whether the General Assembly can grant a fee simple absolute title to the bed or soil of boatable lakes in the State of Vermont.**

1. THE GENERAL ASSEMBLY CANNOT GRANT FEE SIMPLE ABSOLUTE TITLE TO THE BED OR SOIL OF BOATABLE LAKES IN THE STATE OF VERMONT.

The "polestar" case on this issue in the State of Vermont is

Hazen vs. Perkins, 92 Vt. 414, 419 (1918). According to the

Vermont Supreme Court in Hazen:

> "Being public waters according to the test afforded by the Constitution, the grants of land bounding upon the lake pass title only to the water's edge, or to low-water line....The bed or soil of such boatable lakes in this state is held by the people in their character as souvereign in trust for public uses for which they are adapted. Illinois Central R.R. Co. v. People , 146 U.S. 387, 13 Sup. Ct. 110, 36 L.Ed 1018...The defendant did not, therefore, acquire any title to the waters of the lake, as such, nor to the lands covered by such waters, by grants from private sources. And the General Assembly cannot grant to private persons for private purposes, the right to control the height of the water of the lake, or the outflow therefrom, by artificial means, for such a grant would not be consistent with the exercise of that trust which requires the State to preserve such waters for the common and public uses of all. Illinois Central R.R. Co. v. People...The General Assembly being powerless to make such a grant, none can be intended as the basis of the decree."

Hazen at 419-420 (most citations ommited).

The central thesis of the Defendant, Central Vermont Railway

(hereinafter CV), is that the 1827 Wharfing Act and the 1874

Railroad Act conferred upon its predecessors in title fee simple

absolute title to a portion of the bed or soil of Lake Champlain

free and clear of any public trust interest. CV's Trial Brief at

8.

CV goes to great lengths examining the specific wording of the 1827 Wharfing Act and the 1874 Railroad Act to support this contention. CV argues that the words, "heirs or assigns...forever" and "legal title", contained in the Act of 1827 and the Act of 1874, create a fee simple absolute title to these lands in the grantees.

Certainly an examination of the particular wording of an act or statute is an appropriate starting point in any inquiry into the nature of a legislative grant. The shortcoming of CV's approach is its failure to adequately analyze these grants within the broader context of public policy and the public trust doctrine.

In effect, CV has focused on the bark of the tree and failed to adequately examine the entire public trust forest.

The cases CV relies upon to support its argument that the language "heirs or assigns...forever" and "legal title" create a fee simple absolute title are distinguishable from the case at bar because they do not involve lands subject to public trust rights. Hence, these cases are inapplicable to the case at bar.

The language "heirs", when used in connection with a grant of public lands, will pass only a limited conveyance or lease. Johnson v. Town of Salisbury, 120 Vt. 6, 10 (1975). Where a railroad attempts to later convey away such public lands, the conveyance is void. Id. at 10. Jones v. Vermont Asbestos Corp, 105 VT. 79, 94 (1936).

-2-

Defendants have failed to adequately address the underlying question of whether the General Assembly has the power to grant away the bed or soil of boatable lakes in the first place. Amicus Curiae, Citizens Waterfront Group, contends that Vermont law, and particularly the Hazen case, clearly prohibits the outright conveyance of such lands free from the public trust interest of the people of the State of Vermont. Hazen, supra, at 419.

The Supreme Court in Hazen could not be more clear. Even if the General Assembly had intended to grant to private persons the right to raise and lower the level of Lake Morey, it could not do so, "for such a grant would not be consistent with the exercise of that trust which requires the State to preserve such waters for the common and public use of all. Illinois Central R.R. Co. v. Illinois, 146 U.S. 387, 13 Sup. Ct. 110, 36 L.Ed. 1081." Hazen, supra, at 419.

In Hazen, the lowering of Lake Morey by a mere eight inches constituted an aggrievious nuisance. Hazen at 412. Although the nuisance in that instance was the lowering of the lake level, it is quite clear in the Hazen decision that the trust which the court refers to applies equally to "the bed or soil of such boatable lakes." Hazen at 419. See also, State v. Malmquist, 114 Vt. 96, 101 (1944); In Re Water Levels of Lake Seymour, 117 Vt. 367, 375 (1952). It is immaterial whether the bed or soil is exposed by artificial fill or by artificially lowering the level of the lake; public trust law controls.

-3-

This position is entirely in keeping with the earlier finding of the Vermont Supreme Court, prior to the _Illinois_ decision, in _Austin v. Rutland R.R. Co._, 45 Vt. 215 (1872).

> "The right, then, that existed in the testator as owner of lot No. 10, was not a right appurtenant to the lot to build into the lake in front of it. He had only, and at most, so far as the lake was concerned, a right in common with all other persons, to use the waters of the lake in any proper way, and for any proper purposes. As the absolute owner of said lot, he had the exclusive right to use it in passing to and from the lake. But this gave him no peculiar or additional right as to the lake itself. Of course it could not give him title to erections or structures made by others beyond the limits of his own land."

_Id._ at 243-244.

It follows that where a person fills onto the bed or soil of a boatable lake beyond the low water point, it is "as if a man builds on another's land, the building belongs to the owner of the land." _Id._ at 244 (citing _Nicols v. Lewis_, 15 Conn. 136).

The _Austin_ court goes on to state that, "By this expression, I do not understand that the proprietors alluded to were seised, but they had a right of occupation, properly termed a franchise." _Id._ at 244 (citing Ch. J. Hosmer, 7 Conn. 202). Thus, when riparian owners filled onto the bed or soil of Lake Champlain prior to the 1874 Railroad Act, they merely built upon the lands the State was holding in trust for all the people of Vermont, and this filled land belongs to all the people of this State as owners of the bed or soil of Lake Champlain.

The 1874 Act did not change this conclusion, despite the wording used in this statute, for the General Assembly did not

-4-

have the authority to render the public trust null and void by conveying a fee simple absolute title. Hazen, supra, at 419-420.

Hazen has been cited in ten subsequent Vermont Supreme Court decisions, the most recent in 1977. Napro Development Corporation v. Town of Berlin, 135 Vt. 353, 359 (1977). In 1944 and 1952, the Vermont Supreme Court reaffirmed Hazen with identical passages as follows:

> "[T]he bed or soil of the lake is held by the people of the State in their sovereign capacity in trust for the public uses for which it is adapted and the State is required to preserve the water for the common use of all."

State v. Malmquist, 114 Vt. 96, 101 (1944); In Re Water Levels of Lake Seymour, 117 Vt. 367, 375 (1952) (both citing Hazen, supra at 419).

Although these cases involve issues concerning the waters of Vermont lakes, the language employed leaves no doubt that the public trust doctrine applies equally to the bed or soil of such boatable lakes.

No subsequent Vermont decision has overruled or modified the position of the Court in Hazen concerning the public trust. Thus, contrary to Defendant Alden Waterfront Corporation's contention that the "public trust theory is an antiquated legal relic," the public trust doctrine, as set out in Hazen, is the law of Vermont today. Alden's Pre-Trial Brief at 9.

2. THE PUBLIC TRUST DOCTRINE IS INCORPORATED IN THE VERMONT CONSTITUTION AND VERMONT STATUTES.

Hazen and the cases that follow it, frequently rely upon and refer to the hunting, fowling and fishing provision of the Vermont

-5-

Constitution. Hazen, supra, at 419; Malquist, supra, at 101. This portion of the Vermont Constitution secures to all Vermonters the liberty to use all boatable waters as a public right:

> "The inhabitants of this State shall have liberty in seasonable times, to hunt and fowl on the lands they hold, and on other lands not inclosed, and in like manner to fish in all boatable and other waters (not private property) under proper regulations, to be made and provided by the General Assembly."

Vt. Const. Ch. II., Sec. 67.

The right of the people of the State of Vermont to the bed or soil of boatable lakes appears to eminate, at least in part, from this portion of the Vermont Constitution. See, Hazen, supra, at 419; Malmquist, supra, at 101; Seymour, supra, at 375.

This portion of the Constitution guarantees "common passage" on lakes as highways. Malmquist, supra, at 101 (citing Trout and Salmon Club v. Mather, 68 Vt. 338, 345 (1895)). As long as they used the filled lands for public transportation purposes, the railroads served this "common passage" requirement. When the railroads stopped using these filled lands for public transportation purposes (as admitted at trial), they violated not only the public trust doctrine, but also this provision of the Vermont Constitution.

In addition to the Vermont Constitution, the General Assembly has explicitly adopted the concept of the public trust in Title 29, Sec. 401, which provides in part as follows:

-6-

"Lakes and ponds which are public waters of Vermont <u>and</u> <u>the lands lying thereunder</u> are a public trust and it is the policy of the state that these waters and <u>lands</u> shall be managed to serve the public good..."

Vt. Stat. Ann. Tit. 29, Sec. 401 (1981)(emphasis added).

In accordance with the Vermont Constitution, Title 29, Sec. 401, and a long line of Vermont case law, it is clear that the public trust doctrine is alive and well in the State of Vermont and supercedes the specific language of the 1827 Wharfing Act and the 1874 Railroad Act.

B. The Warfing Act of 1827 did not convey title to lands filled into Lake Champlain.

The 1827 Wharfing Act did not give the railroads a right to fill in 42 acres of Lake Champlain. That law provided only a "franchise" to build storehouses and erect wharfs into the lake, <u>Austin</u>, <u>supra</u> at 244.

A great deal of the filling in dispute in the case at bar was not for the erection of storehouses or wharves. Thus, the 1827 Wharfing Act is entirely inapplicable to most of the 42 acres of filled land in question.

The remaining portions, to which the 1827 Wharfing Act was applicable, should revert to the State as trustee for all the people due to the lapse of the franchise granted through non-use. <u>City of Barre v. Perry and Scribner</u>, 82 Vt. 301, (1909). A grant of a franchise of an indefinite duration is restricted to a reasonable time. <u>Id</u>.

-7-

C. **The Railroad Act of 1874 is open-ended and impairs the State's interest in what remains.**

Hazen, the "polestar" case of Vermont public trust law, relies heavily upon Illinois. Hazen at 419 (citing Illinois Central R.R. Co. vs. Illinois, 146 U.S. 387 (1892). The facts of the Illinois case are remarkably similar to the case at bar, both in the form of the legislation enacted by the respective legislatures and the timing of the enactments in question.

In Illinois, the U. S. Supreme Court held that a statute enacted by the Illinois Legislature which purported to convey title to the bed or soil of Lake Michigan was ineffective to convey title to such lands. The railroads were extremely powerful in the latter half of the 19th century and often had an undue influence on state legislators during that time. This was the case in both the State of Illinois and Vermont where large tracks of lakebed were granted to the railroads through legislation enacted in 1869 and 1874 respectively. These grants should be closely scrutinized by this Court due to the historical timing of both enactments during a period of documented graft, corruption and influence peddling by the recipients of these grants.

According to the U.S. Supreme Court, the language of the Illinois statute made the attempted conveyance invalid. The amount of filled land in contention was less than 100 acres, a relatively small portion of the one square mile that the statute allowed the railroad to fill into Lake Michigan. The evidence introduced in the case at bar demonstrates that approximately 42 acres of land have been created by filling Lake Champlain in the

-8-

Burlington harbor. However, under the Illinois test, the amount of actual filling is not determinative. The question is whether the statute purports to convey such a large area of the lakebed that the conveyance impairs the state's interest in what remains. See Illinois at 453 - 455.

Applying the Illinois test, to the case at bar, the answer is a resounding "Yes"! The Act of 1874 purports to "vest" title in the railroads "whenever" they fill into Lake Champlain. Under this phrasing, CV has the audacity to contend that filling undertaken as late as the 1950s is lawful under the authority of the 1874 Act, and hence, CV has fee simple title to such filled lands. See CV's Trial Brief at 11.

CV contends that the only limitation upon its right to fill the lake is that it does not "impede ordinary navigation in passing up and down said lake." CV's Trial Brief at 15.

Under this line of reasoning, CV could continue to fill in the lake unrestrained until nothing but a single channel allowing passage "up and down" the lake remained! This interpretation of the 1874 Act is essentially limitless and clearly impairs the state's duty under the Constitution, statutes and case law to preserve the right of all citizens to boat, fish and fowl upon Lake Champlain.

As in the Illinois case, Vermont's 1874 Railroad Act purports to convey such a large area of the lake bed that it is essentially open-ended and thus, even more suspect than the Illinois statute. As such, it should be declared ineffective to convey title to

-9-

lands filled into Lake Champlain.

D. **Vermont has adopted a _res publicae_ approach to the law of public trust.**

The basic concept behind modern public trust law is ancient with its original roots in the Roman law concept of _res publicae_, belonging to the public. In England, public trust law evolved over a period of centuries, from an earlier rule under which the Crown had the power to grant away public trust rights, to more modern times when Parliament finally prohibited the Crown from alienating submerged lands. Sax, _The Public Trust Doctrine in Natural Resource Law, Effective Judicial Intervention_, 68 Mich. L. Rev. 471, 492 (1970).

Public trust law in the United States has taken different forms depending upon the history of the particular state examined.

Some states adopted the old English approach which allowed the alienation of submerged lands. Thus, the New York Legislature in early times authorized the granting of title to at least small, well defined parcels of submerged land in New York harbor.

New York case law is therefore full of authority to alienate submerged land.

> "[New York State's] right to grant navigable waters is as absolute and uncontrollable (except as restrained by constitutional checks) as its right to grant the dry land it owns. It holds all the public domain as absolute owner, and is in no sense a trustee thereof, except as it is organized and possesses all its property, functions and powers for the benefit of the people."
>
> _Langdon v. The Mayor, Alderman and Commalty of City of New York_, 93 N.Y. 129, 156 (1883).

-10-

The decision of the U.S. Supreme Court in _Appleby v. City of New York_, 271 U.S. 364 (1926), is not surprising in this context. Obviously, the Supreme Court is looking to state law in deciding public trust cases. This may be the only explanation for the divergent results of _Illinois_ versus _Appleby_.

The Spanish form of public trust law was adopted by California. Stevens, _The Public Trust, A Sovereign's Ancient Prerogative Becomes the People's Environmental Right_, 14 U.Cal. Davis L. Rev. 195, 196-197 (1980).

Furthermore, some states have modified public trust rules over time to accomodate circumstances particular to their locality, such as the Massachusetts rule that a change in use of public lands is impermissible without a clear showing of legislative approval. Sax, _supra_, at 492.

It should be noted that even though Massachusetts, our sister state, is far from free to adopt a strict _res publicae_ approach to public trust law, due to the large number of people who have relied upon at least the appearance of valid title to lands filled into Boston harbor over a period of centuries, the Masschusetts courts have nonetheless adopted a farily stringent approach to public trust law.

The Supreme Judicial Court of Massachusetts recently held that,"The land below low water line can be granted by the State only to fulfill a public purpose, and the rights of the grantee to that land are ended when that purpose is extinguished." _Boston Waterfront Development Corporation v. Commonwealth_, 393 N.E.2d

-11-

356, 365 (1979).

Fortunately, very few parties will be adversely affected by a decision, in this case, to reaffirm the extremely strict _res publicae_ approach previously adopted by Vermont in the _Hazen_ case. The only extensive filling of a public body of water in the state is the filled land located in the Burlington harbor.

This filled land is not occupied by private homes or other structures. CV is currently holding the people of this state hostage to its demands for $400,000 per acre, threatening to maintain this land as a wasteland until it is allowed to reap windfall profits for land for which it paid the state nothing. Furthermore, CV has paid very little taxes on this land over the past 113 years.

Contrary to other states, Vermont has never allowed the alienation of public trust lands. Vermont has clearly adopted a strict _res publicae_ approach to public trust law that absolutely prohibits the alienation of the bed or soil of boatable lakes. _Hazen_ at 419.

This is no time to change this rule of law. If fee simple title is confirmed in CV, it will undoubtedly sell this land to the highest bidder, thereby guaranteeing dense private development which would exclude the majority of the people of this state for centuries.

In the event that the public trust is confirmed, this filled land will be put to public uses, including sorely needed urban park space and public facilities for all Vermonters to enjoy for

-12-

generations to come.

At a bare minimum this Court should adopt the approach of Massachusetts where the rights of grantees to such public lands end when the purpose, for which such lands were granted, comes to an end. Clearly CV is no longer using these lands for the same public transportation purposes as they did in the 19th century. The lands should be declared res publicae for the public good of all Vermonters.

E. **Laches and Estoppel are not effective defenses in matters of public trust and environmental law.**

Defendants cite to acts of condemnation and conveyance over the past 100 years from Defendants and their predecessors to various parties, including the City of Burlington. The crux of this argument is that if Defendants did not have title to these lands, why were Defendants compensated for such lands?

The simple explanation is that these public trust rights were overlooked until they were rediscovered and popularized by members of the Citizens Waterfront Group over the past three years.

In environmental law, the doctrine of estoppel cannot be asserted against public lands and the public interest generally. A.L.R.2d 340-341 (1948). For example, the Rivers and Harbors Act of 1899 laid dormant for almost 70 years as industries and municipalities dumped refuse into waterways across the nation. 33 U.S.C. Sec. 407 (1899). By the 1960s, this country's water pollution problem was acute. In 1969, environmentalists dredged up the 1899 Act and were effective in prosecuting discharges

-13-

without the permits required by the 1899 Act.

The result was the enactment of the Clean Water Act of 1972, establishing the "national pollution discharge elimination system" which has led to vastly improved waterways throughout the nation.

Defendants cite to Stone v. Blake, 118 Vt. 424 (1955), to assert that the public is guilty of laches. CV's Trial Brief at 18. The Stone case does not involve the public trust and is distinguishable. The filled lands of Vermont are undeveloped and can be taken without prejudice to Defendants. Laches does not apply to the bed or soil of Lake Champlain.

The public trust doctrine has laid dormant in the State of Vermont for a period of time. But, just like the Rivers and Harbors Act of 1899, it is finally being utilized to save this precious resource for all Vermonters to enjoy for generations to come.

DATED at Burlington, Vermont this 13th day of March, 1987

AMICUS CURIAE,
CITIZENS WATERFRONT GROUP

RICK SHARP, ESQUIRE

-14-

www.ingramcontent.com/pod-product-compliance
Lightning Source LLC
Chambersburg PA
CBHW081156020426
42333CB00020B/2518